INTERNATIONAL HANDBOOK
ON
COMPARATIVE BUSINESS LAW

INTERNATIONAL HANDBOOK ON COMPARATIVE BUSINESS LAW

Edited by

Prof. Dennis Campbell

Director, Center for International Legal Studies,
Salzburg, Austria, and director of European Programs,
University of the Pacific, McGeorge School of Law

1979

SPRINGER-SCIENCE+BUSINESS MEDIA, B.V.

Library of Congress Cataloging in Publication Data
Main entry under title:
International handbook on comparative business law.
Includes index.
1.Commercial law. 2. Business enterprises, Foregn. I. Campbell, Dennis.
K1005.4.I58 346.07 79-16210
ISBN 978-94-017-4401-0 ISBN 978-94-017-4399-0 (eBook)
DOI 10.1007/978-94-017-4399-0

Ursprünglich erschienen bei Kluwer Academic Publishers 1979
Softcover reprint of the hardcover 1st edition 1979

The Center for International Legal Studies is a non-profit and non-stock organization incorporated under the laws of the State of California and with headquarters in Salzburg, Austria. The Center is devoted to the promotion of international legal education, research, information exchange and understanding. It coordinates and supervises various law seminars in Europe and sponsors research in areas of Comparative and International Law.

Inquiries concerning the activities of the Center should be directed to the Center for International Legal Studies, Box 59, A5033 Salzburg, Austria.

THE AUTHORS

Karl Arnold: partner in the firm of Pestalozzi & Gmuer, Zurich, Switzerland; doctor of jurisprudence, University of Fribourg; diplôme de droit comparé, University of Luxembourg; member, Zurich Bar Association, International Bar Association, New York City Bar Association.

Federico Bianchi: Studio Legale Bianchi ed Associati, Milan, Italy; doctor of jurisprudence, Catholic University of Milan; LLM, Harvard Law School; member, Legal Committee, American Chamber of Commerce for Italy; Panel of Arbitrators, American Arbitration Association and Associazione Italiana Arbitrato; member, Italian Bar.

Dennis Campbell: Director, Center for International Legal Studies; director, European Programs, University of the Pacific, McGeorge School of Law; doctor of jurisprudence, University of the Pacific, McGeorge School of Law; graduate diploma in comparative law, Stockholm University; member, Iowa State Bar and International Bar Association; Associate Member, New York State Bar.

Denis Debost: Debost, Borel & Carpentier, Paris, France; LLB, Harvard Law School; licence en droit, University of Paris; member, Association Nationale des Avocats; member, New York State Bar and Paris Bar.

Bodo Haggeney: Gleiss, Lutz, Hootz, Hirsch & Partner, Stuttgart, Federal Republic of Germany; doctor of jurisprudence, University of Cologne; member Stuttgart Bar and International Bar Association.

Sigwart Hübner: Gleiss, Lutz, Hootz, Hirsch & Partner, Stuttgart, Federal Republic of Germany; education, Universities of Bonn and Kiel, Academy for Administrative Science, Speyer, and Berlin Institute of Industrial Management; member, Essen Bar, International Fiscal Association, and Tax Committee of the World Association of Lawyers.

Mads Marstrand-Jørgensen: Holm-Nielsen, Plesner, Holm-Nielsen & Dyekjaer-Hensen, Copenhagen, Denmark; doctor of jurisprudence, University of Copenhagen; assistant professor, Faculty of Law, University of Copenhagen; admitted before the High Court.

Donald Prinz: Member of the faculty, University of the Pacific, McGeorge School of Law; doctor of jurisprudence, University of Michigan Law School; member California State Bar and Nebraska State Bar.

A.H. Puelinckx: Denys & Puelinckx, Brussels, Belgium; doctor of jurisprudence, University of Louvain; master in comparative economic law,

University of Cologne; master in comparative law, University of Chicago School of Law; member, Brussels Bar.

Claude Rohwer: Member of the faculty, University of the Pacific, McGeorge School of Law; doctor of jurisprudence, University of California, Berkeley; Order of the Coif; member, California State Bar.

Henri Swennen: Member of the faculty, University of Antwerp; doctor of jurisprudence, Catholic University of Leuven; doctor of legal science, University of Leuven.

Peter Summerfield: Partner in the firm of Herbert Oppenheimer, Nathan & Vandyk, London, England; MA (Hons.) degree in jurisprudence, Pembroke College, Oxford; qualified as solicitor with honors.

Terry Wittler: Associate, Center for International Legal Studies; doctor of jurisprudence, University of Nebraska College of Law; master in economics, University of Nebraska; member, Nebraska State Bar.

The Editor gratefully acknowledges the assistance of Mr. *Thomas Frame*, Mr. *Keith D. Nunes* and Mr. *Walter Spak*, all interns during 1977 at the Center for International Legal Studies, for their assistance in the preparation of materials upon which the hypothetical case is based.

PREFACE

More than a decade has passed since economist Richard N. Cooper reflected upon the trend toward increasing economic interdependence in the international community:

> During the past decade there has been a strong trend toward economic interdependence among the industrial countries. This growing interdependence makes the successful pursuit of national economic objectives much more difficult. Broadly speaking, increasing interdependence complicates the pursuit of national objectives in three ways. First, it increases the number and magnitude of the disturbances to which each country's balance of payments is subjected, and this in turn diverts policy attention and instruments of policy to the restoration of external balance. Second, it slows down the process by which national authorities, each acting on its own, are able to reach their domestic objectives. Third, the response to greater integration can involve the community of nations in counter-acting motions which leave all countries worse off than they need be ...[1]

Nothing has occured in the 1970s to suggest that Cooper's assessment is inaccurate. Indeed, the process which he identified has accelerated. By the mid-1970s, if one is to mention but one example, exports accounted for twenty per cent of the combined gross national product of the Member States of the European Communities, and exports provided seven per cent of the gross national product of the United States.[2]

Concurrent with the emergence of international economic interdependence—in fact, as a result thereof—legal systems have stepped forward with a process of transnationalization, a movement recognized now by many commentators[3]. In its most telling impact on the legal profession, this linked development of international economic interdependence and the transnationalization of law has resulted in the fact that more enterprises are 'doing business abroad' and involving their domestic lawyers, at the least peripherally, in the complexities of foreign legal systems.

The purpose of this handbook is not to set out a detailed topography of the business law of Belgium, Denmark, England, France, the Federal Republic of Germany, Italy, Switzerland and the United States as each applies to the foreign enterprise. Rather, the intention is to offer a 'core' sample of each of these legal systems as a means of providing a starting point from which the foreign practitioner might attempt a preliminary definition of the legal environment which his client-enterprise seeks to enter.

The authors represent an impressive range of practical legal experience in

1. Cooper, "National Economic Policy in an Interdependent World Economy", 76 *Yale Law Journal* (1967), p. 1273.
2. 80 OECD Observer 19, "The OECD Member Countries", March-April 1976.

their respective countries. To make the most of that experience, it was determined that a two-tier approach to extracting our 'core' samples would be most effective. First, each author has been allowed great latitude in preparing an introductory essay within which he sets out those issues which he believes currently most relevant to the foreign enterprise contemplating entry into his respective domestic market. The breadth of that latitude encompasses the form of the essay as well as its substance, the belief being that the format and approach employed by each author also suggest clues to the nature of the legal system which he represents. Second, each author has been presented a hypothetical case for analysis. These analyses represent a unique opportunity for the practitioner to compare the substantive law of a variety of jurisdictions against a common set of facts molded around the entry and function of a foreign enterprise into a domestic market.

These essays and analyses are prepared under the terms of laws and regulations prevailing in the respective jurisdictions as of July 1979. It has been said that it is the nature of government to create laws and regulations with the inexorability of a rapid and great river. Thus, the December 1978 qualification is a vital one in reference to any particular law or the resolution of any particular issue set out here. However, the essential character of even the swiftest river changes only gradually. Legal systems being of similar nature, it is believed that the essays and analyses contained here will provide a useful basis for examination of the respective jurisdictions.

Dennis Campbell
Salzburg, Austria

3. See, e.g., Macdonald, Morris and Johnston, "The New Lawyer in a Transnational World", 25 *University of Toronto Law Journal* (1975), p. 344; Note, "Foreign Branches of Law Firms: The Development of Lawyers Equipped to Handle International Practice", 80 *Harvard Law Review* (1967), p. 1285.

TABLE OF CONTENTS

INTRODUCTORY CHAPTERS

ANALYSIS OF HYPOTHETICAL CASE

Belgium

A.H. PUELINCKX

HENRI SWENNEN

Introduction

Since the late 1950s, Belgian public policy toward foreign investment has been to welcome and encourage it. There are very good reasons for such a policy. The country is a small one; it has practically (apart from coal) no natural resources and national industry is not, on its own, able to provide for the full employment social policy demands. On the other hand, the country is well-situated within the European Common Market, and it is therefore very attractive to those foreign investors who wish to enter that market.

The Changing Environment for Enterprise

The certain decline which, brought about by the present-day economic crisis, has shown up with regard to investment, and particularly foreign investment, led to increased efforts in governmental action relating to business incentives. In 1977–1978, for example temporary tax provisions permitted depreciation *ad libitum* for specific investments carried out during that period.

But the crisis itself, and the large amount of money needed for helping enterprises in financial difficulties, also led to a reconsidering of the government's industrial policy. The main objectives of the 'new industrial policy', as outlined in the government's 1978 addresses to the Parliament, are as follows:

(a) Continuation of efforts regarding the overall policy and the policy toward separate industrial sectors; the government's industrial policy henceforth also shall aim at specific business areas and business opportunities;

(b) special aid shall be given to small and medium-sized business which was until now somewhat set aside with regard to business incentives;

(c) as to new investments, the government will act as a promoter and a business partner.

In fact, it is felt that the Ministry of Economic Affairs thus far has been merely a ticket office, 'selling' state aids to investors who might show up but leaving it too much up to private enterprise to decide what and where to invest.

Recent legislation has provided the government with the necessary legal instruments for playing a more active role in the national economy. The Law of 30 March 1977, concerning 'the organization of public industrial initiative' has set up the legal framework. The National Investment Company (NIC), which already existed as a semi-public investment bank, has now become the so-called public holding company, the share capital of which will be entirely subscribed by the state. The law provides that the NIC, on its own or in cooperation with other enterprises—either public or private—may take the initiative to found companies and thus create business facilities, if and when the government's economic policy requires it. The address supporting the bill announces initiatives in such areas as energy supply and pipe-lines. It also was announced that a specialized NIC daughter-company will be founded, the object of which shall be to prospect for (foreign) spearhead-technology, patents, and know-how, in order to make it available for licensing to Belgian licensees. Moreover, the bill provides that the NIC shall act in close cooperation with some other government agencies and public financial institutions (including the Regional Investment Companies now to be founded), this cooperation being embodied in a 'Coordination Council'.

It is, of course, too early to judge, but experience in other European countries shows that public enterprises may appear to be good and loyal business partners. The only danger which now appears is that the managers of a public investment company might not be independent enough to resist political pressure and, for the purpose of avoiding politically unacceptable unemployment, might decide to take over out-of-date industries and keep them alive artificially. In fact this is a danger for the public investment company itself. Competitive distortions resulting from such a policy would be prohibited by the European Economic Community (EEC) Treaty provisions concerning state aid. Moreover, European competition law equally applies to both private and public enterprises.

For the government, being in business means having a greater opportunity to take part in the major decisions affecting economic and social structure (for example, the potential development of atomic energy). And this, from that point of view, completes the comprehensive organization of consultation and coordination with private industry and employees' organizations which has been set up since 1945. Consultation, coordination and control are indeed the keywords of much legislation regarding economic and financial policy. Although this concerns first of all the employers' federations, it should be emphasized here that invitations to consult and act in concert with each other reflect the basic attitude of the Belgian government toward private enterprise whenever decisions are to be taken which may affect long-range planning. One might say that in many cases where official authorization to commence business, filing with a government agency or authorization to carry out important business projects is required by law, this is, in fact to be read as an invitation to consult with the government.

This attitude also bears evidence of the government's awareness that carrying on its ambitious social and economic policies is not possible without the cooperation of private enterprise. Therefore, it is merely a matter of course that a 1978 government bill, commonly referred to as the 'crisis-law', apart from provisions relating to the public industrial initiative, also contains provisions which, on the one side, aim to help private industry catching its second breath and, on the other, adjust social security expenditures to what the country now can afford.

As regards relations with the government, one would have to reckon with the regionalization which, as provided by the constitutional reform of 1971 and by the government's program, is to be carried into effect during the next years. Some regionalization already exists. Secretaries of State for each of the three regions handle the economic expansion dossiers. But they are politically responsible to the national Parliament and, though regional bodies advise with regard to relevant aspects of economic policy, legislation concerning regional economic affairs is still to be voted upon in Parliament. Now devolution of powers to institutions representing the cultural (linguistic) communities and the regions must complete this reform. Regional councils will be competent for such matters as, among others, economic expansion and industrial policy. The councils will have some legislative power, and the regions will have a limited financial autonomy.

Matters of national economic interest still will be dealt with at the national level and the Ministry of Economic Affairs' administration has not been divided. Moreover, financial and monetary policy, labor relations and, in some aspects, education are not to be 'regionalized'. Yet the proposed reform must enable each regional executive to carry out its own policy. There are, indeed, significant differences between the two main regions with regard to industrial structure and development and there are different needs to be met. Regional economic policies thus being clearly outlined, direct investment opportunities also will be better profiled.

For many years Belgium has had the reputation of being one of the most open countries for direct foreign investment. Recently, by putting the *Badger* case before the Organization for Economic Cooperation and Development (OECD) Committee, the government has shown its firm will not to make allowances if a multinational corporation, having established itself in the country, does not comply with OECD guidelines.

Entering the Belgian Market

Foreign enterprises wishing to conduct business in Belgium may do so without significant restrictions. As far as authorizations to commence business are required, no distinction is made between foreign and national enterprises.

As regards commercial agency and distribution agreements, the Exclusive Sales Concessionaire Act of 1961 and the Commercial Representative Act of 1961 are to be mentioned. The first act aims at guaranteeing that a reasonable notice or a fair compensation be given to the sales concessionaire (either an individual or a company) when a contract of indeterminate duration is terminated unilaterally by the other party. This notice or compensation is to be agreed upon by the parties at the moment of termination. No notice need be given in the event of serious default of the concessionaire. Not reaching sales quotas reasonably set forth is looked upon by the courts as a serious default. If the contract is terminated for a reason other than a serious fault of the concessionaire or if it is terminated by the concessionaire because of a serious fault of the other party, an additional compensation can be claimed by the concessionaire. The 1961 act related to exclusive dealer contracts of indeterminate duration and regarding products manufactured by the other party. After ten years, new provisions had to be enacted to prevent parties from avoiding the principles of this law by tactics such as subsequent renewal of fixed-term contracts and exclusive dealerships for less than 'all' of the other party's products. Since 1971, the law furthermore applies to concessionaire contracts the termination of which would cause serious losses to the concessionaire, due to important obligations which had been imposed upon him and which were strictly and specially connected with the 'concession'. The act also provides that, notwithstanding any competence-of-court clause, the concessionaire always may sue before a Belgian court, which must apply this compulsory legislation. (It should be noted, however, that, as far as contracts between EEC nationals are concerned, the provisions of the EEC Convention relating to competence-of-court and execution-of-court decisions apply.)

The second act deals with 'commercial representative' contracts. Like a 'commercial agent', a so-called 'commercial representative' has powers of representation, acting in the name and on behalf of a principal. The difference is that an agent is engaged in an independent activity whereas a commercial representative is an employee, soliciting orders from prospective customers by calling on them at the time and in the manner determined by his employer. The main purpose of the 1963 act was to provide a legal presumption that a representative is an employee unless it is proved by the principal that he is not. It may be noted that this presumption, as it is a part of labor relations law, can apply only to individuals.

Foreign enterprises wishing to establish in Belgium may open a Belgian branch, found a Belgian company or seek acquisition of such a company. When opening a branch, which is not a separate legal entity, the foreign company must comply with the company-law provisions regarding 'publicity'. A certified copy of its instrument of incorporation, its articles of association, the decision to open the branch and, furthermore, all decisions relating to delegation of powers to the Belgian branch managing director(s), and the annual accounts must be deposited in the company's file at the Commercial Court's Register. Most of these documents, in whole or in part, shall be published in the Annexes to the official gazette.

When founding a Belgian subsidiary, foreign enterprises in most cases prefer the form of the joint-stock company. This company can be formed either directly by the founding shareholders (at least seven) or by way of public subscription. In fact, the first method is generally adopted, the second being rather complicated. If the shares are to be offered to the general public, this can be done after incorporation, usually by a group of banks who act as an underwriting syndicate. The capital of the joint-stock company, at least Belgian Francs 1,250,000, must be subscribed upon incorporation and the shares representing that capital must be paid up at not less than twenty per cent. The company is managed by a board of directors, acting jointly; the day-to-day management may be entrusted to one or more managers, acting jointly or severally according to the provisions of the company's statutes. The powers of these management 'organs' are specified in the company law. Limitations of powers, arising under the company's statutes, cannot be relied upon against third parties even if these provisions have been disclosed. A company, however, can make special agreements with third persons (a bank) concerning representation powers of its directors.

Prior to the public issuance of securities (also prior to an admission to official stock exchange quotation and prior to a public exchange or purchase offer), a prospectus checked by the Banking Control Commission must be published. The Banking Control Commission was created (1935) to control banking activities and to ensure that correct information is given in the course of a public issue of securities. The Commission will see to it that the public is not misled about the nature of the operation and the rights attaching to the securities. The Commission has the power to postpone the operation for three months if the issuers do not comply with its recommendations. In fact, these recommendations not only deal with correct information but also refer to principles of financial ethics not expressly set forth in the company law (such as the shareholders' right of pre-emption in the course of an increase in subscribed capital).

A foreign company seeking acquisition of a Belgian company, the shares of which are held by the general public, may need the authorization of the Minister of Finance. Such authorization is required for a public exchange or purchase offer with respect to Belgian securities by or for the account of non-EEC nationals. Two other rules regarding acquisitions apply to both national and foreign enterprises. First, prior to every operation involving the transfer of shares representing one third or more of the capital of a Belgian company, the shareholders' equity of which amounts to one hundred million Belgian Francs or more, information must be given to the Ministers of Finance, Economic Affairs and Regional Economic Affairs. Second, there is a recommendation practice of the Banking Control Commission regarding so-called 'private transfers' of a package of shares offering to the holder the opportunity to control a company, the shares of which are held by the general public. The conditions of such transfer may not contravene the principles of equality of all shareholders.

A major reform of the company law is to be carried out during the next years. New provisions will have to be enacted following the EEC directives concerning the harmonization of national laws with regard to mergers and take-overs, the structure of the joint-stock company and prospectuses. In addition, a draft of a new company law has been prepared and is to be considered in Parliament. The draft bill aims at adjusting the legal provisions to the needs of modern business and finance. As an example, it may be mentioned here that a new type of company, the company with variable capital, will be provided for, thus offering a suitable form for organizing multilateral business cooperation. Furthermore, the private limited-liability company, which now is looked upon as the small business' organization (only individuals can be share holders and the shares are not freely transferable) will be converted into an attractive company form for those companies the shares of which are not to be offered to the general public.

Investment incentives, which may be granted to both national and foreign enterprises (either existing or newly established) are provided for by the Economic Expansion Acts of 1959 and 1970. The 1970 act, known as the Regional Expansion Act, provides for two types of state aid: regional aid and additional regional aid. Advantages available as regional aid are interest-rate rebates on loans contracted to carry out investments, state guarantee to back the repayment of such loans, cash grants, employment grants and various tax benefits. These advantages may be granted when investments are carried out in so-called development areas. Additional aid, consisting of additional advantages of the same type, such as additional interest-rate rebates, may be given when warranted by the general economic circumstances. Apart from these incentives, the 1970 act provides for 'contractual planning'. This means that state aid may be granted to an enterprise which, in return, binds itself to fulfill certain obligations implementing targets of the National Five Year Economic Plans. The types of contracts are as follows: progress contracts (covering a long-range development program), management promotion contracts, technological promotion contracts and reorganization contracts.

The 1959 act, known as the General Expansion Act, while regarding investments anywhere in the country, provides for almost the same types of advantages as are mentioned above. Other advantages are: state aid for vocational training, such as cash grants covering part of the remuneration of foreign instructors; assistance of the National Employment Agency with regard to selection and training of personnel, and, last but not least, the infrastructure offered by the government and the local authorities.

As regards the selection of investment projects for which state aid may be granted, priority now is given to:

(a) Investments leading to savings in energy consumption;

(b) Non-material investments (acquisition of know-how, market studies, improvement of management methods), and

(c) Investments leading to new employment.

Labor Relations Aspects

Collective bargaining, 'social peace' and protective legislation are the main features of Belgian Labor Relations Law. Collective labor contracts, agreed upon between the representatives of employers and trade unions in the National Labor Council or, at the sectoral level in the Joint Representatives Committees, can be converted into compulsory provisions and, in the hierarchy of sources of labor law, such contracts come second to the legislation itself, which may supercede the written individual labor contracts.

Usually, these collective agreements provide for so-called social peace, the avoidance of strikes, and the settlement of disputes. This system has proved to be efficient. The major reasons are the high rate of trade union membership and the fact that the three unions present a common front in negotiations with the employers. The employers' acknowledgment of the stability that is brought about by trade-unionism has taken, in some industrial sectors, the form of so-called advantages for trade union members, meaning that the employer pays the employees' contributions to the trade unions.

Another important factor making for stability in industrial relations is the automatic and continuous adjustment of wages and salaries to the cost of living through 'indexation', the linkage between wages and salaries on the one side and the consumer price index on the other.

Protective legislation deals with such matters as hours of work, trial period, and termination of contracts. Except in the event of a serious fault of the other party, contracts of indeterminate duration cannot be terminated unilaterally without giving notice or fair compensation.

In July 1978, a new Labor Contracts Act was voted upon in Parliament. Two major innovations are to be mentioned. First, the new act provides that essential changes in labor conditions are to be agreed upon by both parties. Second, new provisions are enacted with respect to duration, 'places' and functions which such clauses (to be in writing) may cover. A separate provision, however, regards non-competition clauses 'imposed upon' an employee of an enterprise operating in the international market or an enterprise having its own research department. If the employee has special knowledge about the company's business, and if the use of this knowledge outside the enterprise may cause damages to the employer, the specific limitations mentioned above do not apply.

The Belgian social security system covers health care insurance, sickness and disability insurance, pensions and prepension schemes, family allowances, unemployment benefits and holiday benefits. For historical reasons, work-accident risks are not included in the social security system; such risks must be covered by the employer through policies with authorized insurance companies. The social security system is financed by employer's and employees' contributions. Eventual deficiencies are made up by state subsidies.

Tax Considerations

The basic rate of Belgian corporation tax is fixed at forty-eight per cent. A reduced rate, thirty-three per cent or forty per cent, is applied when the company's taxable income does not exceed one million Belgian Francs. It must be noted here that income tax is to be paid in advance. If such prepayments fail to be made, a penalty will be due. This may lead to a surcharge rate of maximum 20.25 per cent.

Taxable income consists of distributed and retained profits, non-allowable expenses, such as abnormal or benevolent advantages granted to a foreign company belonging to the same group, and remuneration of directors. Remuneration of executive directors, exercising real and permanent functions, are allowable expenses in so far as these remunerations exceed bonuses paid to non-executive directors. Dividends received from other companies (Belgian or foreign) and paid out with respect to shares the receiving company has held throughout the period of assessment are excluded from taxable income to the amount of ninety five per cent (ninety per cent when the receiving company's portfolio investments exceed fifty per cent of the shareholders' equity) of the dividends received. Dividends paid out by a Belgian company and interest payments on bonds are subject to a withholding tax of twenty per cent.

Commenting on details of tax legislation is rather hazardous because of the rapid change in this field of the law. Yet especially in this field details are the best indicators with respect to the legal climate. Therefore the following recent provisions, enacted in 1976, 1977 and July 1978 ('crisis law') may be mentioned. To promote the improvement of the financial structure of enterprises, the law provides that profits distributed to shares issued against capital brought in (in cash) in 1979 are, for five years, excluded from taxable income in so far as the distributed profits do not exceed five per cent of the capital paid up with respect to these shares.

To encourage additional investments, an amount equal to fifteen per cent of additional investments carried out (in Belgium) during the 1977 and 1978 periods of assessment also is excluded from taxable income. For the purpose of computing this amount, investments with respect to scientific research are multiplied by a factor of 1.5. Furthermore, capital gains (most of which are already tax immune) are excluded from taxable profits when reinvested in new, fixed assets contributing to the creation of new activities or employment. Interest payments on loans contracted abroad by Belgian companies to finance operations which are considered to be of national economic interest are exempted from the withholding tax (if these loans are not represented by bearer certificates).

Denmark

MADS MARSTRAND-JØRGENSEN

Introduction

The foreign enterprise entering the Danish market immediately encounters basic elements of Danish legal and commercial life—those dealing with formation of contracts, commercial representation, structure and function of companies, negotiable instruments and taxation. It is these elements which are emphasized in the following commentary.

Entering into Contracts

Most contracts of interest are regulated under Act No. 242 of 8 May 1917 on 'Contracts and other legal transactions within the scope of Property Law'. On most points, the law is uniform in Denmark, Norway and Sweden. In general, no formal requirements are attached to the formulation of contracts; however, in exceptional cases, for instance with respect to negotiable instruments and contracts for the formation of companies, certain requirements must be met.

An offer—a promise—is binding as soon as it has come to the knowledge of the recipient of the promise. Thus, the promise may be revoked up to that time, provided that such withdrawal is notified to the addressee before he has knowledge of the offer. It is not a general condition that the promise be accepted, but in many cases an acceptance is required. This applies, for instance, to oral promises and in cases where the recipient must produce something in return (as for instance an ordinary purchase).

The offeror is free to fix a time-limit within which the acceptance shall be given. If no time-limit has been fixed, the offeree must accept without undue delay, provided the promise calls for acceptance. In the absence of such acceptance, the offer lapses and no contract has been made. If the acceptance is advanced too late or contains reservations or amendments, no agreement has been established, but the 'acceptance' is considered a new offer to be subsequently accepted.

In Denmark, contracts for the benefit of a stranger are fully recognized, so that a third person may directly acquire a right from a contract between two other persons.

The Contract Law contains several Provisions aimed at protecting a weaker party against exploitation. These provisions will not be commented upon here. However, it is of interest that the rules aimed at regulating *penalty* clauses quite recently were changed to the effect that the courts may set aside or amend clauses which are deemed unconscionable, especially for the weaker contractual partner.

The conditions pertaining to marketing have been amended of late, and certain rules have been introduced with a view to protecting the consumer, through such devices as obligatory price labelling and prohibition of certain guarantee clauses. Furthermore, a special administrative institution has been introduced, 'the consumer ombudsman' who is in charge of the general lines applicable to relations between tradesmen and consumers. It may be anticipated that administrative and law-court practice will bring about material changes in this field.

Commercial Agency

Under Danish law, different types of Commercial Agency are recognized, ranging from commission agents, who perform transactions in their own names but on the account of someone else, to commercial representatives, being agents or employees. The conditions of commission agents and commercial representatives are regulated under Act Number 243 of 8 May 1917, which is also a common Scandinavian law.

The commission agent must comply with the instructions of the principal insofar as it is possible and shall, if no opportunity is available to procure instruction from the principal, act fairly and reasonably in representing the interests of the principal. The commission agent is entitled to a commission from the transactions concluded by him, but normally the commission is dependent on the factual implementation of the transaction (Article 27).

The principal has the right to dismiss the commission agent, but if the commission agent has been promised to have the object in commission a certain time, or if he has been authorized to conclude a certain transaction, he has a right to compensation for the loss inflicted on him (article 50). The principal is bound by the transactions concluded by the commission agent, even if the commission agent acts outside the orders given to him (unless of course, the purchaser knew of these orders). Furthermore, payment to the commission agent fulfills the purchaser's obligation, unless he has been notified to pay the principal directly. The purchaser obtains protection against the creditors of the principal from the conclusion of the purchase contract. It is not permissible for the commission agent to personally join the transaction unless there is a special agreement to that effect (article 40).

A commercial representative is an individual who, on behalf of another person, has contracted to negotiate the sale of goods, by taking purchase-offers (orders) to the principal, or to sell goods on his behalf, and who is *not* an employee of the principal but practises as an independent trader having either an office or other premises of his own. The commercial representative must safeguard the interests of the principal and incurs liability for damages if he disregards his obligations. If the principal wishes to claim damages, he must advance a claim in this respect forthwith.

The commercial representative has a right to commission from the sales concluded by him, but it is a condition that the purchaser fulfils the contract, the commission being thus entirely dependent on the purchaser's payment. However, the commercial representative is entitled to commission, if the non-fulfillment of the transaction may be ascribed to the principal. The commercial representative is entitled to a special reimbursement for expenses such as postage, telephone and telegrams unless it is expressly agreed that the commission agent shall cover such expenses.

In general, the representation may be terminated freely as no rules as to damages are to be observed. If, however, it is agreed that the representative holds the representation for a definite period and notice is given within that period, the representative does have a claim for damages. In quite exceptional situations, the courts also have granted damages in cases regardless of the lack of a definite term of notice.

For quite some time broader protection of the representative against termination, similar to the practice existing in several other European countries, has been contemplated, but so far no concrete bill to that effect has been introduced.

The representative, without having an express authorization cannot conclude binding contracts on behalf of the principal.

In the event that the representative has reported to the principal on a sale and the principal refuses to approve the sale, the principal, however, shall immediately notify the purchaser to that effect. In the absence of such notification, the principal is bound by the contract. The representative is not entitled to receive payment or to negotiate amendments of the contract unless a separate authorization has been given.

Companies

In 1973, the legislation in this field was materially amended and modernized, partly because of the Danish membership in the European Economic Community (EEC). Whereas the form of the limited company 'A/S' was previously the only form known, there are now two possibilities. On one hand there is the limited company (A/S), which typically operates with considerable capital and a greater number of shareholders; on the other hand there is the private company 'ApS', a typical feature of which is that the contributed capital and the number of participants is smaller. These two types of companies are the most important and common in Denmark when the participants do not want to be personally liable for the obligations of the company. However, there are a few other types of companies of some significance in Denmark, among them the cooperative society.

For the limited company (A/S), the minimum share capital is one-hundred-thousand Danish kroner to be proportioned among at least three shares. There is no special requirement as to nationality of the shareholders. It may be anticipated that the minimum share capital, following an EEC directive, will be increased within the near future. It is a requirement that the company be engaged in commerce or industry. At least three promoters are required for the formation. Until the company is publicly registered, they personally are liable for the obligations of the company. At least two promoters must have their residence in Denmark. However, this requirement often is dispensed with as far as citizens of the Member States of the EEC are involved.

The formation takes place by the promoters signing a formation document containing certain information, as specifically enumerated in the act. If the capital of the company is produced other than by contribution in cash, an exact account shall be given of the facts relevant for the assessment of value.

A notification of registration of the company shall be filed with the Companies Register within six months after formation. Before such notification, at least half of the capital and at least a total of one-hundred-thousand Danish kroner must be paid in full. Furthermore, shares subscribed at the formation shall be paid in full at the latest one year after the registration of the company. Shares without par value are not allowed. The shares are freely megotiable, but the negotiability may be restricted by a special resolution.

The capital in registered companies may be increased either by subscription of new shares or by transfer of the reserves of the company to share capital. Such emission of 'free' shares (representing capital transferred to stated capital) can be effected by transferring to the share capital such earnings which lawfully may be paid out as dividend (typically a part of the net profit of the year), by writing up assets, the value of which is materially higher than the amount with which they figure in the balance, or by transfer from the statutory reserves. It is prohibited for a company to acquire its own shares in excess of ten per cent of the subscribed share capital, and the same applies to acquisitions as security.

The company must have a board of directors of at least three members. If the share capital is below four-hundred-thousand Danish kroner, one or two members may suffice, provided, however, that at least one substitute director be elected. If, during the last three years, the company has employed at least fifty employees, the latter are entitled to elect two additional members for the board of directors (and substitute directors for these two members). At least half of the members of the board of directors must have their residence in Denmark. Also in this respect, certain exemptions apply to citizens from the Member States of the EEC. The same requirement applies to managers.

In companies having a share capital of four-hundred-thousand Danish kroner, or more, the board of directors must engage a board of management consisting of one or more members. In these companies, it also it obligatory that the majority of the members of the board consists of persons who are not general managers of the company. If the share capital is below four-hundred-thousand Danish kroner, there is no necessity of engaging a manager. The manager cannot be the chairman of the board of directors.

The supreme authority in the companies lies with the general meeting. All shareholders have a right to attend this meeting and speak there. At the meeting, the shareholders may vote according to the rules laid down in the articles of association of the company. The share provides a right to vote, but the articles of association may provide that the voting value of certain shares be increased up to ten times the voting value of any other share. The general meeting shall be held at the registered office of the company within six months after the end of each accounting year. The act contains strictly specified rules applying to the conduct of the general meeting, to voting rules, and to protection of minorities.

One or more auditors must be elected at the general meeting. At least one of the auditors must be a resident of Denmark, but to the extent this requirement is contrary to EEC rules there may be deviation. It is a requirement that the auditor be a state-authorized public accountant or a registered accountant. If the shares of the company are quoted on the recognized stock exchange, additional requirements apply. Persons having too close a connection to the company cannot be elected auditors. The requirements regarding the set-up of the accounts are specified in detailed rules. The accounts shall be filed with the Companies Register and are to a wide extent accessible to the public in the Register.

For the Private Company (Aps) the minimum capital shall be thirty-thousand Danish kroner which need not be divided in parts. Generally speaking, similar rules apply to private companies as to limited companies; however, the rules with respect to the board of directors and audit, for example, have been modified on several points in recognition of the fact that the private company typically will be a closely-held enterprise of limited economic extent.

Negotiable Instruments

The following will comment on the rules applying to negotiable instruments under Law Number 146 of 13 April 1938 on instruments of debt. In all material aspects, the said law is common throughout Scandinavia. The law does not comprise the rules applicable to bills of exchange and checks, which rules need not be commented on in this context as they largely follow the international system. The rules to be commented upon apply only directly to the so-called instruments of debt, such as a declaration in writing evidencing mainly unconditional unilateral promises to pay a certain amount. However, the rules apply to a wide extent analogically to, for instance, shares with respect to which no limitations as to transferability have been made.

A special type of document encompassed by the rules is the so-called bond which is closely connected with the peculiar Danish system of credit secured by mortgage on real property.

The rules on negotiable instruments apply to an instrument of debt if it—in addition to being an instrument of debt—is either:

(a) an instrument of debt payable to the bearer or not indicating to whom the debt shall be paid; or

(b) an instrument of debt payable to a definite person *or order* (i.e. an explicit order clause must be stated); or

(c) an instrument of debt secured by mortgage on real property, or registered ship or aircraft (unless the instrument of debt contains a clear reservation); or

(d) an instrument of debt payable to a definite person, when it states unambiguously that it shall be a negotiable instrument.

The fact that an instrument of debt can be grouped under the rules applicable to negotiable instruments has three very material effects:

(a) The issuer forfeits a series of defenses against a holder in due course, i.e. an assignee in good faith, who takes the instrument for value.

(b) A holder in due course sometimes may acquire right, although the assignor was not rightful holder of the instrument of debt or was not of age.

(c) Special rules are applicable in respect of to whom the debtor may or shall direct payment.

It is privided in Article 15 that the issuer of a negotiable instrument of debt cannot set forth against the holder in due course the following defenses:

(a) that the instrument of debt was void according to the law applicable to void contracts;

(b) that the instrument of debt after signature was issued without the intention of the issuer;

(c) that the issuer has not received the payment as agreed or that he has other objections relating to the original legal relationship between the issuer and the first creditor;

(d) that payment had been effected, or that the indebtedness was settled or had been changed, except for such instances, where the issuer has clearly stated his objection on the document itself, even if the endorsement is later removed.

Of course, the issuer always may set forth the defense that the instrument of debt was false, forced by violence, issued in minority, or lacking sense.

As to the acquisition of right by the holder in due course, this applies even if the assignor has appropriated the instrument of debt by theft, compulsion, forgery or the like, but it is of course conditioned upon the assignee being in good faith. He must make such investigations with respect to seller's right as might reasonably be expected in the factual situation.

As regards payment, it is provided that the debtor may pay interest which has fallen due, and sometimes installments, to the assignor unless debtor knew that the assignor no longer held any right to receive payment. By payment of extraordinary installments, debtor, to be protected, must provide for an endorsement on the document itself; at the redemption, the debtor must require that the document be handed over to him duly signed.

A special set of rules applies to passbooks.

Tax Liability for Persons

The fundamental basis of Danish tax is that the total global annual income of the payer is included in the statement of income. A series of bilateral conventions has been concluded with a view to avoiding double taxation.

Unlimited tax liability applies to persons having a permanent residence in Denmark. In deciding this question, it is taken into account whether the individual by establishing a household, renting a residence or by other measures has shown his intention of residing in Denmark. Furthermore, such tax liability applies to individuals who have resided in Denmark within the last four years, unless they prove that they are subject to ordinary taxation in a foreign state. It is also a condition that the previous residence in Denmark has extended over a period of at least four years. Unlimited tax liability applies, furthermore, to individuals who stay in Denmark during a period of at least six months without having, however, a residence in Denmark. The six months must be consecutive, with the exception, however, that short stays abroad owing to holidays or the like are disregarded. Certain exemptions apply to tourists and students. Finally unlimited tax liability applies to state-employees sent abroad, to Danish citizens on Danish ships and to estates administered in Denmark.

Limited tax liability applies to non-resident individuals obtaining an income from Denmark paid by a person who is under an obligation to withhold tax (pay-as-you-earn-system) on that payment, provided that the income arises from activity in Denmark. The main criterion as to whether tax-withholding is obligatory is whether the income is payment for personal work in a contract for employment. This is especially deemed to be the case if the employer has instructional authority vis-à-vis the employee. Furthermore, it is a condition that the employer has venue in Denmark.

Limited tax liability also is relevant with respect to income from Denmark in the form of remuneration for membership on boards of directors, committees, commissions and the like, and pensions.

Limited tax liability also applies to income from business activities attributable to a permanent establishment in Denmark. Whether such a permanent establishment exits is a question which gives rise to difficulties. After the publication of Organization for Economic Cooperation and Development (OECD)'s model tax convention, it may be anticipated that the Danish authorities' decisions on this issue will be influenced by article 5 of the model convention. Firstly, a certain extent of the exercise of economic activity in Denmark is a prerequisite for using the provisions. Thus, ordinary agencies are not encompassed. Secondly, an establishment for business purposes in Denmark is required. Information offices, research departments, purchase offices and the like are not considered permanent establishments. It is doubtful whether service departments and delivery stores are encompassed by the rules, but the criterion is apparently how independent the character of the department is. Thirdly, a certain kind of permanent relationship to Denmark is required. It is not possible in these comments to state the exact temporal condition.

Rules are laid down to the effect that companies are obligated to withhold dividend taxes corresponding to thirty per cent of the dividend paid. The tax is the final tax for individuals with limited tax liability.

Income arising from real estate in Denmark is subject to limited tax liability.

Other capital gains are typically not taxable income for the individuals mentioned in this section. Thus, profit arising from sale of shares is exempt, and the same applies to interest. Furthermore, the same applies to royalties, license fees and the like (unless there is a permanent establishment in Denmark).

Presently, consideration is being given to changing the taxation of interest so that a system is introduced corresponding to the system applicable to dividends from shares.

Tax Liability for Companies

Tax liability under the law on taxable income for limited companies applies to the following companies domiciled in Denmark:

(*a*) Registered limited and private companies. The decisive point in this respect is the actual entry in the Companies Register. The tax rate is thirty-seven per cent.

(*b*) Other companies, in which none of the participants personally are liable for the obligations of the company and who share the profit proportionally to the capital subscribed in the company by the participants. The rules apply to companies not registered but having the same structure, as for instance cooperative societies with limited responsibility and foreign limited companies with headquarters in Denmark. The tax rate is thirty-seven per cent.

(*c*) Cooperative associations with the object of purchasing, procuring or producing goods or to deliver services, fully or partly, for the private use of the members, and who—apart from normal payment of interest from a subscribed share capital—use the turnover with the members as basis for distribution of profits to the members. The tax rate is thirty-seven per cent.

(*d*) Purchase associations, Cooperative production associations, and sales organizations. The income for these organizations is assessed at four or six per cent of the capital, dependent on the proportion of the turnover with members and nonmembers. In distinguishing these companies from those enumerated earlier, the decisive criterion is whether the members exclusively use the goods commercially.

(*c*) Mutual insurance associations which also take over insurance without obligation to participation in the mutual responsibility, and other associations, corporations, institutions, foundations and private foundations *insofar as income from trade or industry is concerned.* The tax rate is thirty-seven per cent, but as the tax liability applies only to income from trade and industry, the taxation is easier than for instance for limited companies. Quite recently, it has been contemplated to subject this category to a higher degree of public control and possibly to a certain form of taxation. It is not possible at the present moment to provide precise details.

As mentioned initially the tax liability applies only to companies domiciled in Denmark. However, it is provided that companies and associations of the nature mentioned above in items (a) and (b), which are domiciled abroad, are subject to taxation in Denmark, if they:

(*a*) exercise trade and industry from a permanent establishment in Denmark or participate in an enterprise with permanent establishment in Denmark or are otherwise entitled to a share of the profit from such an enterprise. In this connection, reference also is made to the interpretation of the words 'permanent establishment' given in several double-taxation conventions.

(*b*) by virtue of being owner, joint owner, user or recipient of income obtain income from real estate situated in this country.

(*c*) receive dividends subject to withholding of dividend tax.

England

PETER SUMMERFIELD

Introduction

The movement toward re-unification of mercantile laws and practices at an international level is engendered by an enormous waste of economic resources involved in proliferation of transactions across national, legal and customary barriers. Even the marked 'dualist' orientation of Britain's stance at international law is forced to recognize the erosion of national sovereignty which participation in multilateral organizations entails. Yet the contractual role of international convention and treaty is no more than a palliative compared with that to be played by emergent supranational bodies, of which the European Economic Communities (EEC) are the most significant.

The EEC is a body '*sui generis*' characterized at present by both the closeness of the union and its restriction to the economic field, resembling nothing so much as a kind of 'thin federation'. The establishment of a common market across national barriers, through the 'four freedoms' of movement, establishment, services and goods and the antitrust provisions of articles 85 and 86 of the Rome Treaty, has general importance for the investor[2]. Its significance goes far beyond immediate structures, however, to the laws of Member States themselves. The 'approximation' of laws of Member States to the extent required for the proper functioning of the Common Market is manifested at a number of points throughout the constitutive treaties[3]. Their most spectacular achievement to date is undoubtedly the harmonization of company laws[4]. Hardly less impressive is the role of the Communities in the conclusion of conventions relating to patents and industrial property[5]. Legislation relating to consumer protection is in prospect.

The mood of critical self-analysis characterizing British society in recent years can be described as a search for new social values commensurate with a long-term reorientation in international affairs. The period of fairly intense legal adjustment which accession to the EEC inevitably has involved is perhaps typified in the problems of enacting legislation to abolish the external form of the corporate *ultra vires* doctrine, commensurate with the First Directive on the Harmonisation of Company Law[6]. Her pragmatic scepticism toward the EEC can be expected to find satisfaction in the realization of her potential role in its development and the consumer benefits which this holds out[7].

Yet, conflicts consequent upon existing divisions between legal systems persist. The cautious liberalism of the English approach is characterized by a 'double *renvoi*' doctrine designed to minimize application of the *lex fori*, where, in the eyes of the English court, some reluctant foreign system of law would have greater relevance. The basic choice-of-law rule has relevance to the foreign investor in two main areas, the law governing status of a corporation and that governing the substance of a contract. With regard to the former, domicile, rather than nationality, is the operative factor. Accordingly, the status of a company as a 'foreign' or 'domestic' enterprise is determinable by its place of incorporation, in sharp contrast to the Continental 'center of management' principle[8]. For purposes of taxation and exchange control, however, its place of residence, determinable by the place or places of its actual control is operative[9]. The choice-of-law principle in contract, expounded by the House of Lords in the *Regla Warehouses Case*[10] continues to move toward application of a 'proper law', which, subject to party autonomy, genuinely reflects the 'closest and most real connection' with contractual circumstance. Illustration is to be found in a recent decision[11] to the effect that, subject to express agreement, the proper law applicable to a commercial letter of credit was not necessarily that of the issuing bank, but that which had the closest and most real connection with the transaction generally. Consequently, although issued by a Spanish bank, a credit opened through a New York bank, payable in United States dollars, against documents presented in New York, should be governed by New York law. It also might be noted in passing that the ailing Uniform Laws on International Sales are operative in English law only as a designated proper law[12].

The recent development most significant to the would-be investor, however, involved a remarkable judicial *volte face* away from the principle, also expounded in the *Regla Warehouses Case*[13], of rendering judgments only in sterling. The recent finding of the Court of Appeal[14] on a statement of account in German Deutschmarks, that national courts of EEC Member States were required to pronounce judgment in the currency of the debtor, has been criticized by the House of Lords for its direct application of Article 106 of the Rome Treaty[15]. The principle was found to be valid, nevertheless, insofar as it would authorize judgment on a contract valid by a Swiss proper law to be expressed in Swiss francs as the designated money of account. This departure from earlier principle already has been followed widely[16]. The Court of Appeal, moreover, has gone further[17] so as to include contracts governed by an English proper law where a foreign currency is given as the money of account. Whether this is susceptible of greater extension is open to doubt. It seems unlikely that the courts will allow a party autonomy circumscribed with regard to the choice of law to find greater freedom in the context of the national currency in which judgment on such law was to be expressed.

Development of Business Law

In an age of corporate multinationalism, foreign investment is a complex, extending through the entire body of business law. Reduced to its essence, the concept involves abrogation of international trading relationships by a partial or complete shifting of the productive base forward into the recipient country. Its main ramifications can be traced through the three essential stages of production, marketing and profit.

If the invention of corporate enterprise was the strength of the Industrial Revolution in England, its subsequent failure to recognize the contribution of labor is the weakness of its technological counterpart. English law recognizes several forms of business organization. Companies limited by shares can be divided into private and public companies, the latter being unquoted or quoted on a stock exchange. Differences between the English and German or French formal styles in this context have led to amendment of the EEC Draft Second Directive to accommodate British requirements.

The current need for recognition of the corporate group as an entity in its own right is becoming especially pressing in relation to the syndicate, the joint venture and the consortium in such contexts as banking, shipping or mineral exploitation. Although such recognition is well established in the field of public law relating to monopolies[18], there is as yet all too little sign of this affecting private law regulation of companies. English and, indeed, German law, unlike the French system, seem content to await the EEC's provision of specific vehicles for concerted enterprise in the form of the European Company (*Societas Europa*) and the European Commercial Group. The Companies Acts 1948 and 1967 give limited specific recognition to the corporate group, in the holding and subsidiary context and in the lesser interconnected relationship[19], whilst myopic judicial peering into the veiled associate mysteries has largely taken place in the context of conglomerate enterprise[20]. Thus, a decision of Mr. Justice Pennycuick some years ago[21] went so far as to suggest that construction of the corporate objects might, in a suitable case, take account of the purposes of the group as a whole. Despite recent hesitations[22], the trend can be expected to continue, not perhaps without some influence from the essentially more flexible civilian laws.

Increasingly complex forms taken by foreign investment in Britain might involve trade by a foreign company subject to Part X of the Companies Act 1948 or the grant of an exclusive manufacturing and dealing license to an otherwise unconnected English company. More frequently, between such extremes, joint ventures identify the wholly-owned subsidiary or the minority shareholding, embellished as necessary by interlocking directorates, profit sharing agreements and the like. Moreover, a loan-based investment often can be coupled with rights to nominate a proportion of the management.

Legal regulation of corporate investment has been a major concern of the legislator for the past century. Designed essentially around the interests of middle class private investors currently in the process of being displaced by institutional investors representing the interests of sectional groups[23], the law is ready for reform.

The characteristically English system of authorized nominal capital for issue piecemeal equates potential liability with the difference between nominal and paid-up capital. The liability of each shareholder remains primary up to the disposal of his holding, but with respect to existing debts continues as a secondary liability for an additional year. Although English law never has recognized a minimum capital, this is likely to be introduced through anticipated legislation of provisions in the EEC draft Second Directive[24] requiring a minimum capital for all public limited companies paid up to at least twenty five per cent. A concommittant requirement for private companies would be unfortunate in an English context which places far greater emphasis than the Continental on the private form of company.

Maintenance of capital, likewise, differs in detail from the archetypal civilian model. Shares may be subscribed for freely[25] except, as suggesting an unreceived financial investment, by the company itself, its subsidiary, or, it would seem, by anyone financing them. Recent decisions on the so-called 'circular check' transactions[26] underline the likelihood of strengthening legislation[27].

Shares may be issued for subscription in cash or in kind. In the case of international investment especially, the issue of shares against investment of industrial property licenses or business contracts is common. Less rigid than many civilian systems, in this respect, English law demands only honest rather than a diligent estimate of the property's value by directors[28]. Proposed legislation giving effect to articles 8, 15 and 17 of the EEC Second Draft Directive on the maintenance of capital requires, *inter alia*, an independent valuation of property taken as payment for shares.

At the same time, the traditional English reliance on risk capital can be expected to abate in favor of a Continental style loan-capital influence, manifested as a further blurring of the distinction between shares and debentures[29].

Subscribers loan capital can be secured directly or indirectly on corporate assets. A characteristic invention of English law in this field is the floating charge designed to allow the company to deal with property charged. Its real nature is *sui generis*, a sort of cross between a present charge, subject to a license to deal, and a mortgage of future assets. Priority of the debt secured is subject to validity of the charge's registration, perhaps, it would seem, where appropriate, retrospectively[30].

The issuance of securities is subject to stringent regulation under the Companies Acts and the Prevention of Fraud (Investments) Act 1956, requiring, *inter alia*, the concurrent issue of a prospectus or statement in lieu thereof conforming with the disclosure requirements of Schedules IV and V of the Companies Act 1948. Statutory penalties for false statements made expressly or by implication are supplemented by the Misrepresentation Act 1967 and the common law torts of fraudulent or negligent mis-statement[31]. Future implementation of the unnamed EEC draft Directive of 1972 on prospectuses would involve several changes of which statutory recognition of the Stock Exchange, its Council, or Quotations Department would be one.

Dealing in corporate securities is a rapidly growing field characterized by the supplementation of the Stock Transfer Act 1963 and the Stock Exchange (Completion of Bargains) Act 1976[32] by the quasi-legal provisions of the Stock Exchange Regulations, the Licensed Dealers Rules and the City Code on Takeovers and Mergers. Developing practices involving takeover bids have led to increasing pressure for introduction of a statutory element into the existing customary machinery. Although it is unlikely to adopt more than minor features of United States securities regulation system this inevitably must make the practice of 'insider trading' a criminal offense in the future[33].

Foreign investors seeking to raise capital locally should be aware that the issuance of bearer shares, unlike debentures, must be in the form of a warrant requiring Treasury permission. For practical purposes, an issue of foreign-bearer securities is covered by non-negotiable share-deposit receipts payable to bearer. Moreover, the practice of takeover bids in conjunction with City institutions offers the foreign investor an opportunity of acquiring an existing business indirectly. In such a situation the EEC Draft Third Directive on internal mergers would require reform of the law applicable to any ensuing rationalization, where this involved universal transfer of business from the absorbed to the absorbing enterprise.

Recent ratification of the Patents Cooperation Treaty, European Patents Convention and Community Patents Convention must be seen as a major, if slightly confusing, step toward the creation of a comprehensive European patent. Together with the Banks Report of 1920, these form the background to the English Patents Act 1977. During a transitional period, extending for over a decade, there will be a 'European Patent (United Kingdom)' granted under the European Patents Convention as equivalent to a national United Kingdom patent; this is, in addition, henceforth, to a 'Community Patent' granted under the Community Patents Convention, subject to local jurisdiction only over matters relating to infringement, as well as the former 'national United Kingdom patent' remodelled along the lines of Continental systems. Accordingly, the new Act extends the period of protection from sixteen to twenty years, replaces the former principle of 'provisional protection' with a system of priorities, introduces an 'inventive step' test of novelty[34], and applies the civilian 'exhaustion of rights' doctrine as part of a new, wide definition of infringement. It also codifies pre-existing loss relating to the employer's interest in inventions by an employee, introducing for the first time an employee's right to claim compensation where the patent has been of outstanding benefit to the employer. A number of familiar concepts are abolished, including extensions of patent, patents of addition, opposition to grant and many of the former grounds of invalidity. Applications for the grant of patent rights under the new system may be made either directly to the patent office of the country where protection is sought or comprehensively through any of several designated offices for the entire Community.

Within the field of copyright, the Whitford Report of 1977 has tackled the scarcely less difficult problems of photographic reproduction in a forthright manner, introducing, *inter alia*, the concept of compulsory license. Despite the 1976 initiative of the EEC Commission in this field, however, Continental influence seems relatively slight.

Supplemented by the tortious action for passing off, the law relating to trade marks, likewise can be expected to develop in the near future. The European Commission's long-expected initiative in this field has been welcomed by a British Government which has offered London as the location for a centralized European office.

It should be borne in mind by the foreign investor seeking to grant a license of industrial property to an enterprise in the United Kingdom that, used as the basis of an exclusive dealing arrangement or intercorporate association, the nationally-based monopoly which it provides potentially could contravene not only English but also Community provisions against restrictive trade and monopoly power.

Structure for Marketing

Protection of the consumer is a relatively new concept to English law, encompassing pre-existing as well as more recent elements. Of the latter, institution of an Office of Fair Trading in 1973 to exercise a general surveillance over the interests of consumers is symbolic of the trend away from a coercive reaction to product liability toward its persuasive prevention. Part III of the Fair Trading Act 1973, in particular, defines a Director General's powers in relation to acts contravening criminal and civil law which are unfair to consumers or detrimental to their legitimate interests, where 'consumers' includes persons receiving goods or services other than in the course of their business from a professional supplier.

The most fundamental form of collective protection is through a criminal law which, in addition to basic crimes of fraud, includes specific statutory protection against misdescription of goods[35], against the manufacture or sale of goods and components in the course of business prescribed by the Secretary of State as likely to be dangerous[36], and against unsolicited sale of goods and services generally[37].

The scope of public policy in English law never has been as comprehensive as in many comparable civilian legal systems. Yet, the economic trend away from free trade and *laissez-faire* has tended increasingly to identify the 'consumer' as object of its protection. Thus, recent consolidation of the law relating to monopolies, restrictive trading and resale price maintenance defines public interest in terms, *inter alia*, of the public as intermediate or ultimate purchasers, consumers or users, and creates specific exemptions having such beneficial effect on consumers as the holding down of prices[38]. In England, however, there is as yet little sign of public law relating to competition giving rise to substantive private rights, as in Germany.

In contrast with the United States position of strict liability, 'product liability' in English law remains essentially part of the general law of tort (or delict) in negligence, imposing liability for breach of a manufacturer's—and perhaps the retailer's—duty to take care that chattels dangerous in themselves, or dangerously defective, do not cause damage to their ultimate consumer or user. The basic principles long have been established[39]. Thus, the defendants may be any or all of the persons whose want of reasonable care constitutes an unbroken causal connection, but it remains uncertain whether, in the case of goods not of an inherently dangerous nature, a mere retailer is liable. The range of products for which liability can be established is comprehensive, perhaps not excluding even housing. Action can be taken by the actual consumer or user of the article, including probably those who merely accept a free sample or innocent bystanders. The little recent development that has taken place largely concerns the remoteness for which compensation can be claimed. This is forcibly illustrated by the case of Vacwell Engineering v B.D.H. Chemicals[40]. B.D.H. was long-term manufacturer and supplier of chemicals to Vacwell. In 1965, B.D.H. had sold boron tribromide to Vacwell in the knowledge of its intended use. Although it had been known generally for over seventy years that the chemical reacted explosively with water, the manufacturer's research revealed only that it would emit a toxic vapor, and they labelled glass ampules containing the chemical accordingly. Subsequently, two of the purchaser's scientists, intending to wash the label off preparatory to using the chemical, accidently dropped and shattered the ampules, causing their contents to react violently with the water in an explosion which resulted in their death and extensive damage to property.

On the issue of negligence, it was held that B.D.H. was liable for failure to take care to ascertain and give warning of possible hazards to customers. The explosion and type of damage being foreseeable, the whole of the damage sustained was susceptible of compensation. Since the chemical could be expected to come into contact with water in ordinary industrial use, Vacwell was not liable for contributory negligence. On the contractual issue, it was held that the condition of fitness for a particular purpose, implied by statute, and the condition, implied from a course of dealing, that chemicals would be supplied with a warning of hazards likely to arise in the normal course of use were both broken. Some explosion was reasonably within the contemplation of B.D.H., but not one of that magnitude. Nevertheless, the whole explosion was caused by supply of boron tribromide without an adequate label and was, therefore, liable to quantification in contractual damages. The provisions of the Unfair Contract Terms Act 1977 are comprehensive and complicating.

Liability for negligence arising in the course of any business or from the use of business premises cannot now be excluded by contractual provision except with regard to such loss or damage, other than personal injury, as could be considered fair and reasonable in circumstances apparently contemplated by the contracting parties. Nor can the liability of a manufacturer or distributor of consumer goods normally be excluded by reference to a 'guarantee' in contracts between retailer and consumer. In this context, the dictum of Lord Pearce in *Young & Martin Ltd. v. McManus Childs Ltd*[41]. is instructive;

'I see great difficulty in extending to an ultimate consumer a right to sue the manufacturer in tort in respect of goods which create no peril or accident, but simply result in substandard work under a contract which is unknown to the original manufacturer'.

Perhaps it is unnecessary to exclude liability for some forms of negligence. A supplier's contractual liability, on the other hand, relating to title, conformity with description or sample, quality and fitness for a particular purpose, cannot be excluded except insofar as, in non-consumer dealings, to do so would be fair and reasonable.

Together with the Secretary of State, the Director General of Fair Trading exercises extensive powers under the licensing provisions of the Consumer Credit Act 1974. This complex piece of legislation brings within its scope all previous forms of consumer credit and introduces a number of new concepts. The main provisions deal with consumer supply agreements requiring credit, whether or not this is made available by the supplier, either as a fixed sum of up to £5,000 or as a recurring account by credit card or other token, consumer-hire agreements not involving credit, with provisions for relaxation of the requirements for agreements involving less than £30. There are also measures to prevent evasion of its provisions through the apparent severance of actually-linked transactions by members of a consumer family. One of its major features is the adoption of a technique of legislating by official example introduced in the Insurance Acts. This is not without attendant dangers of uncertainty and confusion. The Act is being introduced piecemeal to offset the complexity of its provisions.

Profit from Investment

Corporate investments are protected by long-standing rules for the maintenance of capital against losses, other than in the course of a business defined by the objects[42]. Accordingly, the separation of fixed and working capital into capital and revenue accounts allows for declaration of a dividend according to a judicial standard of accounting based on 'current earnings' where losses on the former belie profits accruing to the latter, and 'earned surplus' in the converse situation of profits on the former being impeded by losses on the latter account. This, however, is soon to be qualified by the provisions of article 13 of the EEC Second Draft Directive which prohibits the payment of dividends on unrealised capital gains[43]. Meanwhile, the practice of accounting is moving hesitantly from a historic-cost to a current-cost basis. Reaction to the Sandilands report has been mixed, although the Morpeth Committee was expected to publish revised voluntary standards for 'inflation' accounting during 1978[44]. Moreover, the provisions of the EEC Draft Fourth Directive on corporate accounts represent a workable compromise between the United Kingdom's 'true and fair picture' and the Continental list of obligatory items. Those of the Seventh Draft Directive have involved English law at all stages.

Investor control over the use of assets is based on a comprehensive disclosure philosophy extending from public disclosure of the constitutional documents to public disclosure of directors' business interests at a number of operational levels but placing emphasis on the annual audit and the threat of government inspection. The right of directors to inspect the corporate accounts has been affirmed recently and those of employees or the public have been extended[45]. Moreover, the 1977 government Green Paper on Company Reports recommends introduction of new measures designed to promote energy conservation, good labor relations and a corporate balance in foreign trade. Although this is quite different in philosophy from the French and German commercial register, the provisions of the EEC First Directive enacted under section 9(3)–(7) operate in harmony with the English system.

Separation of corporate ownership and management has reached a point in

Britain where, under standard Table A articles, direct control by the former is limited to very few major items[46] in favor of the latter's exclusive management. Moreover, delegation of the power to manage and represent the company has been reinforced by legal recognition of the constructive director[47] and constructive managing director[48]. Unfortunately, the position of the employed executive director remains anomalous in a number of respects. Although the United Kingdom is committed in principle to the EEC Draft Fifth Directive on employee participation, continued public controversy suggests that its eventual implementation will show a distinctive character, treading a narrow line between 'Bullock' style worker directors (with or without a two-tier board) and an extension of collective bargaining into the sphere of corporate policy[49]. The gap between ownership and management theoretically is bridged in the collective interests of shareholders[50], and prospectively also of employees, by duties which imply a standard of care at common law[51] hardly suited to the age of professional management and a level of integrity in equity[52] which could be thought to inhibit enterprise.

Subject to the general criminal and civil law, the objects and entrenched shareholders' rights, action against breach of a director's duty, other than that sanctioned by a qualified shareholders majority, is reserved to the company itself[53]. However, it has been argued that the representative minority action currently lying against a director's abuse of his majority voting power as shareholder to validate a profit at the corporate expense has been influenced by the United States 'derivative suit'. In *Daniels v. Daniels*[54], two directors married to each other, had sold company land to one of them for £4,250. Only four years later, the same land realized £120,000. Minority shareholders brought an action against the directors, who together controlled a majority of the shares, joining the company as co-defendant. No fraud was alleged in the statement of claim. On application by the defendants to strike out the claim as disclosing no reasonable cause of action, the court held that, where a director's breach of duty had damaged the company, action by a minority shareholder was not precluded by an absence of fraud. This was a preliminary issue and outcome of the trial is awaited with interest. However, definition of the so called 'fraud on a minority' always has been vague. In relation to directors, it consists of the actual or potential abuse of majority voting power to validate what amounts to a breach of their duty to the company. The present decision merely establishes that an actual abuse of voting power need not be established where the position was inherent by reason of an overall majority shareholding and that the directors' act need not be inherently fraudulent where it amounts to a breach of duty. Clearly, this advances protection afforded to a minority without, however, reflecting the derivative suit, which is essentially a shareholder's action in the name of rather than against the company. It does, on the other hand, push English law in the direction of the United States principle that a corporate majority must act in the interests of the company as a whole[55].

The traditional emphasis on various forms of direct taxation on income is undergoing a long-term change in favor of indirect taxation on spending and other transactions. This was initiated by abolition of the old system of purchase tax in favor of the Continental taxation on value-added (V.A.T.) in 1973[56]. The total revenue raised by direct and indirect taxes is currently about equal and the linking of personal taxation with an indexed incomes policy in 1977 can be seen as a further step in the same course. The recent report of the Institute for Fiscal Studies Meade Committee emphasizes the potential importance of this movement for taxation in the corporate field. During a protracted transitional period, the taxation of capital gains and income must be of signal importance for the entrepreneur from abroad. The Finance Act of 1977 introduced no major changes. It extended the 'roll-over' relief applicable to subscribers for shares in kind and bona fide exchanges on shares in corporate mergers and reconstructions. Schedule 7 of the Act also extends the relief on income earned abroad originally introduced by the Finance Act 1974 Schedule 2. Unfortunately, advances made by the EEC in the corporate, industrial property and even consumer fields have not been matched by developments in the field of revenue.

Introduction of current cost 'inflation' accounting threatens to raise issues involving definition of corporate profits. In *Willingdale (Inspector of Taxes) v. International Commercial Bank*[57], the issue was whether a proportion of gains anticipated on the sale or maturity of promissory notes should be considered as accruing towards profit proportionately in years preceding its realization, or whether the entire sum should be allocated to profits for the year of its actual receipt. In a judgment which cannot be regarded as theoretically very cohesive, a majority of the House of Lords took the latter view, equating the acquisition of notes with commodities and contrasting discount with interest. Problems associated with exchange control[58] are likely to be exacerbated for the foreign investor by uncertainties engendered in the ungainly movement towards monetary union, coupled with the euphemistically-named managed floating of exchange rates in the EEC. In accordance with the Treaty of Accession, the United Kingdom's obligation to conform with measures for exchange liberalization was deferred during periods of transition, varying with the type of transaction. The final period elapsed from 1978, when payments for securities quoted on a stock exchange became due for liberalization. Perceptions of immediate economic interest eventually must give way to longer term necessity of a simple joint float against non-member countries[59].

Notes

1. See Schmitthoff, 'The Export Trade', Stevens, 6th ed. (1976).
2. See the *Transocean Marine Paint Case* [1975] *O.T. L286/24*, 2 *CMLR D75* and the *General Motors Continental Case* [1976], 1 *CMLR* 95.
3. See article 3L., Treaty of Rome and articles 27,49/6), 54(3) (g), 57/1), 99, 100–102, 112, 145 and 155.
4. The seven Directives and Draft Directives currently extract, Draft Regulations under article 235 establishing a European Company (*Societas Europea*) and a European Commercial Group, and Conventions under article 220 dealing with Mutual Recognition of Companies, Cross Frontier Mergers, Bankruptcy and Winding up.
5. The Patents Cooperation Treaty. Washington 1970, European Patents Convention, Munich 1973, and the Community Patents Convention, Luxembourg 1975.

6. Section 9(1) European Communities Act 1972 is extremely badly drafted even by modern standards and is likely to be revised before its precise effects can be understood.
7. In fact, it is a tribute to the patience and determination of all parties that the new members have been fully consulted on all major issues, even where this has caused considerable delay in the process.
8. See *Metliss v National Bank of Greece and Athens SA* [1958], *AC* 509.
9. See *De Beers Consolidated Mines Ltd v Howe* [1906], *AC* 455.
10. at [1960]2 *All E.R.* 332, affirmed sub nom *Tomkinson v First Pennsylvania Banking & Trust Co.* [1961] *AC* 1007. See also, *The Assunzione* [1954], 1 *All E.R.* 278; *The Compagnie Tunisionne Case* [1971], *AC* 572; *Vita Food Products v Shipping Co. Ltd.* [1939],*A.C* 277.
11. *Offshore International S.A. v Banco Central S.A. and Another* [1976], 3 *All E.R.* 749.
12 Perhaps the new U.N.C.I.T. R.A.L. draft will prove more successful.
13 Supra, n. 10.
14. *Schorsch Meier v Aeunnin* [1975], *Q.B.* 416.
15. *Miliangos v George Frank (Textiles) Ltd* [1975], 3 *All E.R.* 801.
16. *Krant (Jean) AG v Albany Fabrics Ltd* [1977], 2 *All E.R.* 116 *Q.B.D.*
17. *Federal Commerce and Navigations Co. Ltd v Tradox Export S.A.* [1977], 2 *All E.R.* 41 *CA.*
18. 'Inter-connected bodies corporate' were defined as 'bodies corporate which are members of the same group' under sections 3(1) (c) and 4(1) (c), Monopolies and Restrictive Practices Act 1948.
19. Sections 150–154 of the Companies Act 1948, section 4 of the Companies Act 1967. See, also, sections 31 103 (4) & 332 of the Principal Act.
20. See *Wallersteiner v Moier No.* 2 [1974], 1 *WLR* 991 per Lord Denning MR at 10....; *DNH Food Distributors Ltd v Tower Hamlets London Borough Council* [1976], 1 *WLR* 852; *Camilla Cotton Oil Co. v Granadex SA & Tracomin SA* [1976], 2 *Le R.*10,15. Also Sandals, 'The Dawn of a New Era', 127 *New York Journal* 1022.
21. *Chesterbridge v Lloyds Bank* [1969], 2 *All E.R.* 1185 *at* 1194 *B et seq.*
22. *The Albazero* [1976], 3 *All E.R.* 129.
23. Such as trade union pension funds.
24. During the 1978 Parliamentary Session.
25. Thus, membership includes the original subscribers to the memorandum as have not been relieved of their obligation by over-subscription of the original issue, all later subscribers and their successors in title, plus whatever other interests the articles specify.
26. *Wallersteiner v Moir No.* 2 [1974], 1 *WLR* 991, *Selangor United Rubber Estates v Cradock No.* 3 [1968], 2 *All E.R.* 107.
27. Sections 27 & 54, Companies Act 1948, extending the principle in *Trevor v Whitworth.*
28. *Re Wragg* [1897], 1 *Ch* 796; *Re White Star Line* [1938], *Ch* 458.
29. The convertible debenture already exists, but it has been suggested that a participating debenture would revive interest of the small investor in direct participation on the stock Exchange.
30. Section 95 et seq. Companies Act 1948. *See Re C.L. Nye* [1970], 3 *All E.R.* 1071 *Watson v Duff, Morgan and Vermont* [1974], 1 *All E.R.* 794.
31. *Esso Petroleum v Mardon* [1976], 1 *Q.B.* 801.
32. This has been enacted to enable the 'Talisman' computerized settlement system to be operated effectively by the Stock Exchange subsidiary 'Sepon'.
33. *Section* 209 Companies Act 1948 already deals with dissentients' rights in a take-over situation. The problem with insider trading is to define 'insider'.
34. Section 125 Patents Act 1927. This is likely to increase the difficulty of obtaining protection.
35. Trade Descriptions Act 1965.
36. Consumer Protection Acts 1961 & 1971.
37. Unsolicited Goods and services Act 1971.
38. Section 11 Restrictive Trade Practices Act 1976. See generally the Restrictive Practices Court Act the Restrictive Trade Practices Act, and Resale Prices Act, all of 1976, and the Restrictive Trade Practices Act 1977. The latter was passed specifically to ensure retrospectively that agreements with financial institutions relating to the provision of financial security, loan finance and debit facilities by consortia should not be registerable under previous legislation.
39. *Dominion Natural Gas v Collins & Perkins* [1909], *AC* 640; *Donaghue (McAlister) v Stevenson* [1931], *AC.*

40. [1969], 3 *All E.R.* 1681.
41. [1969], 1 *AC* 454.
42. 'The dominant and cardinal principle of these Acts is that the investor shall purchase immunity from liability beyond a certain limit on the terms that there shall be and remain a liability up to that limit. 'Per Lord McNaughton quoting Buckley on the Companies Act in *Aoregan Gold Mining Company of India v Roper* [1892], *AC* 125.
43. The proposed legislation will amend the 8th Schedule to the 1948 Companies Act. See the Green Paper on Company Reports 1977.
44. See I.C.A. Exposure Drafts 18, 19 and 20.
45. *Conway v Petronius Cloghing Co.* [1978], 1 *WLR* 72. Sections 8–10 Companies Act 1976, the Health and Safety at Work Act 1974, Industry Act 1975 & Employment Protection Act 1975.
46. The main ones are changes in corporate structure, appointment and dismissal of officers, determination of the rights in shares and deployment of a corporate profit.
47. *Selangor United Rubber Estates Ltd v Cradock No.* 3 [1968], 2 *All E.R.* 1073.
48. *Hely Hutchinson v Brayhead* [1967], 2 *All E.R.* 14.
49. Structured but sometimes weak trade union negotiating may force the company to consult on matters of policy from an early stage. Proposed changes in the law to allow directors to consider the interest of employees has been common practice for some time. (Section 99(1)), Employment Protection Act 1975 also is relevant.
50. *Percival v Wright* [1902], 2 *Ch* 421 and compare *Allen v Hyatt* [1914], 30 *T.L.R.* 644.
51. *Re City Equitable Fire Insurance Co* [1925], *CL* 407.
52. *Dorey v Cory* [1901], *AC* 477, *Industrial Developments Consultants v Cooley* [1972], 2 *All E.R.* 162.
53. *Foss v Harbott* (18—) 2 *Hare.*
54. [1978], *WLR* 73, and compare *Heyting v Dufont* [1964], 2 *All ER* 273.
55. See section 210 Companies Act 1948, Re H.R. Harmer & Sons Ltd [1959], 1 *WLR* 62: *Scottish C.W.S. v Meyer* [1959], *AC* 342. See, also, the Companies Bill 1973.
56. Together with changes in the basis of corporation tax on Continental lines.
57. [1977], *All E.R.* 618 *CA.*
58. See Mann 'The Legal Aspect of Money', Oxford 2nd ed (1971) pages 383–87.
59. In this connection, see *Schorsch Meier v Hennin* [1975], *Q.B.* 416; *Miliangos v George Frank Textiles Ltd* [1975], 3 *All E.R.* 801.

France

DENIS DEBOST

Introduction

The French Government generally is favorable to foreign investment in France. A French government agency known as DATAR (*Délégation à l'Aménagement du Territoire et à l'Action Régionale** actively seeks to attract foreign investors, particularly in the lesser developed areas of France, where special incentives are available. These incentives include cash grants, subsidies for the training of personnel, special tax reductions and exemptions and low-interests loans. DATAR welcomes the visit of prospective investors, informs them of the available incentives, helps to select the optimum location and to choose the best incentive program and facilitates contact with the appropriate French authorities.

To encourage multinational companies to establish regional headquarters in France, it also is possible to obtain a ruling from the French tax authorities whereby company income taxation will be limited to a percentage of costs of the French headquarters operations, at a rate of eight per cent to twelve per cent, depending on the type of services rendered by the establishment.

Exchange Control Regulations

Foreign investments in France require the prior authorization of the French Treasury Department. The principal criteria of the Treasury Department itself are mainly financial, such as debt-to-equity ratio and the effect of the proposed investment on the French balance of payments. In addition, however, applications are cleared with other government departments, including the sub-department of the Ministry of Industry responsible for the sector of the economy in which the proposed investment is to be made. It is at this level that difficulties may be encountered in connection with substantial investment projects. The French authorities, for example, may try to obtain certain commitments from the prospective investor in line with current French policies, such as to have investments located in areas where there is unemployment, to create a certain number of jobs, or to carry out research and development in France.

Moreover, when the proposed investment involves the acquisition of a controlling interest in an existing French company, and particularly if such company is one of the few remaining French-owned companies in a sensitive

*Located at 1, Avenue Charles Floquet, 75007 Paris. DATAR maintains offices in most industrialized countries. It can be reached through the nearest French consulate.

sector of the economy, the French authorities may try to find a so-called 'French solution', a group of French purchasers for all or part of the interest which is for sale. These attempts usually fail, however, because the alternatives already have been explored by the sellers or no alternatives exist at the offered terms.

For the establishment or purchase of a distribution or service company in France, or even of a small industrial company in a non-sensitive sector, Treasury Department approval almost invariably is obtained without difficulty, particularly if the foreign investors are from another Common Market country. Although pursuant to the Treaty of Rome the French government cannot obstruct Common Market investments in France, it was authorized in 1968 to reinstate exchange control regulations, and it is on these that the requirement of French Treasury Department authorization is based.

Once a foreign investment has been made in France, Treasury Department authorization also will be required for further parent company financing of the foreign-controlled French company, including financing obtained in France with the guarantee of the foreign parent. There are, however, broad exceptions, such as for increases in capital which do not change the percentages of ownership, parent-company medium-term loans in foreign currency and parent-company guarantees in favor of a French subsidiary whose equity plus long-term debts is at least equal to half of the fixed assets.

Tax Pitfalls

If the proposed investment involves the acquisition of an existing French company, the question will arise whether to acquire its assets or its stock. One substantial factor in favor of the acquisition of stock is that there is a French tax of 16.6 per cent on the transfer of fixed business assets, based not necessarily on the price paid therefor but on their market value as part of a going business, as determined by the French tax authorities. The latter may claim that a purchase of substantially all the stock of a French company amounts in effect to the acquisition of its assets and business. The tax consequences of such treatment are dreadful, not only because of the 16.6 per cent transfer tax but also because, with Cartesian logic, the tax authorities assume that the transaction also involves the liquidation of the original company and the creation of a new one. These risks are minimized if as few immediate changes as possible are made in the name, activities, location, board of directors and management of the company and, above all, if an independent minority of shareholders remains for at least a few years.

In practice, the French tax authorities seldom have applied this unfavorable tax treatment to the acquisition of less than all the stock of a bona-fide company. They reserve such treatment to individual proprietors, such as a corner grocer who incorporates his business merely for tax-avoidance purposes. The possibility of such treatment, however, causes lawyers to worry their clients about it and to then earn the latter's gratitude for having, rather easily, avoided it.

Forms of Business Organization

French company law, which was substantially revised in 1966, provides most of the familiar forms of business organization, including that of a corporation (*société anonyme*), a limited liability company (*société à responsabilité limitée*), a partnership (*société en nom collectif*) and an unincorporated joint venture (*société en participation*). French corporate organization formalities, however, which involve a number of registration, publication, immatriculation and reporting requirements, are probably more complex than in most other countries.

Moreover, a new company only comes into existence when the local Registry of Commerce issues an immatriculation number, which can take several weeks due to a permanent back-log of applications, particularly in Paris. Business may be carried on, however, by the founders prior to immatriculation, as soon as Treasury Department approval has been obtained. The founders who so act on behalf of a company in the process of organization are personally liable unless and until, once the company comes into existence, it adopts the prior undertakings, at which point they are deemed to have been incurred by the company from the outset.

Business, Residence and Work Permits

A traditional obstacle to doing business in France has been the requirement that the chief executive of the French operation, if non-French, obtain a special permit, known as a *carte de commerçant étranger*. This can take years to obtain, at least in the Paris area, and involves pleasures such as completion of a ten-page form designed to discourage illiterate or non-French speaking applicants.

Such a permit no longer is required of nationals of a Common Market country. Moreover, when a foreign investment authorization has been obtained from the French Treasury Department, it is possible to obtain fairly rapidly a so-called temporary permit, pending issuance of the *carte de commerçant*. These temporary permits, however, are issued only on a discretionary basis, so foreign investors are advised to find a Common Market national to manage their French company.

A foreign executive assigned to a French company, other than the chief executive, must obtain a work permit, unless he is a national of a Common Market country. The unemployment situation has led the French authorities to stop practically all immigration into France. Permits can be obtained, however, either on a temporary or semi-permanent basis, for executives with respect to whom it can be shown that there is no registered applicant fitting the job description.

Residence permits are issued as a matter of course to Common Market nationals and to other foreigners who have obtained a business or work permit, as well as to their families.

Marketing

Products usually are marketed in France either:
- through an independent distributor (*concessionnaire*), who buys and resells;
- through a sales agent (*agent commercial*), who obtains orders for the principal without taking title and is usually compensated on a commission basis; or
- through individual salesmen (*voyageurs, représentants, placiers, or 'VRPs'*), who are salaried employees.

Only the last two professions are protected by specific laws.

Sales agents, which can be individuals or companies, are protected by a decree of 23 December 1958 which provides that the termination by the principal of a sales agency agreement of indefinite duration, unless justified by a fault of the agent, entitles the agent, notwithstanding any contract clause to the contrary, to an indemnity in compensation for the damage suffered. This rather vague measure of indemnity has led to frequent litigation and to substantial awards in favor of those whose agencies have been terminated.

Such indemnity is not due in the event of nonrenewal of a fixed term agreement, but if such an agreement is in fact renewed once or twice, a French court may hold that this makes the agreement one of indefinite term, entitling the sales agent to an indemnity in case of nonrenewal. The best precautions for the principal seem therefore to be, first, to impose substantial obligations on the agent, such as quotas, enabling the principal to terminate for fault and, second, to define in the agreement the measure of the indemnity in the event of termination without fault.

The individual salesmen, or VRPs, are a race apart, as are probably their counterparts in other countries. In France, they command considerable political and legislative attention. Many years ago, therefore, the VRPs convinced the legislators, with some justification, that not only did they create a clientèle for their employer but that this clientèle is in a sense theirs. Consequently, if the employer terminates the relationship and supposedly takes over the clientèle, the VRP is entitled to a special indemnity for the clientèle, unless he is guilty of serious fault. (French Labor Code, articles L. 751–1 and following).

The application of the VRP status used to be subject to certain precise conditions, including the exclusive exercise of the profession of salesman. For many years, it was possible to avoid the VRP status by using employees who did not meet one of the conditions, for example by giving them additional duties of a technical or administrative nature. These days are over, due to a 1973 amendment which provides that the VRP status applies to all employees engaged in sales activities.

Foreign investors in France, therefore, must resign themselves to the fact that, if they employ individual salesmen, the latter will have the rights of a VRP upon termination. Unlike the case of sales agents, the VRP indemnity is due even in the event of non-renewal of a fixed term contract. On the other hand, the indemnity is based not on damages but on the creation or development of a clientèle. It is advisable, therefore, to specify upon hiring a salesman who are the existing clients of the employer and the current volume of sales with such clients. It also can be specified that the salesman's compensation includes indemnification for the clientèle created; the successful application of such a clause cannot be guaranteed, but the chances are improved if a special commission is specified for orders from new clients or on increased sales over certain pre-existing levels.

Alternatively, and perhaps more reliably, reference can be made to a nationwide agreement between VRP unions and the French management association (Conseil National du Patronat Français), which provides a precisely calculated indemnity in lieu of the clientèle indemnity (*Convention Collective Nationale Interprofessionnelle* of 3 October 1975).

Distributors have for years tried to obtain legislation like that which protects independent sales agents and salaried salesmen in the event of termination of their contract, so far without success. However, they often have been able to obtain damages in court on the theory that, even though the supplier may have a perfect right to terminate the agreement, in their particular case the principal has 'abused' such right.

A supplier wishing to terminate his relationship with a French distributor, therefore, must not just look at the agreement and terminate in accordance with the usual short-notice clause but must take a number of precautions, including prior warnings and additional notice, and must be prepared to at least repurchase saleable inventory and repay unamortized advertising and promotion costs.

Labor Relations

French labor law allows unions to designate a union representative, chosen among the employees, and provides for the election of employee delegates in enterprises having over ten employees and for the election of a works committee in enterprises having at least fifty employees.

The main difference between employee delegates and the works committee is that the delegates represent the employees, whereas the committee is a joint labor-management body, presided over by the Chief Executive, intended to allow the employees to participate on a consultative basis in the management of the enterprise, particularly insofar as the employees are affected.

The works committee must be informed of the profits of the enterprise and may make suggestions as to the employment thereof. In a corporation (*société anonyme*), the full accounts must be communicated to the works committee and representatives of the committee may attend meetings of the Board of Directors, on a consultative basis.

In practice, it appears that employers who cooperate fully and ungrudgingly with the employee delegates, works committee and union representatives, within the limits of their respective prerogatives, benefit from improved labor-management relations, whereas those who ignore these institutions or merely go through the formal motions often have problems.

French law provides a wide range of benefits, including sickness, maternity, disability and death benefits, old age pensions, family allowances, housing allowances, professional injury or illness insurance and unemployment insurance. In addition, employers often pay approximately one per cent of payroll to the works committee, if there is one, for various welfare, cultural and athletic activities.

Social benefits are financed through employer and employee contributions based on payroll. The whole package of benefits costs approximately fifty three per cent of salary up to a ceiling per employee of 4,000 Francs of which around ten per cent is due from the employee and forty three per cent is due from the employer. On the excess over this ceiling, the cost is around fifteen per cent, of which approximately four per cent is due from the employee and eleven per cent from the employer, except for executives, whose heavier pension plans usually account for another eight per cent above the ceiling, divided equally.

Despite these heavy contributions, the French social security administration seems to suffer from a chronic deficit and the burden of contributions keeps creeping up, through small rate increases and raises in the ceiling.

A number of measures protecting employees in the event of dismissal have been enacted recently, including the right to a prior hearing, the right to require an employer to state causes for the dismissal in writing and the right to indemnities in the event of the employer's failure to follow the proper dismissal procedure or of dismissal without just cause.

Collective dismissals for economic reasons require the prior approval of the employee representatives (the employee delegates in enterprises having between eleven and forty nine employees and the works committee in those having fifty or more) and the prior approval of the local government labor inspector.

If a dismissal for economic reasons has been approved and carried out, authorization of the labor inspector is required to re-hire within the following year.

All these reasons probably account for some of the unemployment in France, due to reluctance of employers to hire persons that they can do without and would have difficulty dismissing.

Use of French Language

A law of 31 December 1975 requires the use of the French language in writings connected with the sale of goods and prohibits the use of foreign terms and expressions when a French expression exists, with certain exceptions. The French text may be accompanied by translations into foreign languages. This law also requires that employment agreements for services to be rendered on French territory be written in French.

A prior decree of 1972 provides for the choice or creation of French words for new products and techniques, by government-appointed Terminology Commissions. The French Academy does not seem to have reacted yet to this apparent trespass into its domain.

Federal Republic of Germany

BODO HAGGENEY

SIGWART HÜBNER

Introduction

One of the main reasons for the fast economic growth experienced in the Federal Republic after World War Two was the fact that this country kept its frontiers open to foreign investment and trade with foreign countries. A great number of manufacturing and trading companies in Germany are foreign-controlled or even wholly-owned subsidiaries.

Foreign Companies Importing into West Germany

Import into and export out of West Germany generally is free and without any restrictions. It is not possible to deal with special problems arising in individual branches. However, aviation law should be mentioned as an example. Aircraft companies must have specific official approval before they can set up business. This approval can be withheld if aircraft are used which are not entered in the West German aircraft register. Aircraft are entered in the register only when they are the exclusive property of a West German national or of legal entities, the majority share of assets and the control of which are in the hands of West German nationals and in which West German nationals form the majority of the representatives.

Contractual relations in Germany may be treated under two different codes, the Civil Code on the one hand and the Commercial Code on the other. The basis is the Civil Code which contains the statutory provisions relating to the law of contracts. The Commercial Code does not enact a complete system of law, but rather supplements the Civil Code. Whether the Commercial Code applies or not is a question of the status of the contracting parties (merchant or not) and the kind of business that is being transacted (commercial transaction). It should be observed that, in general, the contract provisions of the Commercial Code apply even when the contract is commercial business only for one party. When a foreigner is party to a contract with a West German businessman and the contract is governed by West German law, the question as to whether the foreigner is a merchant also is determined by West German law.

Consider the following as an example of the relationship between Civil and Commercial Codes. The general law of contract also applies to commercial contracts and the civil law rules relating to the sale of goods also apply to commercial sales of goods except where the Commercial Code contains special provisions, such as when it imposes on the buyer the duty to examine the goods bought, a duty not imposed on the non-commercial buyer.

The foreign enterprise may set up a liaison or representative office, which exhibits no, or only an incomplete, course of business. These offices need not be registered. They should, however, be reported to the local authorities. In addition, the approval of the State Ministry for Economic Affairs is required and this generally will be granted if the financial situation of the applicant is satisfactory and if reciprocity is guaranteed for setting up such business in the home country of the applicant.

The foreign enterprise may appoint a distributor or an agent. The distributorship agreement may impose restrictions on the distributor as long as the agreement is in writing, subject to the control of the cartel authorities. The same provisions apply to the agency agreement whether the agent is appointed by a foreign or domestic enterprise. Attention may be drawn to the fact that specific provisions in the Commercial Code are for the protection of the agent, such as an indemnity payment upon termination of the agreement. The indemnity is a reasonable compensation based on the fact that the agent has increased the number of the principal's customers and the principal will derive a profit from these dealings after termination.

A non-competition clause prohibiting any competitive activity by the agent for the duration of the contract is valid. It also is possible to apply such a clause, for the time up to two years after termination of the contract but subject to an indemnity payment for the agreed time in the amount of at least half the commission the agent has received before termination of the contract.

The foreign enterprise may grant a patent or know-how license. An exclusive license may be granted for the whole country or part of it. There are no legal restrictions regarding the amount of royalties payable by the West German company. The agreement must be in writing; otherwise, restrictions are not valid. Restraints on the exercise of the protected right or know-how regarding the manner, field of use, quantity, territory or time are permitted. Also permitted are

(a) restraints on the licensee insofar and as long as they are justified by an interest of the licensor in sound technical utilization;

(b) commitments of the licensee regarding price-fixing;

(c) obligations of the licensee to exchange experience or to grant back licenses on inventions improving or applying the original invention insofar as such obligations correspond to obligations of the licensor of the same kind;

(d) obligations of the licensee not to contest the validity of the protected right; and

(e) obligations of the licensee insofar as they relate to the regulation of competition in markets outside West Germany.

Other restrictions infringe the German antitrust law, are not valid, and may be subject to fines.

Foreign Investment in West Germany

Considerations are limited to the joint-stock company (*Aktiengesellschaft, 'AG'*), the company with limited liability (*Gesellschaft mit beschränkter Haftung, 'GmbH'*) and branch offices, as foreigners seldom participate in partnerships.

The joint-stock company is a legal entity which comes into existence by registration in the Commercial Register of the local court. The share capital is at least one-hundred-thousand West German Deutschmark divided into shares, the minimum nominal amount of which must be fifty Deutschmark. At least five persons are required to form a joint-stock company.

In principle, shareholders' resolutions require the majority of the votes cast, a qualified majority being permitted only if specifically foreseen by statute or in the Articles of Association. Each share carries the right to vote. Shares are transferable. Exceptions are possible. The Articles of Association can link the validity of the sale of *registered shares* to the approval of the board of management, which in turn can be made dependent within the company on the cooperation of the supervisory board or the shareholders' meeting. It must be stated that only a few companies have registered shares which are not transferable without the consent of the board. They are common in the insurance business and in the power industry.

Multiple voting-right shares previously were used to create an exception and to assure a majority of votes to individual shareholders not having a majority shareholding. This was declared inadmissible by the Companies Act of 1965. An exception can be granted by the Minister of Economics in each federal state. However, a few multiple voting-right shares still are left over from the time before 1965.

The issuance of non-voting preference shares is possible. In the case of family concerns, capital from persons outside the family may be raised without forfeiting the internal structure of the company. As compensation, these shares enjoy preferential treatment with regard to the distribution of profits.

The Articles of Association may limit the voting rights of a shareholder who owns several shares. Large public companies have applied this method, e.g. largest vote share being ten per cent. Limitation of voting rights can be created by subsequently changing the Articles of Association without the shareholders affected having to give their personal consent.

The company is represented by its board of management, which may consist of one or several persons appointed by the supervisory board.

The joint-stock company basically is chosen in West Germany only if the company is to go on the public money-market and to be registered at a stock exchange. The annual financial statements of each fiscal year must be audited by an independent, certified accountant and filed with the Commercial Register together with a business report. The financial statements also are to be published.

As soon as an enterprise acquires more than twenty five per cent of all the shares in a stock corporation, it shall promptly inform such company in writing;

as soon as an enterprise acquires a majority interest, it shall inform the company; and if the interest held falls below these amounts, the company shall be informed thereof.

The GmbH is a legal entity. The company's name must be derived either from the object of the enterprise or the surnames of the shareholders or the surname of one of the shareholders with an additive (e.g., "& Co.").

The share capital shall be at least twenty thousand Deutschmark and be apportioned to the shareholders. The capital contributions of each shareholder may be different but must be at least five-hundred Deutschmark and divisible by one hundred. If a shareholder makes investments on the share other than in cash, the Articles of Association shall determine the person of the shareholder, the object of the investment and the money value of the consideration stipulated for the investment. In the case of cash contributions, payment of one quarter of the authorized capital suffices.

Two shareholders are required to form a company with limited liability. The second shareholder may, however, transfer his share to the other shareholder immediately after formation. Legal entities also may also be shareholders in a GmbH. A supervisory board is optional but required under the Co-Determination Act (see below).

The GmbH is represented legally by one or more directors (*Geschäftsführer*). These may, but do not need to be, shareholders. They are appointed and recalled by the shareholders' meeting. They may be foreigners. The GmbH is to be registered with the Commercial Register of the local court and comes into existence with registration.

Restrictions also may be introduced in the Articles of Association. Due to the principle of free disposition, which applies in this case, the shareholders have considerable freedom in the elaboration of shareholders rights. The provision, by which the transfer of shares is dependent on the consent of the remaining shareholders with the right of first refusal, is widely used.

Full-trading enterprises—foreign as well as domestic—may maintain independent branches which are to be registered with the Commercial Register. They need their own full-trading establishment and a certain freedom of disposition for the branch manager. Such registered branches bear the name of the head office with or without any additive designating their branch character.

Foreign legal entities require the approval of the State Ministry for Economic Affairs before setting up an independent branch. They need to submit to the Ministry a certified copy of the Articles of Association, the balance sheet for the past year, official certification, and proof that reciprocity is guaranteed for setting up such business between the Federal Republic of Germany and the home country of the foreign enterprise.

Co-Determination

There are three kinds of co-determination in effect in the Federal Republic, the co-determination in the coal, iron and steel industry, the co-determination under the Shop Constitution Act of 1952 and the recent co-determination under the Act of 1976.

Co-determination in the coal, iron and steel industry, commonly referred to as '*Montanmitbestimmung*', applies to companies, the number of whose employees exceeds one thousand. The supervisory board of these companies must comprise an equal number of shareholder and labor representatives and one 'further member', the so-called 'neutral member', on whom the two benches have to agree. A minority of the labor representatives is nominated by the shop council, while the majority is nominated by the trade unions. The board of management has as one member a labor director, the so-called 'Arbeitsdirektor', who is to be appointed and removed only with the consent of the majority of the labor representatives on the supervisory board.

Co-determination under the Shop Constitution Act of 1952 applies to AGs (except family-controlled AGs having less than five hundred employees) which have up to two-thousand employees and GmbHs with between five-hundred and two-thousand employees other than in the coal, iron and steel industry. One-third of the members of the supervisory board of these companies must be labor representatives elected by the employees. The number of members on the supervisory board may be determined by the Articles of Association but must be divisible by three. The first two labor representatives must be employees of the company, the others may be outsiders, which means trade union representatives.

Co-determination under the Act of 1976, called '*paritätische Mitbestimmung* (parity co-determination), applies to companies having more than two-thousand employees other than in the coal, iron and steel industry. The supervisory board comprises an equal number of shareholder and employee representatives. The number of members depends on the number of employees. The employee representatives comprise those from the workers and from the salaried employees' group. Employees in management positions must be represented within the employees' group. Each of the three groups (workers, salaried employees and employees in management positions) is entitled to be represented by at least one member. In addition, there are trade-union representatives within the employees' group. For example, if the supervisory board has twelve members, six are elected by the shareholders' meeting and six are employee representatives; among them, four representatives are employees of the company (at least one representing the workers, one the salaried employees and one the employees in management positions) and two members trade-union representatives. The chairman and the deputy chairman of the supervisory board are elected by the board. A two-thirds majority is required. If this cannot be obtained upon a second ballot, the shareholders' representatives may elect the chairman and the employees' representatives the vice-chairman. This is important because the chairman of the supervisory board has the privilege of casting the tie-breaking vote, which the deputy chairman does not.

The management board has a labor director who is elected by the supervisory board in the same way as other directors. Unlike the situation in the coal, iron and steel industry, the employees' representatives have no specific rights. The responsibilities of the labor director are not specified, but in fact it is clear that his tasks relate to personnel and social matters. The Co-Determination Act also applies to companies which are wholly-owned subsidiaries, or otherwise controlled, by a parent company.

Merger Control

The cartel authority may prohibit a merger if it is to be anticipated that a market-dominating position will thereby result or be reinforced. The following transactions are deemed a merger: the acquisition of the assets and liabilities of another enterprise by merger, transformation or other means; agreements covering the leasing of business, transfer of profits and management; the placing of the same persons, to the extent of one half thereof, on the supervisory board, the board of management or on such other corporate organs that may be authorized to conduct management.

The acquisition of shares is considered to be a merger if such shares alone or together with other shares already owned by the enterprise equal twenty five per cent of the voting capital of the other enterprise, or equal fifty per cent of the voting capital of the other enterprise, or give the enterprise a majority participation within the meaning of Article 16 (1) of the Stock Corporation Law.

To enable the competent cartel authority to ascertain whether a dominant position will be created or reinforced, mergers must be reported when the merger results in a market share of twenty per cent or more of the West German market, or a substantial part thereof; or the participating enterprises have a total (in West Germany and abroad) of ten-thousand employees; or a yearly turnover of five-hundred-million Deutschmark (in West Germany and abroad); or when a participating enterprise has a market share of at least twenty per cent in another market.

Without going into detail, it should be pointed out that the entire structure is to be disclosed for broadly interwoven combines and details concerning number of employees, gross sales profits and share of the market must be given for each company. If a participating enterprise constitutes a dependent or dominating enterprise within the meaning of Article 17 of the Stock Corporation Law or a combine enterprise within the meaning of article 18 thereof, then market shares, number of employees and turnover proceeds are calculated by adding all those resulting from the connected enterprises.

If at least two of the companies participating in a merger have a turnover of at least one-thousand-million Deutschmark the merger must be noticed beforehand to the Federal Cartel Office. If the companies fail to give notice of the merger, the legal transactions nevertheless completed are invalid.

The authority to prohibit the merger presupposes that the enterprises involved have a total turnover of five-hundred-million Deutschmark or more, including both foreign and domestic sales, and the company joining another enterprise has a turnover of more than fifty-million Deutschmark.

To assist the cartel authorities, market domination is presumed to exist when a company has a one-third share of the market, when up to three companies have a fifty percent share of the market, or when up to five companies have a two-thirds share of the market.

When it is proved that market domination exists or the presumption of its existence is not disproved, the companies may overcome the prohibition by proving 'that by means of the merger improvements in the competitive situation will occur and that these improvements will outweigh the disadvantages of the market domination'.

The Cartel Office may prohibit the merger 'as soon as the plan for the merger has been made known to it', even if it already has been completed. As merger control also covers companies which, although not having a turnover of one-thousand-million Deutschmark do reach a total of five-hundred-million Deutschmark, prior notification of the merger is optional. It is therefore advisable to give notice of these mergers beforehand.

The Federal Minister of Economics shall, on application, grant permission for the merger if in the individual case the restraint of competition is compensated by the overall economic advantages of the merger or if the merger is justified by an overriding public interest.

Investment and Foreign-Exchange Laws

Direct capital investments by foreigners in the Federal Republic of Germany are not subject to approval. This applies to the setting up and acquisition of enterprises, branches and permanent establishments as well as to the acquisition of interests in West German enterprises. The extent of foreign participation is not limited.

During the currency crisis of 1972, considerable restrictions were introduced: compulsory cash deposit (*Bardepot*) for borrowing abroad by residents; compulsory approval for the sale of securities bearing fixed interest and shares to non-residents; restraints on investment of foreign capital in West German enterprises; prohibition of interest payments on foreigners' credit balances with West German banks, and compulsory approval for the borrowing of foreign credit. These measures have been cancelled, but the Federal Government is entitled to reintroduce them. Nevertheless, it is necessary to give notice of certain transactions to the state reserve bank. Violation of this duty is subject to fine. However, investments are not prevented by this. Profits and dividends secured in the Federal Republic, as well as royalties and interest, may be transferred in any currency.

Residence and Work Permits

A residence permit is required for any work in the Federal Republic. This is issued in the form of a visa (*Sichtvermerk*) in the passport. A residence permit must be applied for prior to entry, at a West German embassy. The residence permit generally is issued for a limited period of time and may be extended upon application. It may be restricted in terms of area and may contain further conditions and obligations.

No work permit is required for independent work. This is any kind of professional self-employment. A director (*Geschäftsführer*) of a company with limited liability or an executive employee (*leitender Angestellter*) with general authority (*Generalbevollmächtigter* or *Prokurist*) is regarded as self-employed. There is no requirement that a person in such a position be a resident.

For any non-independent work, a work permit is required. The work permit must be applied for together with the application for the residence permit. The application should be accompanied by a written statement from the company that the applicant will be employed.

Foreigners having a residence permit in the form of a visa (Sichtvermerk) must give notice of their residence to the competent authorities immediately after entry.

Social Security

Social security includes health insurance, pension insurance, accident insurance and unemployment insurance. All employees, regardless of their citizenship, must be insured in all of these branches of social security. An exception is made in the case of health insurance for those employees whose annual earnings exceed a certain amount, which varies from year to year.

The contributions for health, pension and unemployment insurance are collected by the health insurance institutions. The accident insurance contribution is levied by the competent professional associations. As to accident insurance only the employer has to make contributions. As far as all the other insurances are concerned, employer and employee each bear half the cost. The employer must pay his contributory shares as well as those of his employees, which are deducted from their wages and salaries, to the appropriate health insurance institution.

Tax Law

Anyone carrying on business in the Federal Republic, irrespective of nationality or residency, whether a natural person, corporation, unincorporated company or branch (permanent establishment), pays on the profits he realizes and on the working capital trade tax amounting to about seventeen to twenty per cent according to the location of the business activity (borough/municipality). The trade tax is an operating expenditure and thus tax-deductible.

There is a tendency toward reducing trade tax by increasing certain allowances or reducing taxation rates.

Natural persons, irrespective of nationality, and whether liable to limited or unlimited taxation, pay progressive income tax on the operating profits up to a rate of fifty-six per cent, which is reached by single persons with an income of approximately one-hundred and thirty-thousand Deutschmark. However, as an allowance has to be taken into consideration, the highest rate of taxation in theory never will be reached. The actual income tax burden on a taxable income of approximately one-hundred and thirty-thousand Deutschmark will be forty seven per cent. Natural persons who participate in a West German unincorporated company also will be liable to income tax on their proportionate profit. In the case of natural persons liable to limited taxation, the rate of income tax will be at least twenty-five per cent. In addition, they, unlike West German residents, do not benefit from certain deductible, personal exemptions.

To summarize, it may be said that the operational profits of natural persons, irrespective of whether they carry on a trade as an individual entrepreneur or via an unincorporated company, will be subject to taxation on earnings in the Federal Republic of Germany in the top bracket of approximately sixty-five per cent, depending on the amount of trade tax.

If the investor is a foreign corporation it will be active in the Federal Republic of Germany either via a branch (permanent establishment) or via a subsidiary corporation. In this case, corporation tax will replace income tax. In Germany, a new corporation tax system, which is characterized by the crediting of corporation tax against the income tax of the shareholder when profits are distributed, has applied since January 1977. When the corporation retains its profit, it pays fifty-six per cent corporation tax on its profit after deduction of trade tax. Distributions of profit are subject to thirty-six per cent corporation tax. If the corporation distributes its retained profit at a later date, it will benefit from a twenty per cent reduction in corporation tax.

When the corporation distributes profits, shareholders who are liable to unlimited taxation will receive, together with their cash dividend, a tax credit of nine sixteenths of the cash dividend which corresponds to a prior burdening of the profits distributed with thirty six per cent corporation tax. In this way, it is guaranteed that the double burden of corporation and income tax on the corporation's profits will be eliminated completely when the profits are distributed.

It is important that only those natural persons and companies benefit from the credit system who are subject to full taxation in West Germany. In the case of foreign shareholders, however, the thirty-six per cent corporation tax on profits distributed becomes a final tax. A reimbursement will not be considered.

This arrangement is extremely controversial. There is great political pressure, in particular from the United States, to alter this in favor of foreign shareholders. It remains to be seen whether a change will be brought about in the near future by modification of the existing double taxation conventions, such as by reducing withholding-tax rates on dividends from the normal twenty-five per cent at present to ten or fifteen per cent.

A permanent establishment (branch) of a foreign corporation is liable to fifty per cent corporation tax. The corporation tax will not be reimbursed in this case either.

Dividends paid by the corporation to foreign shareholders are subject to capital-yield tax of twenty-five per cent if a lower rate is not to be taken into account in accordance with a double taxation convention.

The tax burden on the earnings of a West German corporation with foreign shareholders, when profits are distributed in full, is therefore as follows (when a double taxation convention does not exist):

Profit before deduction of taxes on earnings	100.0
—approximate trade tax	17.0
Profit before deduction of corporation tax	83.0
—36 per cent corporation	29.9
Gross dividend	53.1
—25 per cent capital yield tax	13.3
Net dividend in West Germany	39.8
Total West German tax burden on earnings	60.2
	100.0

If the foreign corporation carries on business in West Germany in the form of a branch, the tax burden on earnings will be as follows:

Profit before deduction of taxes on earnings	100.0
—approximate trade tax	17.0
Profit before deduction of corporation tax	83.0
—50 per cent corporation tax	41.5
Profit after deduction of taxes on earnings	41.5
Total West German tax burden on earnings	58.5
	100.0

In West Germany at present, there are no restrictions on investment by foreigners apart from the obligation to obtain authorization for certain branches of industry, this affecting West German residents as well. Foreign investments normally are notifiable.

There are a great number of investment benefits, which mostly are given in the form of state investment allowances or interest subsidies. These subsidies are given to both West German and foreign trade and business people who invest in West Germany. The same applies for allowances for depreciation.

West Germany has concluded double taxation conventions with about forty countries, including all the important industrial nations of the western world. The network of double taxation conventions is being extended continually. The more recent conventions are orientated on the organization for Economic Cooperation and Development (OECD) standard convention but each has, in addition, very different provisions. Double taxation is eliminated either by the exemption or credit method. If a person liable to unlimited taxation draws income from a non-double taxation convention country, double taxation normally will be eliminated by national measures in the form of tax credit.

Since 1971, West Germany has had an International Transactions Tax Law in which the so-called taxation of additions was created. This essentially provides that the so-called passive income of a West German resident from his shareholding in a foreign corporation in a so-called low-taxation country also will be subject to West German tax even if profits are not distributed.

Apart from taxes on earnings, the Federal Republic of Germany also levies property and transfer taxes. The tax on property amounts to 0.7 per cent of taxable property for corporations and 0.5 per cent for natural persons. West Germany levies a real property transfer tax of seven per cent of the basis of assessment, which normally consists of the original costs of acquisition. In addition, several capital movement taxes are imposed (stock exchange tax, incorporation tax).

West Germany also imposes an all-phase net Value-Added Tax which is levied as a gross tax on domestic deliveries and other deliveries by enterprises and on imports, in conjunction with the right to make pre-tax deductions. Therefore, the Value-Added Tax does not affect profit. At present, the normal tax rate is thirteen per cent. For certain goods (e.g. foodstuffs) there is a reduced rate of 6.5 per cent. The rates of Value-Added Tax are tending to increase.

West Germany has a tax administration which functions quite well and is organized on a federal basis. Recently, a Federal Information Center was opened for the investigation of tax offenses; it will coordinate the activities of the state revenue authorities. The Federal Office of Finance in Bonn collects information for the examination of foreign relations. In West Germany, there is no bank secrecy in respect of tax authorities. Taxpayers are subject to regular auditing, this being carried out on the premises of the taxpayer.

Italy

FEDERICO BIANCHI

Introduction

Problems of foreign investments and operations of foreign enterprises in Italy can be evaluated from two standpoints as regards present and future developments. The first relates to provisions governing foreign capital investments, financing from abroad, as well as tax and other laws and regulations affecting foreign investors and foreign enterprises. The other refers to significant developments and trends of business law which may be influential in regard to relations with foreign countries in general.

Considerations of an economic, social and political nature are beyond the scope of this review, although they certainly have determinant effects for the future of capital investments and operations of foreign companies in this country. It is extremely difficult to make reliable forecasts in this field due to the gravity of problems that Italy now is facing, after having made a rapid post-war reconstruction. In addition to the scarcity of natural resources and overpopulation, which always have played a negative role, recent radical social changes, massive internal migrations, and the attempt to adjust a geographically-unequal and, in many respects, undeveloped structure to an ideal modern society, modelled upon more advanced countries, especially those of the European Economic Community (EEC), have contributed to the present political uncertainties. At the same time, however, and for some of these very reasons, Italy is one of the most attractive markets in Europe. The legal climate and certain developing trends reflect the extent and disparity of the economic and political problems confronting Italy.

Foreign Investments

Thus far, there has been a consistent policy of encouraging foreign investments, especially those aimed at establishing or expanding productive enterprises. Foreign investments still are regulated by Law 43 of 7 February 1956, the purpose of which is to guarantee the transfer abroad of capital invested in Italy and profits and dividends earned on such capital. These rights are unconditional for investments in new productive enterprises (Article 1), although there are certain limitations regarding non-productive enterprises, that is, at least two years for repatriation of capital and no more than eight percent of the amount invested for distribution of dividends and profits (Article 2). Sums exceeding those limits, however, could be made available for transfer abroad if foreign-currency control regulations in force would so permit (Article 2). As a matter of fact, regulations enacted after Law 43 have made those restrictions rather insignificant. Law 43 (Article 5) also contemplates the possibility of investments in the form of equipment and sets forth some limitations as to the capacity of the enterprises, into which the foreign capital is invested, to borrow money from the national market. It may be worth noting that foreign investments under Law 43 can be made either into Italian companies or Italian establishments or branches of foreign companies (Article 4).

Law 43 (Article 6) further guarantees that Italian firms and companies, which are authorized to borrow money from abroad, can obtain the foreign currency needed for paying interest and for reimbursing the principal from the pertinent Government Agency (*Ufficio Italiano dei Cambi*). In this connection, it should be recalled that, according to Italy's commitments to the Organization for Economic Cooperation and Development (OECD) and to the EEC, loans which meet certain requirements (as to duration and interest rates) can be freely taken out by Italian companies under general governmental authorizations.

The above system, which is based on the constitutional guarantee afforded by law, has functioned successfully thus far in spite of the restrictive measures taken in the past few years to protect Italy's balance of payments. Remittances abroad pursuant to Law 43, for instance, were exempt from compulsory temporary deposits of funds with the Bank of Italy, a requirement which in May 1976 was imposed on all payments abroad and later gradually eliminated.

National and foreign investments are encouraged by a special state program aimed at assisting southern Italy in industrializing and in approaching the development level of northern Italy. This program, which was established in 1950 and led to the formation of the state fund called the *Cassa per il Mezzogiorno* (Law 646 of 10 August 1950), originally was designed to cover a fifteen-year period. It subsequently was extended to 31 December 1980 by Law 717 of 26 June 1965. Incentives offered basically consist of tax exemptions, government contributions and low-interest loans. Similar legislation, but with less incentives, was enacted to encourage also industrialization of certain localities of central and northern Italy. Considerable foreign investments were made in the past, especially in connection with the *Mezzogiorno* program.

A positive factor in international business relations is the lack of discrimination between foreign and national subjects, generally speaking. Under corporate laws, no restrictions are set forth regarding participation from abroad in the capital of companies which may be entirely owned by foreigners. No nationality requirements are contemplated for holding corporate offices. Foreign persons holding such offices are facilitated in obtaining permission from pertinent authorities to reside in Italy.

Concerning the application of foreign-exchange control regulations, a basic distinction is made between residents and non-residents, regardless of nationality. The matter is subject to rather complete control by the government either through general authorization given to banks to deal with certain categories of transactions or through special authorization to be granted by government agencies. The whole system is characterized by a considerable amount of flexibility, which is exercised by government agencies according to the conditions of the national economy and the balance of payments. The present trend is rather restrictive, as we shall see, with unfavorable repercussions in regard to foreign trade.

Taxation

An important tax reform was introduced in 1973-74. It replaced more than thirty taxes with a few major ones, both indirect (such as the Value Added Tax, effective as of 1 January, 1973) and direct (a tax on personal income, a tax on corporate income and a tax for the benefit of local public agencies, effective as of 1 January, 1974). Notable improvements thus were achieved also in regard to the assessment of income for enterprises, and self-taxation was expanded. It expressly was stated that international agreements to avoid double taxation in existence at the time of the reform would continue to be in effect. One of the aims of the reform was to simplify procedures and to limit the discretionary powers of the Tax Office, a source of problems and a matter of serious concern.

Subsequent tax provisions were enacted which amended some of the reform and introduced new features. Although this has resulted in some improvements, the rather clear-cut scheme of the reform has been affected adversely by this disorderly legislative proliferation. The trend is expected to continue.

Some internationally-significant tax provisions may be cited here. A person residing in Italy (after six months it is presumed that the individual resides here for tax purposes) becomes subject to taxation for his entire income, including that earned abroad. The same holds true for companies registered or having their main place of business in this country. Tax credits for income earned abroad are given under some conditions, within a maximum limit of two-thirds of the portion of the Italian income tax attributable to that foreign income (Article 18 of Presidential Decree 597 of 29 September 1973 on personal income tax; Article 9 of Presidential Decree 598 of 29 September 1973 on corporate income tax).

Intercompany transactions are the subject of provisions aimed at preventing undue advantage for foreign companies having Italian affiliates or controlling Italian companies. According to Articles 53 and 56 of Presidential Decree 597 above mentioned, the difference between the normal value of goods and services rendered by the Italian company to the foreign company and the actual price received for such goods and services is considered taxable earnings. Conversely, the excess of price paid by the Italian company for goods or services received from the foreign company is not a tax-deductable cost. The definition of 'normal', that is current or market value of such goods and services, may be troublesome. Violations of the above provisions are punishable by rather severe fines.

One of the main features of the new laws on direct taxation is a broader use of the tax withholding method both for payments made in this country and abroad. Concerning withholding rates on interest and dividends due on payments abroad, there are differences in treatment depending on whether international agreements to avoid double taxation are applicable. The taxation of interest and dividends appears to be a fertile field for legislation. Law 904 of 16 December 1977 has revised this field and introduced the principle of avoiding double taxation on company profits, that is the taxation of the company's income and of dividends. This improvement was long expected. The same law, however, contains a new provision dealing with tax withholdings on dividends due to foreign companies having permanent establishments in Italy, which may give rise to uncertainties of interpretation.

Royalties present a special problem. According to certain provisions (Article 19, paragraph 2b; Article 49, paragraph 3b, of Presidential Decree 597 and Article 25 of Presidential Decree 600 of 29 September 1973), royalties and similar compensation paid abroad by a resident for the acquisition or use of property rights and other intangible assets are considered by Tax Offices to be income earned in Italy. Such interpretation is vigorously opposed by some commentators and was not upheld in a tax court decision.

Corporate Law

In some fields of law there have been developments—and further developments are expected—which in some ways may affect foreign investments and operations in Italy. Part of them are in line with common trends of the Western World or more specifically deriving from the enforcement of principles aimed at harmonizing the laws of the EEC Member States (see, for example, Article 100 of the Rome Treaty). Others appear to be more-strictly connected with the country's social and economic situation.

Following extensive studies and public debates on the need to reform the corporate provisions set forth in the Italian Civil Code of 1942, as well as regulations regarding stock exchanges, substantial amendments in these fields were introduced in 1974 (Law Decree 95 of 8 April, 1974 converted to Law 216 of 7 June, 1974). It was a partial reform that constituted progress under several aspects toward bridging the gap with the more advanced laws of other countries.

Reference could be made, among other things, to innovative provisions on conversion of debentures into shares and the issuance of non-voting shares, on the extent of information to be given on balance sheets and corporate reports, on liabilities and disclosure duties of officers of corporations having shares listed on the stock exchange, on the institution of a National Commission of Companies and the Stock Exchange (*Commissione Nazionale per le Società e la Borsa—Consob*). By Presidential Decrees 136, 137 and 138 of 31 March, 1975, the government, pusuant to an authorization set forth in Article 2 of the above Law 216, issued regulations dealing, among other things, with audit and certification of balance sheets of companies having stock traded on the stock exchange, which certification was entrusted to certified auditing firms for the first time in our system.

Several provisions of this reform are aimed specifically at protecting small investors, such as those introducing the category of the so-called savings shares which have a priority in regard to the distribution of dividends but do not allow voting rights, those governing the public offer of shares on the stock exchange and the control of the stock exchange market by *Consob*. An indirect benefit for foreign investment can be envisaged in those provisions which have increased the amount of information to be supplied to shareholders and to the public by capital companies (joint-stock and limited-liability). The insufficiency of previous law provisions in this respect was criticized widely and did allow for abuse, especially as regards closely-held local companies, often resulting in unfair advantages from the standpoint of competition.

Similarly, a new amendment (set forth by Law 904 of 16 December 1977) can be welcomed whereby the minimum company capital has been increased from fifty-thousand Italian lira to twenty-million lira for limited-liability companies and from one-million lira to two-hundred-million lira for joint-stock companies. It was a long-awaited measure, more than justified because of the heavy devaluation suffered by the local currency and it is likely to make investments in limited-liability companies more frequent than those in joint-stock companies. This, however, should not cause inconveniences for foreign investors since, aside from the burden of more formalities concerning the transfer of shares for limited-liability companies, the legal treatment of investments basically would be the same in regard to both kinds of companies. Further amendments to corporate laws are to be expected in accordance with the harmonizing directives of the EEC, and this should ultimately be beneficial from the standpoint of international relations.

Labor Relations

A field in which there has been great evolution and which presents problems that certainly influence business decisions is that concerning labor. Job security and recognition of union power have inspired much legislation in past years. Important limitations on the freedom to dismiss workers were introduced by Law 604 of 15 July 1966, which entitled employees to challenge termination of employment not based either on cause or just motive. This protection was broadened by Law 300 of 20 May 1970 to the point of forcing employers under judicial injunction to rehire employees who were unlawfully dismissed. Law 300, named the 'Workers' Statute', sets forth provisions on the protection of workers' freedom and dignity, on the unions' freedom and activity in places of work and on the placement of workers. It has had a deep impact on the workers' status and especially on the unions' prerogatives.

Another important innovation was introduced by procedural Law 533 of 11 August 1973 which, among other things, gave jurisdiction to a single judge (the *Pretore*) to handle labor cases in rather speedy proceedings and by exercising broad powers.

The above laws are only some of the measures of a legislative trend aimed at improving the protection of employees and remedying other insufficiencies in the labor field. On the other hand, there is little doubt that this radical move in legislation, coupled with recurrent strikes and other forms of protest by workers in the late 1960s in connection with the increase of economic difficulties, did cause serious problems to business activities. The rigidity of the present system, which is an obstacle to the restructurization of companies by collective dismissals or transfers of employees, is also a negative factor for foreign investments. The possibility for companies in difficulty to avail themselves of partial unemployment compensation for a short time as allowed by law is certainly not a decisive remedy.

It is unthinkable that substantial amendments could be introduced in the future in the labor field to increase flexibility as regards amounts of salaries, fringe benefits and social contributions, all matters regulated in detail by compulsory collective-bargaining agreements and laws. Nevertheless, one can hope that the unions, which now have political power and influence in government decisions, will show a willingness to study solutions allowing, among other things, the transfer of workers from one job to another. Symptoms of a new trend appeared by the end of 1976 when unions concurred with a government policy to fight inflation by introducing provisions which have reduced the effect of the sliding wage scale in computing remuneration. Special laws aimed at favoring the mobility of workers in connection with reorganization of enterprises have been enacted in recent years.

It should be added that one of the negative results of the legal-protective scheme for labor is the increase of so-called hidden labor, that is the hiring of persons, usually by small companies which do not comply with all laws and regulations, especially as regards social contributions.

Foreign Exchange

Foreign-exchange control regulation is also a field in which new, important developments occurred in the recent past. New provisions (Law Decree 31 of 4 March 1976, converted to Law 159 on 30 April 1976, and subsequent amendments) were enacted which, without modifying the basic principles of Italian currency-exchange control regulations, have strengthened them by qualifying as criminal offenses violations of more than minor importance. Their purpose was to put an end to past excessive tolerance in the field and to deter the flow of capital abroad. This, in itself should not affect foreign investments and commercial activities in this country by foreign operators. On the other hand, the broadness of definitions of violations contained in this set of laws, the fact that bank employees may incur personal liability for wrong-doings in foreign transactions, and other similar considerations have created problems of interpretation which do not help in the carrying out of international transactions and in the transfer of currency abroad. In line with the above trend, the government agency in charge of this sector (*Ufficio Italiano dei Cambi*) has restricted its current regulations with the result of restricting payments made for international transactions. Some time will be needed to see how these provisions will be interpreted by courts and authorities and whether the government will show more flexibility in its control activities.

Significant Trends

There are some sectors of business activity which have been or are at a sort of standstill. Although they might be only indirectly relevant for investments, they are worth noting as they reflect the country's general situation. Housing, which was characterized by an intense but rather disorderly building activity in the post-war years, starting from Law 765 enacted on 6 August 1967, has become the subject of more and more detailed regulations, greatly limiting owners' rights in relation to the protection of public interest. Law 10 of 28 January 1977 was intended to reorganize the field by, among other things, emphasizing the need for building projects to conform with city zoning and other general planning regulations and by defining the extent of contributions due to town administrations. However, due to the lack of initiative by local public agencies in exercising ample powers which the law grants them for housing projects and the insufficiency of funds needed for such purposes, housing activities are presently rather paralyzed. It would be fair to add that, as regards industrial buildings, the above legislative trend toward setting forth stricter requirements, including anti-pollution measures, has not, generally speaking, caused sizable negative repercussions.

Another field that has been the subject of continuous laws limiting individual rights is that of leases. A rent freeze, coupled with compulsory extension of contracts, was enacted in 1940. It did not, however, affect rentals in buildings constructed in the 1950s. Later, to discourage rent increases, especially in large towns and in response to massive migrations from southern and central regions to northern Italy, a general rent freeze and limitations on the right of the lessor to terminate contracts were gradually introduced between 1963 and 1969. A comprehensive new regulation has been enacted by Law 392 of 27 July 1978. It will be based on the principle of fair rental, allowing the fixing of rentals within maximum and minimum limits calculated on the basis of official parameters which vary according to the category of the building, location, and other factors.

Industrial and commercial activities in Italy are influenced by the state's participation in business enterprises, either through agencies which were created long ago for this purpose or through others which came into existence after World War II to reorganize certain sectors or to help companies in difficulty. In principle, the co-existence of public or semi-public companies and private companies was held to encourage competition. In reality, however, private operators have been adversely affected by competition with companies having public or semi-public capital or funds.

Moreover, large private companies or groups of companies which expanded their activities and shareholdings without restrictions due, among other things, to the absence of cartels and antitrust laws, and sometimes even with the encouragement of public powers, are today putting pressure on the state to find a solution to their economic problems and to help avoid unemployment. This last factor largely accounts for the proliferation of recent laws to subsidize companies which operate in fields especially hit by the economic crisis. Unfortunately, they often help to keep unprofitable activities alive.

To conclude, various and at times contradictory factors are met when considering the general climate in regard to foreign investments and operations in Italy. The more negative ones might diminish in the future, but radical changes appear unlikely, notwithstanding the fact that Italy is in need of capital investments from abroad. One could hardly expect that free trade will be entirely accepted in a country where public intervention is sought for the solution of serious social problems and restrictive measures are required to protect the balance of payments. However, as noted at the beginning, Italy constitutes an important market. Although massive industrial foreign investments as were made in the past will hardly be repeated, Italy will nevertheless probably continue to induce foreign operators to intervene, either through moderate investments of a commercial nature or through other arrangements. The fact that Italy belongs to the EEC may be considered as a guarantee of gradual progress towards the more advanced economies of its European partners.

Switzerland

KARL ARNOLD

Introduction

Switzerland accomodates a great number of foreign-controlled enterprises, including manufacturing enterprises, holding companies created to hold foreign based investments, and service and finance companies coordinating international interests of multi-national groups. However, for those companies based in countries which tax profits of Swiss subsidiaries, Switzerland may have lost, to a certain extent, its former attraction as a tax haven.

Entering the Swiss Market

The foreign enterprise exporting to the Swiss market basically will encounter no barrier other than the Swiss or foreign competitor trying to gain its own share of the market. The only regulation affecting the flow of commerce into and out of Switzerland involves the requirement of import licenses for some commodities and tariffs. Except for agricultural products, import licenses are available. The customs duties are low compared to most other countries.

A further step toward entering the Swiss market may involve the establishment of a representative office. A representative is not engaged in business but merely acts as an information officer between the foreign enterprise and the actual or prospective Swiss customers. For tax reasons, the representative has no general power to negotiate and conclude contracts on behalf of the foreign enterprise.

The legal framework for a long-term exporting relation may be a distributorship or an agency agreement. The Swiss distributor purchases goods from the foreign enterprise and then sells them in his own name for his own account. The agent sells the goods in the name and for the account of the foreign manufacturer.

In case a foreign manufacturer does not wish to export to Switzerland, he may choose to grant a Swiss company a manufacturing license. There are no legal restrictions regarding the amount or the remission of royalties payable by Swiss companies. As a rule, exclusive manufacturing licenses for the whole territory of Switzerland do not present any problem under the Swiss antitrust legislation.

The principal or manufacturer often requires the agent or distributor to sign a non-competition clause prohibiting any competitive activity not only for the duration of the contract but also for a time after termination of the contract. In an agency contract, such a provision may be enforceable to a limited extent only and always gives the agent the right to reasonable compensation. Under an agency contract, the agent or his heirs are entitled further to a reasonable compensation if the agent has substantially increased the number of the principal's customers and the principal derives a profit from the dealings of his agent with the customers.

In Switzerland, the government attitude is not unfavorable toward wholly-owned subsidiaries of foreign enterprises. Therefore, equity joint ventures are not as common as in other countries. A further reason against sharing ownership with another firm in a company may be that minority stockholders are not well protected under Swiss corporate law. A foreign enterprise which nevertheless decides to become a minority stockholder often tries to protect its interests by pooling them with those of another minority stockholder or with the majority stockholder in a stockholders' agreement (covering such areas as board membership and dividend policy). Non-equity joint ventures where participation extends to manufacturing process, patents, trademarks and managerial knowhow are frequent.

Any foreign enterprise legally established in its own country may choose to enter the Swiss market by opening a branch office. The branch office may consist of a sales office or a more complex operation. The manager of the branch office need not be a Swiss citizen, but at least one manager must be a Swiss resident and have full authority to conduct the business of the branch.

Engaging in any kind of commercial activity in Switzerland on a long-term basis usually requires creating a Swiss joint-stock corporation (*Aktiengesellschaft, Société Anonyme*). The structure of the corporation is flexible enough to suite the purposes of the individual businessman desiring to reduce his potential liability as well as those of the financing or manufacturing group having a great need for capital. Out of the one-hundred-thousand corporations in Switzerland, only about fifty per cent exceed the minimum share capital of Swiss francs fifty-thousand required by law. It would lead too far to comment in this context on the various types of shares, the commercial accounting and the dissolution of the corporation. A member of the board of directors must own at least one share and the majority of the members must be Swiss citizens. It is therefore common practice for a foreign shareholder of a hundred per cent Swiss subsidiary to enter with a Swiss citizen into a qualifying share agreement whereby the shareholder sells one share to the trustee board member but retains an option to buy it back. The trustee board member in turn binds himself to act only upon instruction of the principal.

Employment of Swiss Citizens and Foreigners

For many years, Switzerland experienced a significant shortage of labor. The number of foreign residents in Switzerland reached one million, thus exceeding fifteen per cent of the total population. The majority of the foreigners are employed as construction, industrial or agricultural workers or as hotel employees. The following remarks will be restricted to executive personnel.

A foreigner has no right to accept employment in Switzerland without first securing a work permit for himself and a residence permit for the whole family. The fact that only a small number of work permits are available may present a major stumbling block to establishing a foreign-controlled enterprise in Switzerland.

The granting of permits is left to a great extent to the discretion of the competent cantonal and federal authorities. The federal government allocates to each canton each year the number of permits available. Owing to political factors, the cantonal quotas are very limited. Applications for work permits for executive personnel need careful consideration and preparation. The cantons grant the permit mostly based on economic considerations. In recent years, it has become more customary to discuss the proposed set-up of a Swiss establishment with the authorities beforehand in order to make sure that the needed permits will be available. It is no secret that multinational enterprises choose to establish a subsidiary in one canton rather than in another because of the availability in that particular canton of the needed permits. Securing of permits often requires negotiation and may take several months.

The employment relationship is governed by the provisions of the Federal Code of Obligations (*Obligationenrecht, Code des Obligations*). Strikes are exceptional. The employment contract may be terminated by either party by giving one month's notice. When an employee has served for a period exceeding one year, the period of notice is usually two months. Employer and employees may agree on extended-notice period. The Swiss social security system is compulsory and provides for benefits in case of old age, death and disability. The contributions are ten per cent, paid in equal parts by employer and employee. The Swiss Parliament has considered a bill which will make it compulsory to provide on a private basis a minimum pension scheme. This bill provides for minimum benefits in case of old age, death and disability. The employer will have to pay at least fifty per cent of the contributions. This bill is likely to be enacted and become effective within two or three years. On the other hand, most Swiss enterprises already have created pension funds which exceed the minimum benefits compulsory under the new law.

Banking and Finance

The monetary unit of Switzerland is the Swiss franc. The central bank in Switzerland is the Swiss National Bank (*Schweizerische Nationalbank, Banque Nationale Suisse*). There is no exchange control in the usual sense. The Swiss National Bank is more concerned about the inflow of foreign currency than about the outflow of Swiss francs. Foreign investments, loans or royalties and other capital transactions are uncontrolled. The remission of earnings and the repatriation of foreign investments in Switzerland are unrestricted. Other temporary controls to keep foreign money out of Switzerland have been abolished. Until January 1979, the purchase of Swiss securities by foreigners was, as a rule, subject to approval by the Swiss National Bank, and the amount of foreign bank notes allowed to be brought into Switzerland was limited to the equivalent of twenty-thousand Swiss francs.

Until May 1979, loans and similar credits extended by foreigners to Swiss residents were subject to approval by the Swiss National Bank.

Since 1974, new funds entering Switzerland and deposited in a Swiss bank have been subject to a negative rate of interest of ten per cent per quarter, provided that the amount of the deposit exceeds one-hundred-thousand Swiss Francs. The Swiss government recently has restricted the inflow of foreign currency by limiting the amount of foreign bank notes allowed to be brought into Switzerland to an equivalent of eight-thousand Swiss Francs.

Local capital is easily available in Switzerland. The rates vary according to demand and offer. They have a tendency to be substantially below the rates usually applicable in other countries. Swiss banks engage in the capital, money, foreign-exchange and gold markets. Many of them are experienced in the multinational commercial banking business. All the banks are subject to the supervision of the Federal Banking Commission (*Bankenkommission, Commission des Banques*) under the federal banking law (*Bankengesetz, Loi sur les Banques*) of 1934.

The most active stock exchange is in Zurich. On the Zurich Exchange, brokers buy and sell securities for their own account only. Even when executing a customer's order, the broker acts as principal in the transaction.

Here we cannot avoid commenting on the most-discussed feature of Swiss banking, banking secrecy and the numbered account. Article 47 of the Banking Law reads as follows:

> 1. Whoever divulges a secret entrusted to him in his capacity as officer, employee, authorized agent, liquidator or commissioner of a bank, as a representative of the Banking Commission, officer or employee of a recognized auditing company, or who has become aware of such a secret in this capacity, and whoever tries to induce others to violate professional secrecy, shall be punished by a prison term not to exceed six months or by a fine not exceeding fifty-thousand Swiss francs.
> 2. If the act has been committed by negligence, the penalty shall be a fine not exceeding thirty-thousand Swiss Francs.
> 3. The violation of professional secrecy remains punishable even after termination of the official or employment relationship or the exercise of the profession.
> 4. Federal and cantonal regulations concerning the obligation to testify and to furnish information to a government authority shall remain reserved.

Any bank client therefore is protected by law against disclosure of confidential information. He is as much protected as the holder of a numbered account. Numbered accounts are clients' accounts designated by a code number rather than by the real name of the customer. In the case of a numbered account, the identity of the client does not remain unknown to the management of the bank. It is basically just an additional administrative safeguard against illegal disclosure of information protected under the law.

In case of criminal proceedings, the banks must disclose the requested information on clients. Their officers testify and give evidence to the competent authorities in case of criminal proceedings in Switzerland; in foreign criminal proceedings testimony may be required to the extent an international treaty on mutual assistance in criminal matters provides for such disclosure. The treaties as a rule do not provide for disclosure of information in cases of tax evasion, antitrust or securities exchange law violations, which under Swiss law as a rule are not considered crimes. The rules of civil procedure of some cantons provide for the obligation to testify also in cases of civil litigation. The establishment of accounts and deposits maintained under numbers or passwords affects in no way the obligation of the bank officers to give evidence to the competent authorities.

The Swiss Bankers Association as well as the Swiss National Bank have been trying to prevent clients from misusing the secrecy provisions. The Swiss Bankers Association on behalf of all its members and the Swiss National Bank entered recently into an agreement under which the banks consented to prevent the improper use of the banking secrecy provisions. Whenever a new account is opened, the banks now may request information as to whether the account holder is acting for his own account or for somebody else. If he is acting as agent legally bound by professional secrecy or as trustee, he must confirm that he knows the beneficial owner of the assets to be deposited with the bank and that, in ascertaining the origin of such assets with all reasonable care and diligence, he has not become aware of any circumstance that would point to any improper use of banking secrecy by the beneficial owner, in particular to criminal acquisition of the assets in question.

Taxation

Taxes in Switzerland are levied at three levels: federal, cantonal and municipal; only the federal tax remains constant for all Swiss corporations. Cantonal and municipal taxes depend on the particular canton in which a corporation is registered and doing business. Taxes vary to some extent in each canton. Switzerland has a classical system of corporate taxation which taxes income of companies at the corporate and individual levels. There are, however, exceptions and concessions granted under federal or cantonal laws.

The federal tax (*Wehrsteuer, impôt pour la défence nationale*) is payable by all Swiss corporations. If a company owns more than twenty per cent or holds an investment of more than two-million francs in another Swiss or non-resident company, then dividend income received from the subsidiary is exempt from Swiss taxation at federal level. Most cantons and municipalities grant a similar concession to their companies under the holding-company privilege. Some types of corporations are exempt from cantonal and municipal but not from federal taxes. These are holding companies owning less than twenty per cent of the stock of other companies, domiciliary companies which do not engage in any trade within Switzerland, and mixed companies or auxiliary companies which either are eligible for a reduced tax rate or an exemption from cantonal and municipal taxes but on qualifying income only.

To illustrate the overall tax burden we will consider a few examples based on the 1978 tax rates.

A company with capital and reserves of one-million Swiss francs showing an annual net profit before taxation of (a) one-hundred-thousand Swiss francs or (b) five-hundred-thousand Swiss francs paid for 1978 the following aggregate direct tax (federal, cantonal, municipal):

Place of incorporation		Operating Company	Holding Company	Domiciliary Company
Zurich	a)	24,300	2,400	24,300
	b)	189,300	2,400	189,100
Geneva	a)	20,900	3,700	9,300
	b)	160,100	3,700	65,000
Zug	a)	19,900	1,600	7,500
	b)	120,600	1,600	57,000
Lucerne	a)	22,300	1,300	7,400
	b)	156,800	1,300	57,000

In Switzerland, the tax treatment of foreign-source income is similar to that of domestic income. There are no tax credits available. Foreign income however, may be totally or partially exempt if the income represents the net profit of a foreign branch of a Swiss company, originates from foreign real estate, from a substantial holding in a foreign company or is received by a Swiss domiciliary, mixed or auxiliary company.

If the foreign income is derived from a country which is a party to a double taxation treaty with Switzerland, the provisions of the treaty will apply to the Swiss company whether or not the Swiss company is entitled to partial or total exemption on its income on the federal, cantonal or municipal level. The reduced rates of withholding taxes levied by parties to these treaties on dividends, interest and royalties transferred to Switzerland often are more favorable compared with other countries.

In case dividends received by Swiss company are redistributed to a parent company, the dividend payments are subject to a thirty-five per cent Swiss withholding tax. This thirty five per cent rate may be reduced if the dividend payment goes to a double taxation treaty country. The Swiss legislation against the abuse of tax treaties usually requires that a Swiss company controlled by non-residents must pay out as dividends at least twenty-five per cent of income benefiting from the use of double taxation treaties.

In addition to the income tax imposed on resident individuals and the profit tax on companies engaged in business, there is a small tax on the net wealth of individuals and the capital of companies. Other taxes on capital are an immovable-property tax (in a few cantons), an inheritance tax (in most cantons), a gift tax (in some cantons) and an estate tax (in a few cantons). In addition, there is a federal stamp tax (*Stempelsteuer, droits de timbre*) on the issuance of domestic stocks and shares in domestic investment trusts, a duty on the transfer of securities, and a duty on the payment of certain insurance premiums. The federal turnover tax (*Warenumsatzsteuer, impôt sur le chiffre d'affaires*) is a single-stage sales tax levied on domestic turnover and on imports of movable goods. The present rates are 8.4 per cent on the wholesale value and 5.6 per cent on the delivered price if the merchandise is not for resale.

United States

DONALD PRINZ

CLAUDE ROHWER

Introduction

One can state generally that, by the standards of most countries in the world, the United States legal and political climate is and will remain favorable to foreign investment and foreign business enterprise. There are a number of factors which contribute to this situation.

The United States has a history of encouraging foreign investment. Before the First World War, this policy was in part the product of the great need for investment capital which could be met only with the participation of foreign investment. More recently, it may be a reflection of the fact that such investment has the immediate result of reducing the dollar 'drain'. For whatever reason, the historical pattern is clear and consistent and, like all traditions, will not be lightly discarded.

The United States has a generally consistent record of minimum controls and taxes upon imports. The United States Constitution prohibits discrimination by the individual states against imported goods, and the implementation of that provision produces some minor local taxation advantages for imported goods over domestic goods. At the consumer level, there never has been a discernable inclination to favor domestic goods over imports. On the contrary, there is a prestige value associated with the purchase of foreign goods which exists even in areas where the functional quality of domestic goods may be superior.

There is a deep-seated animosity in the United States toward government regulation of personal affairs and conduct. While the significance of the impact of this philosophy ebbs and flows with the times and the relative importance which the public attaches to other goals and objectives, it is nonetheless clear that the public has an ingrained distrust and dislike for government control. While it is obviously true that an individual citizen will be much more concerned with government controls over his or her activities than with government controls over the activities of foreigners, controls per se are not highly regarded.

In addition to basic attitudes and historical tradition, there is an intellectual commitment to foreign investment and trade which is predicated upon the perceived best interests of the United States and the world in general. For selfish interests and to fulfill our commitments and responsibilities as a major force in world economics, the United States must continue and expand its commitment to free investment and trade. It is difficult to discern the degree to which these thoughts are appreciated or shared by the general public, but they certainly influence the position of our society's leaders.

Readjusting the Economy

There is no doubt that the United States is undergoing a period of substantial readjustment in both its domestic economy and its position in and relation to the rest of the world. These readjustments have been moderately painful and will become more painful in the near future. As Americans attempt to identify the source of this pain, many will focus upon the activities of foreigners, including their domestic investments and trade, as the real or imagined source of particular problems. Therefore, we are witnessing and will continue to observe some significant arguments and proposals concerning these activities.

Foreign imports have an adverse effect upon certain domestic business and employment as well as upon the balance of payments. In general, there has been no substantial or concerted effort by the business community as a whole to restrict imports via quotas, taxes or discrimination to protect United States business. Obiously, particular industries, ranging from textiles to sugar beet production, have been very vocal from time to time and have had an impact which, in some cases, has placed significant limitations or burdens on imports. Viewed as a whole, however, these activities have not had a substantial effect upon imports. Labor unions probably constitute the most vocal interest group in the country on this issue. Aside from occasionally intense efforts in a particular industry, however, the basic thrust of the unions' efforts has been to amend tax laws to discourage United States corporations and multinationals from 'moving' their business activities to foreign countries and thereby 'exporting jobs'. Given the relatively limited political power of labor unions in the United States today, it would not seem likely that they will focus any great portion of their political efforts on attempting to restrict imports, but it probably is accurate to state they constitute the largest organized pressure group which exhibits some negative attitudes toward the importation of foreign goods.

A relatively new force in American politics is organized consumer groups. In various forms and varieties, existing and new organizations have become active in reflecting the interests of the consumer which, as they continually remind everyone, includes us all. It is difficult to predict whether this is a permanent addition to the American political scene, but one of the many areas of interest and activity of consumer groups is free trade to provide the consumer with the widest choice of products and the best price competition. They have had a significant impact in defeating proposals which would impede free trade.

The effect of imports upon the United States balance of payments does not seem to be advanced by anyone as a basis for restricting trade. One might surmise that those with sufficient understanding of economics to appreciate the problem also understand that there are adverse consequences which would result from restricting imports.

Regarding imports, one can summarize by noting that there have been and will continue to be concerted efforts by particular industries, both from employee groups and employers, to restrict imports which cause domestic dislocations. The prevailing trend, however, is to resist these efforts. One would expect to see some limited restrictive action from time to time with respect to certain types or categories of goods but no general shift toward restricting trade.

Foreign Investment

With respect to foreign investment in the United States, some different considerations are present. As previously noted, historical patterns and philosophical attitudes mitigate against restricting such investments. Investments in United States industry (as distinguished from passive investments such as purchase of land) have the effect of boosting employment in the United States. For the same reason that the unions oppose 'overseas' investment in plants and factories by United States corporations, they favor foreign investment in such facilities in the United States. These investments produce jobs. There is no significant voice in opposition. This position is reflected in past and current treaties which rather uniformly promote investment and provide safeguards and remove impediments thereto.

Since the First World War, there had been no substantial foreign ownership of United States property. In the last few years, such foreign investment has expanded rapidly, particularly in such areas as real property, and there is every indication that this will continue. Under these circumstances, caution dictates that one use care in predicting future American attitudes and legal policies with respect to these investments because total foreign investment is still relatively small, and the public attitude really has not been tested yet.

If foreign ownership and control began to assume substantial significance in such areas as domestic energy sources, financial institutions, transportation, news media or other key industries, it could well produce a significant reaction from our public and government. The only area which can be described as a 'trouble spot' today is ownership of farm land.

There has been significant foreign investment in American real estate in general. There is no available source which provides accurate statistics on this subject as there generally has been no control, reporting requirements or record keeping. However, there has been significant buying activity by foreigners and foreign investment entities, and this had produced a degree of concern.While few Americans are involved in farming today, many trace their antecedents to a farm family. For this or other ill-defined reasons, the American public has a great attachment to farm land. Before foreign purchases became an issue, there was a substantial shift away from the small, family farm toward large individual or corporate farming operations which produced a great public concern over the 'concentration of ownership of farm land'. The perceived threat of substantial foreign ownership of farmland has produced a significant outcry which has resulted in the adoption of a federal law imposing some reporting requirements upon foreign nationals who purchase land. There also is isolated state legislation purporting to restrict or prohibit such foreign investments.

It can be anticipated that this will remain a significant issue and may result in further legislation. To accomplish the objective which some seek, however, the United States would have to overhaul drastically its laws concerning ownership of property by other than natural persons or its laws concerning the obligation to divulge the identity of investors in partnerships, corporations and other forms of business organizations. We believe it unlikely that the United States will take the far-reaching steps required to effectively preclude beneficial ownership by foreigners of farm land in this country.

As countries such as Canada have found it appropriate to restrict foreign ownership and control of certain basic resources and industries, the United States might be moved to such action if such investment or control reaches levels perceived to be threatening. While this is a matter of some public discussion, it seems unlikely that the problem will develop to the point that it produces such a reaction in the foreseeable future. In this regard, it is significant to note that dollar-rich foreign interests are reported to be investing heavily in such assets as government bonds and shares of large publically-traded corporations. It would appear that this is a conscious policy to avoid the American reaction which might be produced by heavy investment in a key United States industry or resource, such as coal.

All business, domestic or foreign, which desires to construct new factories or production facilities in the United States faces substantial new environmental and land-use controls. Discussion of problems in this area are not within the scope of this work because they impact upon foreign and domestic business interests equally.

In conclusion, there have been no significant recent changes in the legal climate with respect to foreign investments or foreign imports, and we do not expect any fundamental changes in the foreseeable future.

The Hypothetical Problem

DENNIS CAMPBELL

TERRY R. WITTLER

Introduction

The purpose of this hypothetical legal problem is to illustrate solutions which would result in different legal systems to a common set of facts; to highlight the interplay of legal systems when confronted by such international transactions, and to compare the various outcomes. The contributing authors have emphasized legal considerations but also have noted relevant commercial (or political) considerations where appropriate. It is assumed that the international transactions in this problem do not violate relevant antitrust or foreign-exchange laws and that all technical know-how and patents have been registered properly or protected. Each contributing author has been requested to analyze the hypothetical situation by assuming that the corporation or company is entering the jurisdiction in which he practices. (For example, a United States attorney might assume that the Solar Collector and Solar Generator are produced by two companies in the European Communities attempting to penetrate the United States market; a French attorney might assume that the Solar Collector and Solar Generator are produced by two corporations in the United States attempting to penetrate the French or European Communities market.)

Facts

A. Background

Two corporations (domestic-market corporations) produce Solar Energy Electrical Units. When properly installed, these units provide individual homes with an alternative source of electricity. The unit consists of two basic component parts: a Solar Collector and a Solar Generator. Each of the two corporations has individual patents on each component part. It is recognized that the Solar Collector of Corporation *A* is superior to that of Corporation *B*; the Solar Generator of Corporation *B* is superior to that of the patented model of Corporation *A*. However, the advantages and disadvantages of each respective Solar Energy Electrical Unit are about equal and, therefore, the two models are competitive in their domestic market. Both Corporation *A* and Corporation *B* have developed a lucrative domestic market. They separately have exported models through independent Foreign-Market agents, Agent *Y* and Agent *Z*, respectively. At the present time, however, the number of foreign sales is relatively low.

B. Cooperation in the Foreign Market

Corporation *A* and Corporation *B* wish to increase sales in a Foreign-Market Country. As a result, Corporation *A* and Corporation *B* have decided to cooperate in the selected Foreign-Market Country. By combining the Superior Generator with the Superior Collector, the quality of the entire energy unit will be increased substantially, improving its marketability and allowing for increased sales and profits. The two corporations, however, are concerned about tax consequences and product liability in the Foreign-Market Country.

C. Plan of Action

1. Liberian Corporation

Corporation *A* and Corporation *B* have determined to form a Liberian corporation. They want this corporation to be properly formed, organized and functioning; ownership of this corporation to be shared by allocating fifty per cent of the share capital to Corporation *A* and fifty per cent to Corporation *B*; the board of directors of this corporation to consist of two directors, one from Corporation *A* and one from Corporation *B*; no record of their involvement in this corporation, and the names of the directors to be anonymous. The Liberian Corporation is to have only a minimal amount of capitalization but will hold rights to the technological know-how of the two component parts of the Solar Electrical Unit, namely the Superior Collector and the Superior Generator. This technological know-how is to be purchased for a nominal price from Corporation *A* and Corporation *B*, respectively, upon formation of the Liberian Corporation.

2. Foreign-Market Country Representatives

The Liberian Corporation upon formation is to contact Agent *Y* and Agent *Z* in the Foreign-Market Country. The Liberian Corporation and the Agents are to agree that the latter will be authorized to act as the former's representatives in all matters related to the Superior Units; that the agents are to find a Foreign-Market Country company to patent the device, assemble and distribute the product in the Foreign-Market Country; that the said company must promise to purchase all of the Superior Components from the Liberian Corporation; that the agents will receive a five per cent commission on all sales; that said company will retain twenty-five per cent of all sales, and that the agents will transfer to the Liberian Corporation the costs of the Superior Components plus overhead and shipping expenses but will deposit the remainder of all sales into a Swiss bank account (anonymously held by the Liberian Corporation).

3. Foreign-Market Company

The Foreign-Market Company to be contacted by the agents must agree that the company will patent the Superior Generator, the Superior Collector and the Solar Energy Electrical Unit as a whole in its own name in the Foreign-Market Country; purchase all Superior Units from the agents; assemble the units, package and translate instructions for installation in appropriate foreign languages, and transfer to the agents seventy-five per cent of all sales.

D. Operation in Action

The Foreign-Market Company, after the above steps were completed, received one-thousand orders for the new Superior Unit in the first month. Corporations A and B were duly contacted. Corporation *A* produced one-thousand Superior Solar Collectors and sold these to the Liberian corporation at a price of cost plus overhead and shipping expenses; Corporation *B* produced one-thousand Superior Solar Generators and sold these to the The Liberian Corporation at a price of cost plus overhead and shipping expenses. The Liberian Corporation transferred these one-thousand Superior Collectors and one-thousand Superior Generators to the Foreign-Market Agents at cost plus overhead and shipping expenses.

The Foreign-Market Agents then transferred these Superior Collectors and Generators to the Foreign-Market Company for a promise to pay the Liberian Corporation seventy-five per cent of all sales. The Foreign-Market Company assembled the Superior Unit merely by attaching the two basic component parts with eight bolts, packaged the entire Superior Model and supplied instructions in the Foreign-Market Country language. The Company sold each Model at a price equal to ten-thousand dollars. The Company had costs equal to one-thousand dollars per Unit. The Company transferred to the agents an amount equal to seven-thousand five-hundred dollars per Unit, as required by contract terms. The agents retained the equivalent of five-hundred dollars per Superior Model, paid the Liberian Corporation two-thousand dollars (the cost of the Liberian corporation plus overhead and shipping expenses) and deposited the remaining five-thousand dollars per Unit in the Liberian Corporation's anonymous Swiss bank account. The Liberian Corporation paid the equivalent of seven-hundred and fifty dollars per Solar Collector and seven-hundred and fifty dollar per Solar Generator (the cost of production plus overhead and shipping expenses) to Corporations *A* and *B*.

The summary of the financial details of the business operation is as follows in United States Dollar equivalents:

Solar Collector production costs	$ 500
Solar Generator production costs	500
Overhead/shipping to Liberia expenses	500
Overhead/shipping from Liberia to Foreign-Market Agents expenses	500
Foreign-Market Company costs	1,000
Foreign-Market Company retains	1,500
Foreign-Market Agents' share	500
Swiss bank account	5,000
Retail Price of the Superior Unit (equivalent)	$10,000

E. Malfunctioning of the Superior Unit

Of the thousand Solar Energy Models sold in the Foreign-Market Country, all functioned perfectly except one unit. In either the Solar Generator or the Solar Collector of the Superior Unit, there was a malfunction which, despite the best quality control on the part of the Foreign-Market Company, could not have been detected beforehand. The Foreign-Market Company performed all other functions without fault (*culpa* or *dolus*). The Superior Unit was installed and, after two months, overheated, causing a fire which destroyed the home of the purchaser, injured the owner's spouse and a visiting neighbor, and killed the child of the owner.

Issues Presented

A. Corporation Formation

Domestic-Market Corporations *A* and *B* decided upon the formation of a Liberian Corporation. Please explain steps to be taken to form such a corporation and the required structure; suggest alternative locations for the formation of such a corporation and steps to establish such corporation, and discuss advantages and disadvantages of forming the corporation in Liberia and in any suggested alternative, as compared with forming the corporation in the country in which you practice.

B. Contractual Considerations

How would your courts view the nature of the contract whereby the Foreign-Market Company registers the patents in its own name but pays seventy-five per cent ot the Liberian Corporation through the agents? In particular, please discuss the nature of payments as described through the appropriate contracts; the various parties' interests in the patents as described through the appropriate contracts, and any alternative contractual arrangement which you believe would more adequately protect the parties with respect to product liability and tax liability.

C. Tax Liability

What tax consequences do you foresee for each of the parties in the instant case. Will either Domestic-Market Corporations *A* or *B* have Foreign-Market Country taxable income? Will the Liberian Corporation pay tax on any of the amounts received or placed in the Swiss bank account? Will the Foreign-Market Agents be taxed on their profits or the amounts which they transfer (to the Liberian Corporation and the Swiss bank account)? Will the Foreign-Market Company be required to pay taxes on any amounts?

D. Product Liability

Which party to the international transactions will be liable for the personal injury and property damages caused by the defective component part of the Superior Electrical Energy Unit: the Domestic-Market Corporations, the Liberian Corporation, the Foreign-Market Agents, the Foreign-Market Company?

The Model In Action

Legal systems are best understood by observing them in action. Thus, the authors of the following chapters discuss the functioning of their respective domestic legal systems with respect to the preceding hypothetical problem. The Model involves an attempt by two exporting corporations to minimize their taxable income by concentrating it in an intervening corporation domiciled in a so-called tax-haven country, in this case Liberia[1]. Tax havens can be divided into four categories:

(a) jurisdictions which impose no taxes at all;
(b) those which impose very low taxes;
(c) those which do not tax foreign source income, and
(d) those which grant special privileges[2].

Liberia is in the third category. Under the Liberian Internal Revenue Code, 'in the case of a nonresident person, gross income shall include only gross income derived from Liberia'[3]; thus, taxation of income from sources outside of Liberia implicitly is excluded. The key phrases in this exclusion are 'nonresident person' and 'income derived from Liberia'. For purposes of these analyses, a 'nonresident person' is defined as a Liberian corporation which '(i) is foreign-owned, (ii) is not regularly engaged in the ownership of Liberian real property..., (iii) is not regularly engaged in... a contractual arrangement with the Government of Liberia,... and (iv) is not carrying on operations in Liberia'[4]. A corporation will be considered 'foreign-owned' if 'not more than twenty-five per cent of the total combined voting power and not more than twenty-five per cent of the total value of the outstanding equity stock is owned, directly or indirectly, by resident persons'[5]. Since the Model provides for the projected Liberian corporation to be owned in equal shares by two non-Liberian corporations, the 'foreign-owned' requirement of the statute easily can be met under the conditions of the hypothetical fact situation.

Because the Model does not provide for ownership of any real property within Liberia nor for contractual arrangements with the Government of Liberia, the second and third requirements of the law can be met.

The fourth requirement is that the Liberian corporation not carry on operations in Liberia. This condition is commonly found in taxation statutes and treaties and often is difficult to apply to specific fact situations. However, the Liberian tax code provides that the following activities carried out within

Liberia will not constitute carrying on operations in Liberia:
(a) maintaining an administrative, management, or statutory office;
(b) holding meetings of directors or share holders;
(c) investing in Liberian securities;
(d) maintaining a bank account, and
(e) registering a vessel or aircraft[6].

The Liberian corporation envisioned in the Model can comply with these limitations and, thus, qualify for taxation as a non-resident person. As noted above, this means only income derived from Liberia will be subject to taxation in Liberia. Since the Model does not contemplate such activities, no tax liability should be incurred in Liberia. Further, if the corporation has no Liberian-derived gross income, it need not file a Liberian tax return[7].

Formation of a Liberian Corporation

Forming a corporation in Liberia is not a difficult task. The International Trust Company of Liberia will provide copies of the Liberian Business Corporation Act, the Internal Revenue Code, two pamphlets, *A Service for Attorneys* and *Documentation Requirements and Schedule of Fees*, and model forms of articles of incorporation and bylaws[8]. If these draft forms are used with only minor variations, the trust company will make necessary local arrangements upon receipt of telexed instructions and advise of corporate existence by telex within two business days[9]. The company will provide original incorporators who will relinquish their shares to designated persons after incorporation. It also will arrange for original directors to hold an initial board meeting to adopt bylaws and appoint officers. These directors then customarily resign and new directors take control. The corporate minutes of these transactions need not be public[10].

If the incorporators wish, the incorporation also can be carried out by mailing the required documents to the trust company or one of its agents[11]. Four sets of the articles of incorporation are required, and each must be signed by the incorporators and duly acknowledged[12]. In addition, if these documents are signed outside of Liberia, two of the copies must be attested to by a consul of Liberia or by a consular official of another government which has diplomatic relations with Liberia[13]. The trust company will provide resident incorporators to avoid the necessity of having the signatures of the incorporators authenticated[14]. Notice of incorporation is to be telexed within two business days of receipt of the necessary documentation[15].

Characteristics of a Liberian Corporation

Liberia has a modern business corporation act designed to accommodate the needs of international business. Under this act, the Model's requirements of joint control, minimum capitalization, and anonymity can be met.

A corporation can be organized in Liberia for any lawful business purpose[16]. Unless limited by the articles of incorporation, the corporation will have a broad range of powers, including the right to sue and be sued, the right to buy and sell real and personal property, to have a corporate seal, to make contracts, and to issue and acquire its own shares[17]. Its duration is perpetual[18]. These general powers need not be enumerated in the articles of incorporation[19].

Every corporation must designate a registered agent in Liberia for service of process and reception of notices[20]. For a domestic corporation not having a place of business in Liberia, the registered agent must be a domestic bank or trust company which has a paid-in capital of fifty-thousand dollars and which has been authorized by the Legislature to act as an agent[21]. A corporation may change its registered agent by sending notification to the Ministry of Foreign Affairs[22], but no new designation will be recognized until all charges due to the former agent have been paid[23]. Any corporation which fails to maintain a registered agent will be dissolved[24].

A Liberian corporation can be formed by one or more persons or corporations, regardless of nationality[35]. All required documents must be in the English language, but the corporation's name can be in any language so long as it is written in Roman letters[26]. The corporate name must contain the word corporation or some other word or abbreviation indicating limited liability[27]. The name must not conflict with any existing name on an index of corporate names kept by the Ministry of Foreign Affairs[28].

A limited set of articles of incorporation is required. Basically, they must include the name of the corporation and the name and address of its registered agent; a statement of purpose, such as 'any lawful business purpose'; a description of the number and classes of shares to be issued including par value, if any, and whether they are to be issued as registered or bearer shares; the number of original directors; the names and addresses of original incorporators, and any provisions limiting the powers otherwise granted under the Act to the corporation[29].

After the articles have been filed with the Ministry of Foreign Affairs[30], a meeting of the incorporators must be held within a reasonable time. This meeting may be held in person or by proxy and need not be within Liberia[31]. The incorporators listed in the articles may transfer their stock subscriptions prior to such meeting so that the transferees shall hold the organizational meeting of incorporation[32].

The directors are to adopt bylaws for the corporation consistent with the Business Corporation Act and the articles of incorporation[33].

The Act provides for a flexible corporate structure. Several classes of shares may be issued, either with or without a stated par value, and they may have either full or limited voting power[34]. Shares may be convertible[35] or redeemable[36] and fractional shares may be issued[37]. Restrictions upon the transfer of shares may be imposed by the articles of incorporation, the bylaws, or an agreement among shareholders[38]. Such restrictions may include a right of first refusal or an obligation on the part of the corporation or another person to buy the shares at a specified price[39], but absolute prohibitions on transfer are ineffective[40]. Transfer restrictions must be noted on the stock certificates[41].

Subscriptions for shares are irrevocable for six months unless the agreement specifies otherwise or the other subscribers unanimously consent to the withdrawal of a subscription[42]. Subscription agreements must be in writing[43]. Payment for the shares subscribed shall be as directed by the board of directors, unless the subscription agreement specifies otherwise[44]. Calls for payment shall be uniform within classes of shareholders[45]. Failure to pay for the shares upon call can result in loss of the subscription rights, although the defaulting subscriber may receive all or part of his payments back if the shares are subsequently sold[46]. Subscription rights are transferable[47].

Shares may be paid for in cash, tangible or intangible property, or services[48]. The judgment of the board of directors as to the value of the consideration received is final, absent evidence of fraud[49]. Certificates may not be issued until the shares have been paid in full[50], and obligations of the subscriber for future payment or services are not sufficient[51]. The reasonable costs of the formation of the corporation and underwriting expenses may be allowed out of the proceeds of the sale of stock[52].

If the corporation issues shares with a stated par value, the consideration received to the extent of the par value shall constitute the stated capital of the corporation and any excess received shall be surplus[53]. If shares without a stated par value are issued, all of the consideration received shall be considered stated capital unless the board of directors, within sixty days of issuing the shares, votes to allocate a portion of the proceeds to surplus[54]. The stated capital may be increased by the board by transfers from surplus to capital at any time[55].

Shares in the corporation shall be represented by stock certificates bearing the signature of the president or vice president of the corporation, and another corporate officer[56]. Any limitations upon the rights of the shares must be indicated upon their face, or a statement must be printed upon the certificate to the effect that a statement of such limitation will be provided to the share holder by the corporation upon request[57].

The corporation may pay dividends in cash, stock or property. Dividends may be declared out of the corporate surplus or, if there is none, out of the profits for the present and preceding fiscal years[58]. Dividends may be paid from profits arising from the exploitation of natural resources, patents, and other wasting assets, without any deduction for depletion of such assets, so long as any share holders with a preference are protected[59]. Share dividends are allowed as long as stated capital is adjusted accordingly[60] and the dividend is approved by a two-thirds vote of the shares of each class of share holders that might be adversely affected by the distribution[61]. The unrealized appreciation of any assets may not be included in the surplus for purposes of distribution[62].

The corporation also has the power to purchase or redeem its own shares[63]. Shares purchased out of stated capital are to be cancelled[64]. Other shares may be held as treasury shares and disposed of as the directors see fit[65].

The board may reduce the stated capital of the corporation by any amount of surplus that had been transferred to capital, but no reduction may prejudice preferred shareholders[66].

The powers of the corporation are vested in the board of directors[67]. Directors may be of any nationality and need not be residents of Liberia or share holders of the corporation[68]. Furthermore, non-resident corporations are allowed to have other corporations as their directors[69]. Unless otherwise provided, the corporation shall have three directors[70]; if there are fewer than three shareholders, the number of directors shall equal the number of shareholders[71]. The number of directors can be increased or decreased by the shareholders and, if the bylaws so provide, by the directors, as long as such action is by the majority of the entire board and the term of an incumbent director is not reduced[72].

Directors are elected at the annual shareholders meeting[73]. Directors may be divided into up to four classes to allow for staggered terms[74]. If a director is removed without cause, he or she must be replaced by a vote of the shareholders[75]. Otherwise, vacancies are filled by a majority vote of the board[76].

The Act fixes a quorum of the board at a majority of the entire board, but the articles or bylaws may reduce this to not less than one-third of the entire board[77]. Directors are allowed to vote by proxy given in writing[78]. As an alternative to a full meeting, action can be taken if board members unanimously agree in writing and this is entered on the corporation's minutes[79]. Meetings also may be held over a conference telephone line or by other similar method of simultaneous communication[80]. The bylaws or articles may require a larger quorum for specific actions[81].

Board meetings may be held within or without Liberia[82]. Notice of regular meetings need not be given if their time and place are specified in the bylaws[83]. Notice may be waived in writing either before or after the meeting[84]. The work of the board may be carried out by one or more executive subcommittees, if the bylaws or the articles so provide[85].

No limitations are placed on transactions between the corporation and the directors or companies in which the directors have a financial interest so long as there is full disclosure to the board of the director's interest[86]. However, further restrictions may be placed in the articles[87]. The corporation may agree to indemnify directors and other persons for any liability they might incur as a result of actions taken on behalf of the corporation in good faith[88]. The corporation also may insure such risks[89].

The corporation shall have a president, secretary, and a treasurer appointed by the board unless otherwise provided[90]. The same person may hold two or more offices unless specifically prohibited[91].

Both officers and directors are held to a standard of care of 'ordinarily prudent men' acting under similar circumstances[92].

An annual meeting of shareholders must be held, either within or without Liberia[93]. Shareholders are entitled to written notice of the meeting not more than sixty nor less than fifteen days before the meeting[94]. Such notice may be waived in writing either before or after the meeting, or by attendance at the meeting without objection as to lack of notice[95]. Action also may be taken by the shareholders by unanimous written consent without a meeting[96]. Shareholders may be represented by proxy, which shall be valid for eleven months after signing, unless it specifies a different period of validity[97]. Quorum requirements are similar to those of the board of directors[98].

Non-resident corporations need not keep records and accounts in Liberia[99]. Records and minutes may be kept in written form, or in any form capable of being reduced to writing within a reasonable time[100].

The Act protects minority shareholder interests in several ways. Shareholders have the right to dissent from any mergers or any sale of substantially all of the assets of the corporation[101]. In such a case, the dissenting shareholder is entitled to the fair value of his shares[102]. The Act also provides for the dissolution of the corporation in case the board of directors or the shareholders should become deadlocked and incapable of acting[103].

Liberia as the Corporate Domicile

It is clear that the Liberian Business Corporation Act will facilitate the formation of a corporation which fulfills the requirements of the Model.

The corporation can be formed quickly and with a minimum of formalities. If the services of the International Trust Company of Liberia are used, corporate existence can be obtained in as little as two days[104]. The trust company will provide initial incorporators and directors, thus preserving the anonymity of Corporation *A* and Corporation *B*[105]. Once the corporation is formed, these nominal corporate officials can appoint successors as directed by Corporations *A* and *B*, and resign[106]. In fact, since directors of non-resident companies need not be natural persons, and there will be only two shareholders[107] Corporations *A* and *B* could direct that they themselves be named directors, with no fear of disclosure[108].

Corporate records need not be kept in Liberia[109] and shareholder and directors meetings may be held anywhere in the world[110]. Both the board[111] and the shareholders[112] may act without meeting by unanimous written consent and provision is even made for the board to act by conference telephone call[113], all of which should make transacting corporate business rather easy. Similarly, only three corporate officers are required, and an individual may hold more than one position[114]

The cost of incorporating in Liberia is not substantial. The trust company estimates that, for a corporation with minimal capital (up to fifty-thousand dollars) the first year cost will be under seven-hundred dollars and the annual costs thereafter two-hundred and fifty dollars[115]. The United States dollar is legal tender in Liberia, and there are no currency restrictions placed upon non-resident corporations[116].

Other Jurisdictions

There are, of course, many other tax-haven jurisdictions. Bermuda is a popular base for multinational companies. It is one of those countries which imposes no tax on incomes, capital gains, or turn-over[117]. There is no requirement of local ownership[118] and there are no external exchange controls[119]. However, at least a quorum of the directors must be Bermuda residents, and corporate records must be maintained in Bermuda[120]. Bearer shares are not permitted, but nominee share holdings are[121]. Finally, an annual audit is required, and a share registry must be made available to the public[122].

Panama is also an often-mentioned tax haven. Its corporation act has many features similar to Liberia's. A corporation can be formed in Panama using local founders, so that it is not necessary to be present in Panama[123]. There is no requirement of Panamanian ownership and directors and officers may be of any nationality, only a resident agent is required[124]. Bearer shares and no-par shares are permitted[125]. The articles of incorporation may be executed in any language[126]. However, unlike Liberia, Panama requires that corporate directors be natural persons[127].

Taxation in Panama is similar to that of Liberia. No tax is levied upon income from operations carried on outside of the country[128]. The law clearly outlines that, as long as foreign merchandise does not enter Panama, foreign sales operations conducted within Panama will not be subject to local taxation[129].

Finally, it should be noted that most tax havens are not party to double taxation treaties, since they impose no tax themselves on foreign-source income. This may be an advantage in some cases, in that these countries are not required to disclose information to tax authorities of other countries[130]. However, it also means that tax-haven corporations are denied whatever benefits these treaties might provide. Liberia tries to compensate for this problem by giving the tax authorities discretionary powers to reduce Liberian taxes ((w)here a foreign country does not allow appropriate relief from double taxation. . . .)[131]

Panama and Bermuda, along with Liberia, are only three examples of jurisdictions which can be used to minimize the taxation of international transactions. In every case, however, the advantages to be gained from the use of a tax-haven corporation depend to a great extent upon the tax laws of the jurisdiction in which the original corporation is formed, and of those in which the ultimate sales are made[132]. Care must be taken to ascertain whether these two jurisdictions will respect the corporate formalities of the transactions. It is possible that certain expenses will be disallowed for tax purposes, or that certain foreign-source income will be attributed to the corporate share holders and taxed locally, even though it was earned and remains outside the jurisdiction[133]. Since such considerations are beyond the scope of this article, it only can be noted that the successful operation of the Model in any given tax jurisdiction will depend heavily upon the precise nature of the domestic tax laws.

Notes

1. No attempt is made to present a recommended plan or scheme for minimizing taxes, but rather to provide a reasonable model, based upon past experience, which can be used to observe the operation and interrelation of the various legal systems.

2. See, for example, Stebbings, 'Panama and the Multinational Corporation: Tax Haven and Other Considerations', 8 *International Lawyer* (1974), pages 626, 629.

3. Section 11.83(1), Internal Revenue Code of Liberia (1977).
4. *Id.*, Section 11.81(3).
5. *Id.*, Section 11.81(3)(b)(i).
6. *Id.*, Section 11.81(4).
7. *Id.*, Section 11.91(2)(b).
8. The International Trust Company of Liberia is located at 80 Broad Street, P.O. Box 292, Monrovia, Liberia. It is represented by the following international agents: Liberian Corporation Services Inc., 5 West 45th Street, New York, New York 10036, U.S.A.; Liberian Services S.A., Pelikanstrasse 37, 8001 Zürich, Switzerland; Liberian Services Ltd., 33 Cork Street, London W1X 1HB, England; and Liberian Services (Far East) Ltd., 11th Floor, American International Tower, 16–18 Queens Road Central, Hong Kong.
9. *A Service for Attorneys*, The International Trust Company of Liberia, page 7, paragraph 3(a).
10. *Id.*, page 8, paragraphs 3(c) and (d).
11. *Id.*, page 8, paragraph 4.
12. *Id.*
13. Section 1.4(5)(c), Business Corporation Act of Liberia (1976).
14. *A Service for Attorneys, Supra*, note 9, page 8, paragraph 4.
15. *Id.*
16. Section 2.1, Business Corporation Act of Liberia (1976).
17. *Id.*, Section 2.2.
18. *Id.*
19. *Id.*, Section 4.4(1).
20. *Id.*, Section 3.1.
21. *Id.*
22. *Id.*, Section 3.1(4).
23. *Id.*, Section 3.1(3).
24. *Id.*, Section 3.1.
25. *Id.*, Section 4.1.
26. *Id.*, Section 1.4(2).
27. *Id.*, Section 4.2(1)(a).
28. *Id.*, Section 4.2(1)(b).
29, *Id.*, Section 4.4.
30. *Id.*, Section 4.6.
31. *Id.*, Section 4.8(1).
32. *Id.*, Section 4.8(2).
33. *Id.*, Section 4.9.
34. *Id.*, Section 5.1(1).
35. *Id.*, Section 5.1(2).
36. *Id.*, Section 5.1(3).
37. *Id.*, Section 5.1(4).
38. *Id.*, Section 5.2(1).
39. *Id.*, Section 5.2(2).
40. *Id.*, Section 5.2(1).
41. *Id.*, Section 5.3.
42. *Id.*, Section 5.3(1).
43. *Id.*, Section 5.3(2).
44. *Id.*, Section 5.3(3).
45. *Id.*
46. *Id.*, Section 5.3(4).
47. *Id.*, Section 5.3(5).
48. *Id.*, Section 5.4(1).
49. *Id.*
50. *Id.*, section 5.5(2).
51. *Id.*, Section 5.5(1).
52. *Id.*, Section 5.6
53. *Id.*, Section 5.7(1).

54. *Id.*, Section 5.7(2).
55. *Id.*, Section 5.7(3).
56. *Id.*, Section 5.8(1).
57. *Id.*, Section 5.8(3).
58. *Id.*, Section 5.9(1).
59. *Id.*, Section 5.9(2).
60. *Id.*, Section 5.10(1).
61. *Id.*, Section 5.10(4).
62. *Id.*, Section 5.10(2).
63. *Id.*, Section 5.11(1).
64. *Id.*, Section 5.12(1).
65. *Id.*, Section 5.12(3).
66. *Id.* Section 5.12(1) and (2).
67. *Id.*, Section 6.1.
68. *Id.*, Section 6.2.
69. *Id.*
70. *Id.*, Section 6.3(1).
71. *Id.*
72. *Id.*, Section 6.2.
73. *Id.*, Section 6.4(1).
74. *Id.*, Section 6.5.
75. *Id.*, Section 6.6(2).
76. *Id.*, Section 6.6(1).
77. *Id.*, Section 6.8(1).
78. *Id.*, Section 6.8(3).
79. *Id.*, Section 6.8(4).
80. *Id.*, Section 6.8(5).
81. *Id.*, Section 6.8(6).
82. *Id.*, Section 6.9(1).
83. *Id.*, Section 6.9(2).
84. *Id.*, Section 6.9(3).
85. *Id.*, Section 6.10(1).
86. *Id.*, Section 6.11(1).
87. *Id.*, Section 6.11(3).
88. *Id.*, Section 6.13(1).
89. *Id.*, Section 6.13(5).
90. *Id.*, Section 6.15(1).
91. *Id.*, Section 6.15(5).
92. *Id.*, Section 6.14.
93. *Id.*, Section 7.1(1) and (2).
94. *Id.*, Section 7.2(1).
95. *Id.*, Section 7.3.
96. *Id.*, Section 7.4.
97. *Id.*, Section 7.6(1) and (2).
98. *Id.*, Section 7.7(1).
99. *Id.*, Section 8.1(1).
100. *Id.*, Section 8.1(3).
101. *Id.*, Section 10.7.
102. *Id.*, Section 10.8.
103. *Id.*, Section 11.2.
104. *A Service for Attorneys*, *Supra*, note 9, page 7, paragraph 3(a).
105. *Id.*, paragraph 3(b).
106. *Id.*, page 8, paragraphs 3(c) and (d).
107. Section 6.3(1), Business Corporation Act of Liberia (1976).
108. *Id.*, Section 6.2.
109. *Id.*, Section 8.1(1).
110. *Id.*, Sections 6.9(1) and 7.1(1).

111. *Id.*, Section 6.8(4).
112. *Id.*, Section 7.4.
113. *Id.*, Section 6.8(5).
114. *Id.*, Sections 6.15(1) and (5).
115. *A Service for Attorneys*, *Supra*, note 9, page 3, paragraphs 6(a) and (b).
116. *Id.*, page 2, paragraph 5(a) and page 3, paragraph 8.
117. Ellison, 'Bermuda as a Base for Multinationals', 53 *Boston University Law Review* (1973), pages 367, 369.
118. *Id.*, page 367.
119. *Id.*, page 371.
120. *Id.*, page 370.
121. *Id.*
122. *Id.*
123. Stebbings, *Supra*, note 2, pages 626, 628.
124. *Id.*, page 628.
125. *Id.*
126. *Id.*
127. *Id.*
128. *Id.*, page 629.
129. *I.*, page 630.
130. *Id.*; See generally Hadari, 'Tax Treaties and Multinational Enterprise', 20 *American Journal of Comparative Law* (Winter 1972), page 111.
131. Section 11.84(5), Internal Revenue Code of Liberia (1977).
132. For example, see a detailed explanation of the tax laws of Switzerland and an explanation of their interaction with the tax laws of the United States, Braun, 'The Swiss Base Company: Tax Avoidance Device for Multinationals', 50 *Notre Dame Lawyer* (1975), page 645.
133. Tillinghast, 'Tax Aspects of International Transactions' (1978), Section 8.3, pages 182–199.

Appendix I

ARTICLES OF INCORPORATION PURSUANT TO THE LIBERIAN BUSINESS CORPORATION ACT.

The undersigned, for the purpose of forming a corporation pursuant to the provisions of the Liberian Business Corporation Act, do hereby make, subscribe, acknowledge and file in the Office of the Minister of Foreign Affairs this instrument for that purpose, as follows:

The name of the Corporation shall be:

The purpose of the Corporation is to engage in any lawful act or activity for which corporations may now or hereafter be organized under the Liberian Business Corporation Act. (*Although not required by Section 4.4 of the Business Corporation Act, detailed purpose or power clauses may be stated if desired.*)

The registered address of the Corporation in Liberia shall be 80 Broad Street, Monrovia, Liberia. The name of the Corporation's registered agent at such address shall be The International Trust Company of Liberia.

The aggregate number of shares of stock that the Corporation is a authorized to issue is (*identify number of registered and/or bearer shares. If bearer shares are to be issued, state the manner of giving notice as required by Section* 1.9 *of the Business Corporation Act.*)

The Corporation shall have every power which a corporation now or hereafter organized under the Liberian Business Corporation Act may have.

The name and mailing address of each incorporator of these Articles of Incorporation is:

Name	Post Office Address	No. of Shares of Common Stock (*Optional*)

The number of directors constituting the initial board of directors is:
(*If the initial directors are to be named in the Articles, give names and addresses—at least* 3, *or not less than number of shareholders.*)

The board of directors as well as the shareholders of the Corporation shall have the authority to adopt, amend or repeal the by-laws of the Corporation. (*optional*)

Corporate existence shall begin upon filing these Articles of Incorporation with the Minister of Foreign Affairs as of the filing date stated on these Articles.

IN WITNESS WHEREOF, I (we) have made, subscribed and acknowledged this instrument on this day of , 19 .

____

____

)
)SS.:
)

On this day of , 19 , before me personally came to me

known and known to me to be the individual(s) described in and who executed the foregoing instrument and he (they severally) duly acknowledged to me that the execution thereof was his (their) act and deed.

____

Appendix II

BY-LAWS

As Adopted , 19

ARTICLE I

OFFICES

The principal place of business of the Corporation shall be at . The Corporation may also have an office or offices at such other places within or without Liberia as the Board of Directors may from time to time appoint or the business of the Corporation may require.

ARTICLE II

SHAREHOLDERS

Section 1. *Annual Meeting*: The annual meeting of shareholders of the Corporation shall be held on the ____________ day of ____________________ __ at ______________________ .M. in each year or on such day and at such time and place within or without Liberia as the Board of Directors may determine for the purpose of electing Directors and of transacting such other business as may properly be brought before the meeting.

Section 2. *Special Meeting*: Special meetings of shareholders, unless otherwise prescribed by law, may be called for any purpose or purposes at any time by the President or by the order of the Board of Directors or by the President or Secretary or an Assistant Secretary whenever requested in writing to do so by shareholders owning not less than one-tenth of all the outstanding shares of the Corporation entitled to vote at such meeting. Such request shall state the purpose or purposes of the proposed special meeting. Such meetings shall be held at such place and on a date and at such time as may be designated in the notice thereof by the officer of the Corporation calling any such meeting. The business transacted at any special meeting shall be limited to the purposes stated in the notice.

Section 3. *Notice of Meetings*: Notice of every annual and special meeting of shareholders, other than any meeting the giving of notice of which is otherwise prescribed by law, stating the date, time, place and purpose thereof, and in the case of special meetings, the name of the person or persons at whose direction the notice is being issued, shall be given personally or sent by mail, telegraph, cablegram, telex or teleprinter at least fifteen but not more than sixty days before such meeting, to each shareholder of record entitled to vote thereat and to each shareholder of record who, by reason of any action proposed at such meeting would be entitled to have his shares appraised if such action were taken, and the notice shall include a statement of that purpose and to that effect. If mailed, notice shall be deemed to have been given when deposited in the mail, directed to the shareholder at his address as the same appears on the record of shareholders of the Corporation or at such address as to which the shareholder has given notice to the Secretary. Notice of a meeting need not be given to any shareholder who submits a signed waiver of notice, whether before or after the meeting, or who attends the meeting without protesting prior to the conclusion thereof the lack of notice to him. If the Corporation shall issue any class of bearer shares, notice of all meetings shall be given in the manner provided in the Articles of Incorporation.

Section 4. *Quorum*: At all meetings of shareholders, except as otherwise expressly provided by law, there must be present either in person or by proxy shareholders of record holding at least a majority of the shares issued and outstanding and entitled to vote at such meetings in order to constitute a quorum, but if less than a quorum is present, a majority of those shares present either in person or by proxy shall have power to adjourn any meeting until a quorum shall be present.

Section 5. *Voting*: If a quorum is present, and except as otherwise expressly provided by law, the affirmative vote of a majority of the shares of stock represented at the meeting shall be the act of the shareholders. At any meeting of shareholders each shareholder entitled to vote any shares on any matter to be voted upon at such meeting shall be entitled to one vote on such matter for each such share, and may exercise such voting right either in person or by proxy. Any action required or permitted to be taken at a meeting, may be taken without a meeting if a consent in writing, setting forth the action so taken, is signed by all of the shareholders entitled to vote with respect to the subject matter thereof.

Section 6. *Fixing of Record Date*: The Board of Directors may fix a time not more than sixty nor less than fifteen days prior to the date of any meeting of shareholders, or more than sixty days prior to the last day on which the consent or dissent of shareholders may be expressed for any purpose without a meeting, as the time as of which shareholders entitled to notice of and to vote at such a meeting or whose consent or dissent is required or may be expressed for any purpose, as the case may be, shall be determined, and all persons who were holders of record of voting shares at such time and no others shall be entitled to notice of and to vote at such meeting or to express their consent or dissent, as the case may be. The Board of Directors may fix a time not exceeding sixty days preceding the date fixed for the payment of any dividend, the making of any distribution, the allotment of any rights or the taking of any other action, as a record time for the determination of the shareholders entitled to receive any such dividend, distribution, or allotment or for the purpose of such other action.

ARTICLE III

DIRECTORS

Section 1. *Number*: The affairs, business and property of the corporation shall be managed by a Board of Directors to consist of not less than three Directors unless the shares of the Corporation are owned beneficially and of record by less than three shareholders in which case the number of Directors may equal the number of shareholders. Within the limits fixed by these By-Laws the number of Directors may be determined either by the vote of a majority of the entire Board or by vote of the shareholders. The Directors need not be residents of Liberia or shareholders of the Corporation. Corporations may, to the extent permitted by law, be elected or appointed Directors.

Section 2. *How Elected*: Except as otherwise provided by law or Section 4 of this Article, the Directors of the Corporation (other than the first board of Directors if named in the Articles of Incorporation or designated by the incorporators) shall be elected at the annual meeting of shareholders. Each Director shall be elected to serve until the next annual meeting of shareholders and until his successor shall have been duly elected and qualified, except in the event of his death, resignation, removal or the earlier termination of his term of office.

Section 3. *Removal*: Any or all of the Directors may be removed, with or without cause by a vote of the shareholders. Any Director may be removed for cause by action of the Board of Directors.

Section 4. *Vacancies*: Vacancies in the Board of Directors occurring by death, resignation, creation of new directorships, failure of the shareholders to elect the whole Board at any annual election of Directors or for any other reason, including removal of Directors for cause, may be filled either by the affirmative vote of a majority of the remaining Directors then in office, although less than a quorum, at any special meeting called for that purpose or at any regular meeting of the Board, or by vote of the shareholders. Vacancies occurring by removal of Directors without cause may be filled only by vote of the shareholders.

Section 5. *Regular Meetings*: Regular meetings of the Board of Directors may be held at such time and place as may be determined by resolution of the Board of Directors and no notice shall be required for any regular meeting. Except as otherwise provided by law, any business may be transacted at any regular meeting.

Section 6. *Special Meetings*: Special meetings of the Board of Directors may, unless otherwise prescribed by law, be called from time to time by the President, or any officer of the Corporation who is also a Director. The President or the Secretary shall call a special meeting of the Board upon written request directed to either of them by any two Directors stating the time, place and purpose of such special meeting. Special meetings of the Board shall be held on a date and at such time and at such place as may be designated in the notice thereof by the officer calling the meeting.

Section 7. *Notice of Special Meetings*: Notice of the date, time and place of each special meeting of the Board of Directors shall be given to each Director at least forty-eight hours prior to such meeting, unless the notice is given orally or delivered in person, in which case it shall be given at least twenty-four hours prior to such meeting. For the purpose of this section, notice shall be deemed to be duly given to a Director if given to him personally (including by telephone) or if such notice be delivered to such Director by mail, telegraph, cablegram, telex or teleprinter to his last known address. Notice of a meeting need not be given to any Director who submits a signed waiver of notice, whether before or after the meeting, or who attends the meeting without protesting, prior to the conclusion thereof, the lack of notice to him.

Section 8. *Quorum*: A majority of the Directors at the time in office, present in person or by proxy or conference telephone, shall constitute a quorum for the transaction of business.

Section 9. *Voting*: The vote of the majority of the Directors, present in person or by proxy or conference telephone, at a meeting at which a quorum is present shall be the act of the Directors. Any action required or permitted to be taken at a meeting may be taken without a meeting if all members of the Board consent thereto in writing.

Section 10. *Compensation of Directors and Members of Committees*: The Board may from time to time, in its discretion, fix the amounts which shall be payable to members of the Board of Directors and to members of any committee, for attendance at the meetings of the Board or of such committee and for services rendered to the Corporation.

ARTICLE IV

COMMITTEES

Section 1. *Executive Committee and Other Committees*: The Board of Directors may, by resolution or resolutions passed by a majority of the entire Board, designate from among its members an executive committee to consist of two or more of the Directors of the Corporation, which, to the extent provided in said resolution or resolutions, or in these By-Laws, shall have and may exercise, to the extent permitted by law, the powers of the Board of Directors in the management of the business and affairs of the Corporation, and may have power to authorize the seal of the Corporation to be affixed to all papers which may require it. In addition, the Board of Directors may, by resolution or resolutions passed by a majority of the entire Board, designate from among its members other committtees to consist of two or more of the Directors of the Corporation, each of which shall perform such functions and have such authority and powers as shall be delegated to it by said resolution or resolutions or as provided for in these By-Laws, except that only the executive committee may have and exercise the powers of the Board of Directors. Members of the executive committee and any other committee shall hold office for such period as may be prescribed by the vote of a majority of the entire Board of Directors, subject, however, to removal at any time by the vote of the Board of Directors. Vacancies in membership of such committees, shall be filled by vote of the Board of Directors. Committees may adopt their own rules of procedure and may meet at stated times or on such notice as they may determine. Each committee shall keep a record of its proceedings and report the same to the Board when required.

ARTICLE V

OFFICERS

Section 1. *Number and Designation*: The Board of Directors shall elect a President, Secretary and Treasurer and such other officers as it may deem necessary. Officers may be of any nationality and need not be residents of Liberia.

The officers shall be elected annually by the Board of Directors at its first meeting following the annual election of Directors, but in the event of the failure of the Board to so elect any officer, such officer may be elected at any subsequent meeting of the Board of Directors. The salaries of officers and any other compensation paid to them shall be fixed from time to time by the Board of Directors. The Board of Directors may at any meeting elect additional officers. Each officer shall hold office until the first meeting of the Board of Directors following the next annual election of Directors and until his successor shall have been duly elected and qualified, except in the event of the earlier termination of his term of office, through death, resignation, removal or otherwise. Any officer may be removed by the Board at any time with or without cause. Any vacancy in an office may be filled for the unexpired portion of the term of such office by the Board of Directors at any regular or special meeting.

Section 2. *President*: The President shall be the chief executive officer of the Corporation and shall have the general management of the affairs of the

Corporation together with the powers and duties usually incident to the office of President, except as specifically limited by appropriate resolution of the Board of Directors and shall have such other powers and perform such other duties as may be assigned to him by the Board of Directors. The President shall preside at all meetings of shareholders at which he is present.

Section 3. *Treasurer*: The Treasurer shall have general supervision over the care and custody of the funds, securities, and other valuable effects of the Corporation and shall deposit the same or cause the same to be deposited in the name of the Corporation in such depositories as the Board of Directors may designate, shall disburse the funds of the Corporation as may be ordered by the Board of Directors, shall have supervision over the accounts of all receipts and disbursements of the Corporation, shall, whenever required by the Board, render or cause to be rendered financial statements of the Corporation, shall have the power and perform the duties usually incident to the office of Treasurer, and shall have such powers and perform such other duties as may be assigned to him by the Board of Directors or President.

Section 4. *Secretary*: The Secretary shall act as Secretary of all meetings of the shareholders and of the Board of Directors at which he is present, shall have supervision over the giving and serving of notices of the Corporation, shall be the custodian of the corporate records and of the corporate seal of the Corporation, shall be enpowered to affix the corporate seal to those documents, the execution of which, on behalf of the Corporation under its seal, is duly authorized and when so affixed may attest the same, and shall exercise the powers and perform such other duties as may be assigned to him by the Board of Directors or the President.

Section 5. *Other Officers*: Officers other than those treated in Sections 2 through 4 of this Article shall exercise such powers and perform such duties as may be assigned to them by the Board of Directors or the President.

Section 6. *Bond*: The Board of Directors shall have power to the extent permitted by law, to require any officer, agent or employee of the Corporation to give bond for the faithful discharge of his duties in such form and with such surety or sureties as the Board of Directors may deem advisable.

ARTICLE VI

CERTIFICATES FOR SHARES

Section 1. *Form and Issuance*: The shares of the Corporation shall be represented by certificates in form meeting the requirements of law and approved by the Board of Directors. Certificates shall be signed by the President or a Vice-President, and by the Secretary or an Assistant Secretary or the Treasurer or an Assistant Treasurer. These signatures may be facsimiles if the certificate is countersigned by a transfer agent or registered by a registrar other than the Corporation itself or its employee.

Section 2. *Transfer*: The Board of Directors shall have power and authority to make such rules and regulations as they may deem expedient concerning the issuance, registration and transfer of certificates representing shares of the Corporations's stock, and may appoint transfer agents and registrars thereof.

Section 3. *Loss of Stock Certificates*: The Board of Directors may direct a new certificate or certificates of stock to be issued in place of any certificate or certificates theretofore issued by the Corporation alleged to have been lost or destroyed, upon the making of an affidavit of that fact by the person claiming the certificate of stock to be lost or destroyed. When authorizing such issue of a new certificate or certificates, the Board of Directors may, in its discretion and as a condition precedent to the issuance thereof, require the owner of such lost or destroyed certificate or certificates, or his legal representative, to advertise the same in such manner as it shall require and/or give the Corporation a bond in such sum as it may direct as indemnity against any claim that may be made against the Corporation with respect to the certificate alleged to have been lost or destroyed.

ARTICLE VII

DIVIDENDS

Section 1. *Declaration and Form*: Dividends may be declared in conformity with law by, and at the discretion of, the Board of Directors at any regular or special meeting, Dividends may be declared and paid in cash, stock, or other property of the Corporation.

ARTICLE VIII

CORPORATE SEAL

Section 1. The seal of the Corporation, if any, shall be circular in form, with the name of the Corporation in the circumference and such other appropriate legend as the Board of Directors may from time to time determine.

ARTICLE IX

FISCAL YEAR

Section 1. The fiscal year of the Corporation shall be such period of twelve consecutive months as the Board of Directors may by resolution designate.

ARTICLE X

AMENDMENTS

Section 1. *By the Shareholders*: These By-Laws may be amended, added to, altered or repealed or new By-Laws may be adopted, at any meeting of shareholders of the Corporation by the affirmative vote of the holders of a majority of the stock present and voting at such meeting provided notice that an amendment is to be considered and acted upon is inserted in the notice or waiver of notice of said meeting.

Section 2. *By the Directors*: If the Articles of Incorporation so provide, these By-Laws may be amended, added to, altered or repealed, or new By-Laws may be adopted, at any regular or special meeting of the Board of Directors by the affirmative vote of a majority of the entire Board, subject, however, to the power of the stockholders to alter, amend or repeal any By-Law as adopted.

The Belgian Analysis

A. H. PUELINCKX

HENRI SWENNEN

Contractual Considerations

Having registered in Belgium the patents for the generator, the collector and the combination of these two, the payments by the Belgian Foreign-Market company still can be made for two considerations: (a) payment for delivery of goods, i.e. delivery of the generators and collectors by the Liberian company or its agents; and (b) payment in consideration for receipt of know-how (the concession of intellectual property rights), which according to the definite or temporary nature of the concession will·be considered either a sale or a lease of movables.

It then will be necessary to substantiate the bearing of the know-how agreement since the Belgian company will have registered the Belgian patents in its own name and the Belgian courts can set aside the qualifications proposed by the parties in their agreement. The court may want to know why the holder of a patent needs to sign a know-how agreement for the same product. The know-how agreement therefore could, for instance, specify that the know-how concerned will enable the Belgian company to register the patents in the Belgian market.

Alternatively one can consider the entire operation as a mere sale between the Liberian and Belgian company, through Agents Y and Z. In both cases however, one must conclude that the operation would be incompatible with Common Market regulations, specifically Article 85, paragraph 1, of the European Economic Community (EEC) treaty. If a court concluded that the operation was an exclusive-purchase commitment, it would easily find Article 85, paragraph 1b and c applicable: the undertaking to buy only from the agents or the Liberian company is a (prohibited) way to limit or control production, markets, technical development or investment (Article 85, paragraph 1b), and to share markets or sources of supply (Article 85, paragraph 1c). The general exception granted to exclusive agreements by regulations 17/65 (Council) and 67/67 (Commission) is of no avail since the role of the Belgian company is not limited to resale.

In the case of a joint know-how purchase agreement, one more ground of incompatibility will be found where the tying of both elements (know-how licensing and purchase commitment) can be qualified as making 'the conclusions of contracts subject to acceptance by the other parties of supplementary obligations which, by their nature, or according to commercial usage, have no connection with the subject of such contracts' (Article 85, paragraph 1e). Here, however, a loophole can be found in the Commission's official notice on patent licensing agreements (O. J. Number 179, 24 December 1962, page 2922) which permits under littera IC 'Standards of quality or obligations imposed upon the licensee with respect to obtaining supplies of certain products, insofar as they are indispensable for a technically proper utilization of the patent' and reads under littera III 'there is therefore no longer a reason to give notification of agreements of this nature'. This notice goes even further than Regulation 27/65 (Council), Article 42 ii b, generally excluding from notification (and thereby granting automatic exemption under Article 86, Section 3 of the treaty):

> restraints on the exercise of the rights of any person acquiring or using industrial property rights ... or entitled under contract to acquire or use ... knowledge relating to the utilization or application of industrial techniques and of which the sole object is (a) the development or the uniform application of *standards and types*, ...

It, of course, is mandatory to avoid a notification procedure which would lead eventually to full disclosure of the reason for the existence of the Swiss bank account.

Patent Interests

Companies A and B hold the United States patents for the collectors and generators. The Belgian company holds the Belgian patent for the collector, the generator and the unit as a whole. Through the know-how agreement it is possible for: the Liberian company to impose certain obligations on the Belgian company as to the use of the component parts (Council Regulation 17/65 Article 4 (2) b and the Commissions's official notice on patent licensing agreements) and to impose certain limitations on the utilization of the patent in time and area (point I A of the Commission's notice). It would be even better if the agreement between the Liberian company and the Belgian company were an outright patent licensing agreement because then it would squarely fall under the official notice on patent licensing agreements.

Both Belgium and the United States are parties to the Paris Union and the Madrid Arrangement. According to Article 2 of the Paris Convention, they both can claim national protection in each of the member states of the Union. Article 4 establishes a one year priority right in favor of the oldest registration. Consequently, A and B will be able to safeguard their rights by making use of their priority rights in each of the member states except Belgium. They do not have a title to the unit as a whole however and this patent could therefore be registered by the Belgian company throughout the union in case no sufficient limitations have been written into the know-how agreement between the Liberian and the Belgian company. The extent of the patent rights of the various parties having been established, the question remains: what can they do with them?

After the *Deutsche Grammaphon*, *Café Hag*, and *Sterling Drut* decisions of the European Court of Justice (the first relating to author's rights, the second to trademarks and the third to potential drugs), it appears clear that within the EEC parallel imports can no longer be prevented through the use of identical patents held by different persons but having a common origin. The exception provided for in the *EMI/CBS* case (ECJ 51/75) is not applicable since apparently there will not be a sole proprietor of the trademark for the entire Common Market. This will cause severe problems if other local companies within the EEC set different prices. Their know-how agreement with the Liberian company may indeed be held sufficient proof of the common origin of the patent. The risk will be excluded only when the Belgian company is the only one within the EEC (or the only one whose link to the Liberian company can be established) or when the different EEC companies apply the same prices.

Normally, the holders of the EEC patents will be able to prevent imports from the United States since a common origin cannot be established at first. However, the omission by the United States companies to avail themselves of their priority rights under Article 4 of the Paris Convention will cast serious doubts on the legitimacy of the situation. Finally if the United States corporations were to work directly in any of the EEC countries parallel imports of such United States installations into Belgium could be prevented in the same manner but with the same caveat.

Alternative Arrangements

From a contractual point of view, the weakness of the scheme lies mainly in the tightness of the loophole through which the Liberian—Belgian agreement escapes the obligation of notification to the EEC Commission and in the apparent contradiction between the need for a different origin of the Belgian—Liberian and United States devices and the refusal of the United States companies to avail themselves of their priority rights under the Paris Convention. To streamline the operation from an EEC point of view, the conversion of the agents into exclusive distributors in the sense of the Belgian laws of 27 July 1961 and 13 April 1971 seems to be one step forward. The know-how agreement, signed directly between the Liberian company and the Belgian company, would make more sense and could still make the use of the concessionaries' component parts obligatory. As already stated, a straightforward patent licensing agreement between these two parties (the Liberian and Belgian companies) would be even better. An exclusive distributorship agreement between the Belgian company and the Agents, since it concerns only resale, would fall under the general exceptions of notification to the commission granted by regulations 17/65 (Council) and 67/67 (Commission).

The change would have certain advantages in the fields of tax and product liability, too. As to tax liability, the danger of the Liberian company having a permanent establishment in Belgium would be totally excluded and the profit and cost ratio in Belgium would become reasonable:

	Receipts per unit	Costs	Profit
Corporation A	750	750	0
Corporation B	750	750	0
Switzerland	5,000	0	5,000
Liberia	2,000	1,500	500
Concessionaries Y Z	5,500	5,000	500
Belgian Company	10,000	8,500	1,500

The direct receipts of the Liberian company would be either pursuant to the know-how agreement (as in the schedule) or pursuant to the know-how agreement and pursuant to the sales to the distributors Y and Z. (For example, the Belgian company pays one-thousand to Liberia and six-thousand five-hundred to Y and Z who forward one-thousand to Liberia and five-thousand to Swiss bank account).

As to product liability, the sales concessionary, being the last link in the Belgian chain subject to Belgian jurisdiction and legislation, has no access to the know-how and no rights to the patents. Therefore, it should be easy for him to prove that he could not possibly have detected a hidden defect which eventually led to damages. The disadvantage of making the agents sales concessionaries lies in the extensive protection granted to them under the 1961 and 1971 laws. After three renewals these agreements automatically become of indefinite duration and, in the absence of a serious fault committed by the concessionnary, can only be ended by giving a 'just' period of notice (amounting often to three years after only ten years contract duration) or paying the gross profits, calculated on the basis of the last three to five contract years, which the concessionnary can expect to earn during such a period and by paying a client indemnity, often equal to the net profits of the concession over a duration equal to two-thirds of what is supposed to be the just period of notice (which would amount to two years of net profits in the above example). The concessionnary must also be reimbursed for redundancy payments to the personnel he let go pursuant to the termination of the concession, and for that portion of his investment that will continue to benefit the grantor beyond the termination of the concession.

And, since Liberia is not an EEC country, there is no way to escape the imperative character of this law on the basis of the 1967 Brussels Convention on competence and execution of judgments in civil and commercial matters that makes a choice of forum possible where the grantor resides in another EEC state. The application of the New York arbitration convention has been denied by the court in these cases.

Moreover, the whole scheme remains very weak. It would be sufficient for the real cost of the component parts to become publicly known (for instance pursuant to a parallel imports case) in order to shift the burden of proof to the Belgian company and to the concessionnary. The same applies to the question of common origin of the patents about which sufficient information can be found at the International Bureau of the Paris Union. The lack of action by the United States companies to avail themselves of their priority rights is too obvious. Any serious investigation, therefore, will quickly result in the taxation of the amounts paid to the Swiss bank account as back commissions or benevolent advantages. The fact that a tax haven like Liberia is included will certainly not be advantageous. And once this is revealed, Community action will be inevitable (the above does not take into consideration the Commission's *de minimis* rule).

I must conclude that it would be very hazardous for any business lawyer to endorse the scheme as proposed.

Tax Liability

The Domestic-Market Corporations A and B would not incur any tax liability in Belgium. Belgian internal law, as well as the double taxation treaties, requires the presence of an 'establishment' in the country as point of contact for the local authorities to levy a non-resident corporate tax. This 'establishment' is very broadly defined in Article 140, paragraph 3 of the income tax code. 'Even in the absence of any representative authorized to bind the (foreign) company vis-à-vis third parties: (presence in Belgium of) the offices of effective management, branch offices, manufacturing works, workshops, agencies, stores, offices, laboratories, purchase or sales offices, depositories [or], likewise all permanent installations with a productive character' will be sufficient to prove the existence of an 'establishment'.

Depending upon the exact contractual relationship with Agents Y and Z, there could be a tax exposure in Belgium for the Liberian company, doing business in Belgium through an agency. An independent agent, representing several other foreign and domestic companies, and acting in his own name and in the normal course of his business, will not be considered as a permanent establishment. An agent who acts in Belgium in the name of the Liberian company and is in fact dependent upon the foreign company, will be classified as such an establishment. There is one exception though, provided by the income tax code. The foreign company will not be subject to Belgian non-resident corporate tax, if the agent's role is limited to merely taking orders, provided the foreign country grants the same exemption (Article 141, 5° C.I.R.).

The royal decree implementing the income tax code gives the Belgian tax administration the authority to assess such a foreign company on a comparative basis in case no accounting documents can be produced to establish the exact profit.

The Liberian company could, under this provision of Article 146 of the above mentioned royal decree, be taxed on eight per cent of the gross sales income or on a minimal basis of one-hundred and forty-thousand Belgian francs at a rate of fifty-four per cent (assuming the tax has been paid properly in advance).

In the assignment, the sales volume was fixed at two-thousand dollars.

$2,000	Taxable basis: (without import T.V.A.) × 8%		$160
tax: $160 × 54%		$86	
increase for lack of prepayment: $86 × 20.25%		$17.40	$103

As it is a new activity, the temporary contribution to the solidarity fund, introduced by the law of 30 March 1976 and fixed at 4.8 percent on the part of the profit exceeding one hundred and ten percent of the profit realised in the year 1975, is not applicable. The Liberian company will not be held liable for taxation on the five-thousand dollars commission paid by the Belgian company to the Swiss bank account, for the simple reason that the amount is paid anonymously. The Liberian company is not known as beneficiary.

The situation of the foreign company looks as follows:

cost price of the product		$ 2,000
sales price		10,000
gross revenue		8,000
production cost	1,000	
agents' commission	500	
secret commission	5,000	
		6,500
net profit		$ 1,500

The secret commission of five-thousand dollars can be taxed either in the name of the company or in the name of the agents. As a general rule, the commission cannot be deducted as operating expense when the name of the beneficiary is not disclosed (Article 47, paragraph I. C.I.R.). The company can pass the problem to the agents by mentioning the name of the agent as beneficiary of the payments and thus apply for the deduction of the commission because the agents are liable for personal income tax on this amount. However, even by disclosing the name of a beneficiary, the authorities could reject the deduction of the commission which is twice as high as the income price, as exceeding manifestly the normal professional standards (Article 50 bis 2° C.I.R.).

In case the agents will not permit the company to indicate them as beneficiary, the commission will be subject to tax as 'secret commission' at a rate of sixty-five per cent (Article 132 C.I.R.) instead of the normal rate of forty-eight per cent.

In some cases, the Belgian tax authorities recognize that 'secret commissions' have to be paid in order to develop a particular industry (for example, the port). The tax payer can file a request for the deduction of secret commissions which can be allowed, provided the amounts remain in normal limits and the company pays a forfeiture tax, fixed by the Ministry of Finance in an individual decision (article 47, paragraph 2 C.I.R.).

By disclosing the name of the beneficiary, the company could eventually avoid the application of the special rate, but the commission could still be added to the taxable basis as an abnormal and benevolent advantage granted to a company established in a country where it is subject to a tax regime which is notably more advantageous than the Belgian system (a tax haven) (Article 24 al. 2). The law does not even require a special link with the beneficiary; the only criterion being the place of establishment and the tax regime to which the beneficiary is subject.

From a tax point of view, the scheme does not seem to be realistic. Payments from Belgium to a tax haven are regarded with suspicion. Under Article 46 C.I.R. it is still possible to pay interest and royalties to a holding company, provided however that the operations correspond to reality and that the amounts can be considered normal. However, as a general rule, a withholding tax of twenty per cent is due, unless there is a double taxation treaty exempting the royalty payment from withholding tax. Double taxation treaties with tax haven countries do not exist, and even the treaty with Luxemburg excludes the holding company from the scope of the treaty.

Product Liability

Upon the assumption that no sales intermediaries intervene between the Belgian corporation (the Belgian company) and the purchaser, that the alleged defect[1] of the Superior Unit was hidden[2], and that the Belgian company in good faith could not detect the malfunction before the product left the factory, Belgian law would consider the liabilities involved according to two specific aspects; the contractual liability, and the liability based on the law of torts. A claim may be brought on both grounds, but a plaintiff cannot recover on both; he must make a choice, according to such elements as the importance of the damages suffered, the statute of limitation (short for contractual liability) and so on.

As a general rule of contractual liability, when a defect appears, the professional vendor is presumed liable vis-à-vis the purchaser. The seller is supposed to know of all consequences due to the functioning of each individual product he offers for sale[3]. A defect is a vice rendering the product improper for its use or diminishing the use in such proportion that the buyer would not have acquired it, or only at a lesser price[4]. Such a presumption would exist on the condition that the hidden defect exists before the sale takes place; but the slightest beginning of a vice is enough to activate the presumption[5]; also a normal and regular use by the buyer, even if the vice appeared later, could reinforce the presumption[6].

If the seller can prove that it would have been absolutely impossible for him, even with the most diligent behavior to have had knowledge of the defect, he might escape from liability[7]. An important issue in this respect is the destination of the product contemplated by the buyer and the performance expected[8]. In other words, the goods must be appropriate to what the buyer is entitled to obtain. The pamphlets and explanatory notices delivered by the supplier would play a prominent role in the appraisal of the situation.

For hidden defects, such exoneration clauses are commonly held to be invalid[9], except when the purchaser is a professional. This jurisprudence is not followed by the authors[10] who emphasize the unfairness of the rule toward the final seller (possibly a small corner shop) who would be liable vis-à-vis the purchaser, but who could not bring an action in guarantee against the supplier or the manufacturer because of an exoneration clause in favor of the latter. A change in the jurisprudence can be expected in the forseeable future, toward a non-rebuttable presumption against the seller, who could in turn bring a claim against his predecessor in the chain of supply. Another source of exoneration might arise if the vendor specifically mentions in writing, at the time of the sale, the possibility of defects, provided the buyer has full, prior knowledge of the nature and the extent of such possible vices[11].

Concerning compensation, the purchaser can bring an action '*rédhibitoire*' (claim for reimbursement of purchase price) or '*estimatoire*' (in order to obtain a reduction of price), at his option, but will never obtain the replacement of the item nor its repair[13]. In addition, the purchaser is entitled to all indirect damages sustained[14]. The action must be filed within a very short period of time, taking into account the nature of the defect, and the location where the sale took place[15]. What in each case is to be considered as a satisfactory short term is left to the decision of the courts[16]. If the petitioner fails to meet the requirement, the vendor can assert the expiration (statute of limitation) of his obligation to guarantee against hidden defects. Prior negotiations can suspend the term, but the failure to come to an agreement would restore it[17].

Who may be liable? Obviously, the final seller stands first. But also liable may be all suppliers who intervened in the sales chain. The original manufacturer of the defective part can be sued directly by the final purchaser, despite the absence of contractual relationship[18].

Practically, and generally speaking, the purchaser will sue the final vendor (the Belgian company) who will in turn move a recurrent action against his own supplier, who will ultimately seek recourse against the actual manufacturer of the defective item. The requirement of factual extraneity was strongly argued by the attorney general and definitely followed by the court[26]. This decision, although not unanimously welcomed, was expressed in an opinion of our highest court, and must be considered part of Belgian law[27].

As to recoverable amounts on tortious grounds, all computable damages are included, even damages that might appear later on, after the accident occurred, whether the action is grounded on Articles 1382, 1383 or 1384 al. 1 of our Civil Code. The statute of limitation in torts is thirty years from the time the accident occurred. Note that, through the mechanisms described above, the Belgian company, the Liberian corporation, and the Domestic-Market corporations could be sued, either initially or by recourse; the agents would not escape either, provided they acted on their own behalf and invoiced the Belgian corporation.

Tort liability, based upon Articles 1382 and following of the Civil Code[19], could be sought by the injured third party who could sue the party responsible for the single or concurring cause of the damage. Therefore, the visiting neighbor, the heirs of the child, and the spouse, (provided she is not a party to the contract) can sue the author of the damage[20], (for example the Domestic-Market corporation that manufactured the part, if the damage was caused by a defect of the part and/or the Belgian company if the defect is due to an assembling mistake). A firm trend in our jurisprudence holds that a fault committed by a professional in the performance of a contract can result in liability based on tort vis-à-vis injured third parties[21]. These persons (generally, the spouse also) might, instead take the opportunity offered by Article 1384 al. 1[22], of the Civil Code to sue the holder of the defective product (the purchaser) on the grounds that he is responsible for the things under his custody. This is a strict liability even in absence of personal fault on the part of the purchaser.

The possibility of recourse by the purchaser against the party responsible for the defect used to be a disputed issue. Many jurisdictions allowed recovery by the purchaser on the basis of tort, provided he failed to fulfil an obligation imposed upon anyone[23] (or infringed an economical legislative regulation—safety regulations, testing final products, harmful nature of components). Otherwise, when the liability found its origin and its motivation strictly in the contract, the action could only be brought on contractual grounds[24], with the consequences noted above.

A widely commented upon decision of the *Cour de Cassation*[25] ruled that the victim of damage due to the failure to perform a contract cannot invoke liability based on tort unless he can prove a fault and a damage extraneous to the performance of the contract. The dispute arises when it comes to whether liability in tort implies extraneity in law or extraneity in fact.

Notes

1. A defect is a permanent element, inherent to the product, exclusive of any party extraneous to its manufacture, and to its delivery, as such, in view of a specific usage (Cass. 19/1/1978, J.T. 1978, page 434);
2. The vendor cannot be held contractually for apparent vices (article 1642, Civil Code).
3. Article 1643, Civil Code—Cass. 4/5/1939, Pas. I, 223—Cass. 13/11/1959, Pas. I. 1960, 313.
4. Article 1641, Civil Code.
5. De Page T. IV, page 177.
6. Comm. Brux. 20/5/1958, J.C.B. 1959, 58.
7. Cass. 13/11/1959 cited here above, Bruxelles 5/2/69, J.T. 1969, page 298, Bruxelles 16/3/1972, J.T. 1972, page 606, Bruxelles 9/5/1972, R.W. 1972-1973, col 20/6, Grand 22/10/70, R.W. 1970-1971, col 893, Liège 21/5/74, Jur. Liège 74-75, page 81, Civ. Anvers 17/2/72, JPA 1972, page 228, Comm. Charleroi 6/1/72, JT 1972, page 286, 't Kint a Horsmans, Annuales de Droit CCL, 1971, page 239.
8. Comm. Tournai 23/1/1969, JT 1969, page 245, Comm. Bruxelles 14/09/71, JCB 1972, page 664, Comm. Bruxelles 15/11/71, JCB 1972, page 668.
9. Simont and De Cavre, Examen de Jurisprudence, RCJB 1976, page 418, sur les contracts spéciaux.
10. Ibid, page 418—Corner Harmonisation dans la rigueur des vices cachés à la charge du vendeur professionnel, Rev. Trim, Dr. Civ., 1975, page 126.
11. Civ. Nivelles 26/3/1969, JIT 1969, page 463.

12. Article 1646 Civil Code—Cass. 21/11/1974, Pas. 1975, I. 322.
13. Contra: Brux. 6/10/75, JT 1975, page 696; decision apparently isolated.
14. Cass. 13/11/1959, Pas. 1960 I, 313 applying article 1645, Civil Code in case of faultive negligence in the execution of the contract.
15. Article 1648, Civil Code.
16. See e.g., Comm. Brux. 27/5/1967, J.C.B. 1967, 311: Such would be considered as a later and irreceivable court action, a filing made thirteen months after a contradictory expert has terminated his report, considering no negotiations were introduced between the parties during the period (Bruxelles 31/10/68, Pas. 1970, II 20).
17. Comm. Liège 18/12/70, Jur. Liège 70-71, page 220.
18. Brux. 27/11/1963, Pas. 65, I, 52-53.
19. Article 1382 of the Civil Code very pragmatically reads as follows: any fact caused by a human being that inflicted somebody else a damage compels the one because of whom it occurred to repair it. Article 1283 restates the same rule for the person responsible by negligence or inprudence.
20. The jurisprudence is largely in favour of a such liability. See cases cited by: Fagnart, Examen de Jurisprudence, 1969-1976, JT 1976; Dalcq, Traité de la Responsabilité Civile, page 573, T.I, n° 101 et 399 ss; Dalcq, Examen de Jurisprudence, RCJB 1968, page 195 n° 3.
21. Fagnart, op. cit. number 5. Dissenting jurisprudence: Brux. 26/9/1974, RGAR n° 9375.
22. This recourse exists only in favor of the victims and no one else (Cass. 2/9/1976).
23. Fagnart, ibid.
24. Cass. 4/6/1971, Pass. I 940. Van Ryn, RCJB 1957 page 302.
25. Cass. 7/12/1973 (Pas. I, 1974, page 376). The decision was heavily criticized. See Fagnard, op. cit.: Rasir in JT 1976 page 164; note, Herbots, R.W. 1973-1974, col. 1587 ss.

The Danish Analysis

MADS MARSTRAND-JØRGENSEN

Corporation Formation

As an introduction to this question, it should be pointed out that Danish law accepts foreign companies regardless of their structure in the home-country. The foreign companies may even be taxable in Denmark without being registered formally in Denmark (see below). On the other hand it is possible for foreign companies to register a (daughter) company in Denmark, provided that the regulations in the Danish company laws are followed (see general section). It also is possible for foreign companies to register affiliates in the Danish Companies Register, provided the company has legal existence in its home-country, and provided that the foreign company is a limited company (Limited-Companies Act, Section 147).

It must be underlined that Danish law does not contain rules concerning the formation of foreign companies outside Denmark, and thus the technicalities concerning the formation of such companies will not be discussed. Several rules concerning foreign-exchange naturally have to be considered. However, as stated in the introduction, it is assumed that the transactions mentioned do not violate such regulations. It must be underlined that the Danish laws on foreign-exchange are very detailed and thorough care must be taken to ensure that the transactions conform with these regulations.

Turning to alternative locations, other 'tax havens' may be suggested. Danish corporations do, to some extent, use holding companies or daughter companies situated in Luxemburg, or Liechtenstein, but it must be considered that the reputation of the latter may not be too good in the eyes of the tax authorities. The same consideration may be valid even in the relation to any other 'tax-haven'.

Recently, there has been some discussion of severely extending control over companies formed by Danish citizens or companies outside Denmark, but at the moment there are no rules directly regulating the formation of companies in these countries (apart from the rules of foreign-exchange). In the case presented where the Liberian company is formed by foreign companies no Danish authorities probably will wish to discuss the question.

The main advantage of forming the company in Liberia or the above mentioned countries is that the names of the board members need not be disclosed, the taxation may be lighter, and the balances of the company will not be available to the public. The Danish rule concerning limited companies is that the names of the members of the board are open to the public, and that the yearly balances will be available to the public in the edition in which they have to be handed over to the companies register every year.

The taxation of Danish companies is thirty seven per cent. The demands for capitalization are, for limited companies (A/S) one-hundred thousand, Danish kroner, and for Private Companies (ApS) thirty-thousand Danish kroner.

Below it is discussed whether agents *Y* and *Z* are 'independent' agents, and it is pointed out that if the agents are not independent enough from the Liberian corporation or corporations *A* and *B* this may lead to these corporations being taxable in Denmark, and may lead to the application of Danish law in all matters concerning the Danish foreign-market company (the Danish company). Further, in this connection, it must be mentioned that if the agents are not independent, the Liberian corporation or corporations *A* and *B* may be deemed to be acting through an affiliate in Denmark. According to the Limited-Companies Act, Section 151, affiliates must be registered with the Companies Register before commencing business in Denmark, and according to Section 161 they will be punished if they commence business in the form of an affiliate before being registered. There are no written laws to decide whether an agent is independent or not in this respect and the question has not been brought before the courts.

Contractual Considerations

In Denmark, there are no restrictions on who may apply for a Danish patent. It is, however, a requirement that the name of the inventor be indicated in the patent application. This requirement is taken quite literally so it is necessary to indicate the person(s) who made the invention. The insertion of, for instance, a corporation as inventor is not acceptable. Further, the two United States patents presumably will be known to the Danish Patent-authorities, so the applicant will have to prove his right to the patents. Disputes relating to rights to patents are settled, not by the patent authorities, but by the ordinary courts (the High Court) (Patents Act 1967, Sections 9, 17, 64). Since the Danish Patents Act—as probably most patent-laws throughout the world—requires that the invention be new, the United States patents may prevent the granting of a Danish patent, as the invention is already known. If however, the Danish patent is applied for within twelve months from the date of the United States application, a Danish patent may be granted (Patents Act 1967, Section 6).

The right to the patent under Danish law is freely assignable and, thus, there is nothing to prevent the Danish corporation from filing an application to have the invention patented (Patents Act 1967, Section 44). If the applicant is not domiciled in Denmark, it is provided in Section 12 of the Patents Act that he shall appoint a local agent to represent him in all matters pertaining to the application. Corporations *A* and *B* must satisfy themselves that the agreement with the Danish corporation provides that the right to the patents is re-assignable if the corporation ceases to exist, and it is important that the contractual relations between the inventors and the Danish company give the inventors the possibility to have the Danish patents transferred to them. It is stated that the Liberian company has purchased the technological know-how of the two component parts of the Solar Energy Electrical Unit. A special agreement between the Liberian corporation and the Danish company to protect this know-how in different circumstances should be considered. The Danish laws on unfair competition do, to some extent, offer protection of know-how, but this rather vague protection may be widened considerably by entering into a written contract describing the various aspects.

The idea of letting the Danish company patent the devices in its own name will demand thorough contractual regulation. Therefore it is questionable whether it would not be better to let corporations *A* and *B* or the Liberian corporation patent the devices. Many disputes might be avoided in this manner, where the Danish company merely acts as licensee.

Provided that the Exchange Control Act is duly observed, no objections can be raised to the principle of a payment to the Liberian corporation through the agents. Further, the payment from the Danish parties and/or the obligation to buy does not seem to violate any Danish rules in themselves, it being quite ordinary to pay a price corresponding to a percentage of the sales sum or a license in this manner. Also no EEC rules on unfair competition seem to be violated as there seems to be no restrictions on export of the devices from Denmark to other EEC countries. If, however, corporations *A* and *B* were Danish companies who had formed a Liberian corporation as described, the Danish tax authorities would most certainly show this arrangement more than ordinary interest. In fact, the Danish tax authorities would state that there is no reason—aside from the tax planning—that the seventy-five per cent should be paid to the Liberian company there being no actual work done by said company. Therefore it is believed that the seventy five per cent would be deemed taxable in Denmark, and further the companies *A* and *B* (if they were Danish) would risk involvement in a criminal prosecution according to the tax-laws and according to Law Number 372 of 23 December 1964 on foreign-exchange.

In order to try to avoid taxation in Denmark, the following alternative contractual arrangement should be considered. Corporations *A* and *B* or the Liberian corporation themselves patent the devices in Denmark. The said companies then grant a license to the patents to an independent Danish company (the Foreign-Market Company).

The purpose of granting the license is described above, and the fact that a foreign company owns patent rights in Denmark, from which it earns license fees, does not in itself make the company taxable in Denmark. The purpose of excluding the agents is to avoid tax liability in Denmark for the Liberian or United States companies. If these companies are doing business in Denmark through an independent representative (the Danish company), and provided that the representative is performing business as usual, only the Danish company will be taxable in Denmark. The amounts paid by the Danish company such as license fees and money paid for the goods will not be taxable in Denmark but will be deductable from the income of the Danish company.

The tax authorities, however, might argue that the price paid to the foreign companies is too high, but in a case like this, where the Danish company is totally independent from (not owned by) the foreign companies, this would not give the authorities reason for taxation in Denmark of the foreign corporations. If business, on the other hand, partly is performed through the agents there is a severe risk that the foreign company will be considered taxable in Denmark. This depends upon how independent the agents are from the foreign companies. From the informations given it is not possible to decide whether the agents are so independent that (limited) taxation in Denmark can be avoided.

This is, in my opinion, the second major point (the first being the question about the patents), in the contractual considerations, and to avoid difficullties the best thing may be—as mentioned—to do business directly between the foreign companies and the independent Danish company.

Tax Liability

Neither Corporation *A* nor *B* will have any taxable income in Denmark as they are not domiciled in Denmark, and they are not 'doing business' in Denmark. As mentioned above, there is the risk that the corporations will be considered (limited) taxable in Denmark if they are represented by non-independent agents. It is not possible to decide whether the agents are independent enough, but if they are dependent the whole profit in Denmark will be taxable in Denmark. In this case it is, therefore, of major interest that there is no double taxation agreement between Liberia and Denmark. It must be noted that the fact that the foreign companies *A* and *B* have patents in Denmark (as proposed above) does not in itself imply taxability in Denmark, and no tax will have to be withheld from license fees.

The agents will—if they are independent—be taxed on their profits. If they are not independent they will be taxed on their profits *and* the Liberian corporation and/or the domestic-market corporations will also be taxed. It is impossible to give precise information on the amount that will be deemed taxable. It has only to be considered that the Danish tax authorities have rather wide discretion to decide this question.

The Danish Company is taxable on its profit from the sales. This means that the twenty five per cent will be considered as income of the company while the amounts paid by the company will be deductable.

Product Liability

It appears that the Danish company has exercised the best possible quality control, and that the defect could not have been detected beforehand and further that the Danish company has performed all other functions without fault. It also is assumed that the buyer, his spouse, child, and neighbor neither suspected nor ought to have suspected that the devices were defective, as this might otherwise reduce their compensation. If they should have had doubts about the risk, they may be held to have accepted this risk, and thus recover no compensation. If the owner knew of the defect, but did not warn the persons injured, the owner may be held totally or partly responsible.

In Denmark, it has been discussed whether the fact that the defendant can show that at the time of production or of being put into circulation the product conformed to an officially approved standard concerning safety or did not have a defect according to the state of knowledge of safety, might influence the result. It is the general opinion that compliance with official standards is not an absolute defense, but that it may of course be taken into consideration. Further the defendant probably will not be held liable if the defect was not known to the average technician when the device was marketed. On the other hand the defendant may be held liable if the danger becomes known later, and he fails to give warning about it.

The legal position in Denmark with respect to product liability is not easily explained, and is, as a matter of fact still developing. The basic point of Danish law is definitely still the general so-called 'culpa-principle', that is responsibility only in the event of negligence, but with a *marked* tendency to make this responsibility more stringent by easing the burden of proof.

Product liability in Denmark is based on contract only when there is a warranty. The Danish Sale of Goods Act is not applicable in these cases. In Denmark product liability also may be based on tort and normally is placed on the link in the chain of manufacture and marketing where the defect occurred. In the present case the Danish Company functions partly as middleman and partly as partial manufacturer, due to the fact that the company has assembled the units.

In the event that the United States manufacturer is culpable, there is no doubt that the middlemen, the Danish company, the agents and the Liberian Company, can be held liable for the fault of the manufacturer, regardless of whether the fault is attributable to the middleman or not. In other words, any link in the chain is held vicariously liable for the act committed in the previous links.

As the case is presented, it is not clear whether there is fault on behalf of Corporations *A* and *B*. If this is the case, two questions arise. Can the injured parties hold the United States and Liberian companies or the agents responsible in Denmark? Can the Danish company hold the manufacturer and/or the Liberian company responsible, and sue them in Denmark?

There is some discussion in Denmark as to whether the person who sustained the damage will be able to levy a damage claim directly against the manufacturer, thereby leaving out one or more of the intervening links. A clear answer cannot be given to this question, but there seems to be a tendency for the courts to permit the person who sustained the damage to bring his claim directly against the manufacturer, thus leaving out the middleman, or against the manufacturer and middleman jointly.

The next question is whether the non-Danish parties involved can be sued in Denmark. The main rule here is that only persons/companies 'living' in Denmark can be sued in this country. However, there are several exceptions. Cases where suits are brought for damages caused by non-contractual acts may be heard by the courts at the place where the damage or injury happened

(Code of Procedure, Section 244), and in some cases, foreigners can be sued in Denmark if they own property here (Code of Procedure, Section 248). Thus, it is possible for the purchaser, his spouse, the visiting neighbor, and the estate of the child to sue all the companies involved before the Danish courts. the Danish courts.

On the other hand these exceptions will probably *not* allow the Foreign-Market Company—if convicted alone—to sue the manufacturer before the Danish courts, the Foreign-Market Company not being directly damaged or injured. The only possibility for the Foreign-Market Company to sue the manufacturers in Denmark would be to prove that the foreigners owned property in Denmark. This will be possible with respect to both the domestic-market corporations and the Liberian corporation provided that the Danish Company can show that the Liberian company, and Corporations *A* and *B* are creditors concerning amounts owed to them by the agents.

There is no doubt that the agents can be sued in Denmark. If—see alternative contractual considerations above—there are no agents in Denmark, the question is whether the fact that the Liberian company and corporations *A* and *B* have money in Denmark owed to them by the Danish company will allow them to be sued before the Danish courts according to Code of Procedure, Section 248. This probably is the case provided that the Danish company has not withheld payments solely in order to establish the situation mentioned in Section 248.

If the Liberian corporation or corporations *A* and *B* have patent-rights in this country, this will be considered property in Denmark and enable the Danish Company to sue in Denmark according to Section 248.

The next question that can be discussed is which law the courts will apply, there being a conflict of laws. This question has never clearly been decided by the Danish courts. It is the ordinary assumption that the Danish courts will use *lex loci delicti*, in this case Danish law with a possibility to use the law of the country where the devices were produced if this leads to a more favorable result for the injured parties.

The question is complicated by the fact that Denmark has signed the Hague Convention of 15 June 1955, concerning which law to apply in international sales. According to this convention it is the law of the seller which has to be applied. In this case this may lead to the use of non-Danish law. There is however, in the convention mentioned, another rule saying that if the goods are ordered at a place of business belonging to the seller the rules of the country where the business is situated must be applied. This rule may again lead to discussion of whether the agents are independent agents or not. If the agents are not considered independent, this may well lead to the application of Danish law *also* in the relation between the Danish Company and the domestic-market corporations. This again leads to the thesis put forward above that the seemingly unnecessary agents *Y* and *Z* should be avoided.

The Danish Company in its terms of sale may have included conditions to avoid product liability. In contract, a disclaimer may be effective, but before the courts there will be a tendency to apply very strict limitations when the parties were not equal in bargaining power; therefore a defense based upon such a disclaimer is unlikely to succeed when the claimant is a consumer. Even if the 'ordinary' consumers have signed such conditions, there is a major risk that the courts will not accept them. This result is almost certain concerning injuries to persons, but the rule may well be applied also concerning damage to things, although in the case of consequential damages such contractual conditions may have some effect.

While the possibility of avoiding product liability in the relation between the Danish company and the consumer (including the neighbor and others) is not great, the situation is different between the Danish company and the agents and/or the Liberian company and the manufacturer. Anyway, it is generally agreed that such contract clauses seeking to avoid product liability may be accepted by the Danish courts between the 'professional' links in the transactions, especially when concerning accidents where no persons have been hurt. Therefore, including such clauses in the contracts between these links should be considered. Such clauses may well lead to the result that even if the Danish company is held liable on the grounds that the manufacturers (*A* and *B*) have been shown to have been negligent the company will be cut off from having the other companies held liable.

To avoid the discussions mentioned above of which set of laws that are to be used between the 'professional' links, a clause on this in the contracts should be discussed and would be legal. In the same way, consideration should be given to agreeing upon where the different parties in the transactions can be sued.

The general Danish rules of compensation apply in cases of product liability. Consequently claims normally can be raised for physical damage to property, indirect financial loss, pain and suffering incidental to personal injury, and so on. However, it must be noted that there is a major difference in the amounts of compensation obtainable in Denmark compared with the United States. Compensation in Denmark by the courts is standardized and limited to a simple average. The compensation for total disability lies around two-hundred-thousand Danish kroner and compensation for pain and suffering around thirty Danish kroner for each day in bed and around twelve Danish kroner for additional days lost through sickness. This of course must be seen in connection with free Danish health-care and the well developed social security system. It may even be assumed that the estate of the child will get no compensation apart from financial expenses, as the child has no family to keep. There will be no compensation to the parents for mental sufferings. Another factor which makes product liability cases much different from what is common in the United States is that according to Danish law the losing party must compensate the winning party for their costs. Further, the lawyers in Denmark do not act on a contingent fee base.

The English Analysis

PETER SUMMERFIELD

Introduction

On the basis of the common set of facts (the model) as applied to England and Wales[1], it can be concluded that the courts would apply English domestic law as the proper law both of the contracts, with one exception, and of tort. The exception is the contractual relationship between the Domestic-Market Corporations (the Corporations) and the Liberian Corporation (which contract I will call the 'sales contract').

Further, the courts would view the nature of the contractual relationships between the parties (to transfer the components and to patent, assemble and sell the Superior Units in England) as an agency agreement or series of agency agreements (the English agreement) with the exception of the sales contract. The sales contract would be held to comprise the sale of goods, unless there was a clear inference of agency on the basis of the *modus operandi* in the model, for example, on 'commission merchant' or 'corporate veil' principles of agency (or perhaps even of partnership).

Contractual Considerations

The view which the courts would take of the nature of the English agreement and the sales contract already has been outlined. Thus only the patent aspects of the model will be dealt with here. There are no restrictions on who may apply for a United Kingdom patent, the initial assumption being that the applicant is entitled to the patent; however, the applicant will have to satisfy the Comptroller of Patents of his right to apply before grant of the patent (see sections 7(2)(b) and (c); 7(4); and 13(2)(b) Patents Act 1977). Thus, before grant, the Liberian Corporation will have to assign or licence the United Kingdom rights in the Superior Units to the agents, who will in turn have to sub-assign or sub-license them to the Foreign-Market Company (the English Company). Note that the consideration for passing the rights would be derived under the English agreement, that is the commission arrangements, and the assignment or sub-assignment would take place under that agreement; as such it is registrable with the Comptroller of Patents (see section 33(3) *ibid*).

Both before and after the grant of the patent, the Comptroller of Patents has wide discretion and authority to determine disputes relating to rights to patents (see sections 8(1) and 37(1) *ibid*). There is a similar procedure as regards disputes concerning entitlement to foreign applications for United Kingdom patents and for patents at the European Patents Office or through international patent conventions (see section 12(1) – (5) *ibid*). In the event that a patent application is withdrawn, amended, or refused, or a patent has been granted to a person found not to be entitled to it, the Comptroller may make an order permitting the person who referred the question to him to make a new application relating to the whole or any part of the invention originally contained in the earlier application (see sections 8(3) and 37(4) *ibid*).

A unified system of appeals was created by the Patents Act 1977, which establishes a Patents Court with High Court status. The Patents Court will hear appeals from decisions of the Comptroller, and thereafter appeals will be to the Court of Appeal (see sections 96 and 97(3) and (4) *ibid*). Thereby, the Agents or the English Company could enforce their patent interests under the English agreement, if registered, to which Corporations A and B (*quaere*, also as regards patents, the Liberian Corporation) would not be a party. The Liberian Corporation's interest in the patents, if any, would also come under the English agreement, but it would have none under the sales contract.

The nature of the payments, as described in the model, would be viewed factually by the courts in each case.

Corporations *A* and *B* sell the component parts to the Liberian Corporation, upon its undertaking to pay after being paid itself 'at a price of cost plus overhead and shipping expenses'. Whether or not the sales contract would be viewed as the sale of goods by the courts depends upon confirmation of three issues in favor of such view. The price, which is fixed by the sales contract as above, is sufficient consideration in money, paid or promised (sections 1(1) and 8(1) Sale of Goods Act 1893). However, there must be an agreement as to the exact price[2]. Secondly the Liberian Corporation must be an outright buyer, not taking the goods on 'sale or return';[3] and thirdly, delivery must take place and title must pass to the Liberian Corporation outside the United Kingdom[4].

The agents 'will receive a five per cent commission of all sales'. Therefore, they are clearly to be seen as 'commission agents'[5] since they are acting in relation to the English company for a disclosed principal under the exclusive agreement to 'purchase all of the Superior Components from the Liberian Corporation'. (But *quaere*, under C3(b) if the English Company is to 'purchase all Superior Units from the agents', might the agents be acting for an undisclosed principal as 'commission merchants' and thus liable on their contract with the English Company?).

The English Company '... will retain twenty five per cent of all sales'. Therefore, it is a 'mercantile agent'[6], factor, or distributor because of its duty, implicit in the model, to account for its receipt of the profit on the proceeds of sale to its principal(s), either the agents or the Liberian Corporation. The Model provides that 'the agents will transfer to the Liberian Corporation the costs of the Superior Components plus overhead and shipping expenses, but will deposit the remainder of all sales into a Swiss bank account (anonymously held by the Liberian Corporation)'. Therefore, the Liberian Corporation accepts payment as principal, unless the sales contract is one of agency (in which case it would be a 'commission merchant' trading on behalf of an undisclosed principal).

As set out above, if the English Company is granted the relevant patent in the Superior Unit, it will have satisfied the Comptroller of Patents of its right to apply. Subject to any dispute as to its rights, thereafter the English Company will be the patent owner who can legally prevent others from taking and using the invention in the United Kingdom. The other parties' interests in the patent will then be derived from the English agreement and through its terms, as expressly disclosed or implied in the model. The respective interests in the patents also follow the parties contractual rights in the alternative solution put forward, whether as licensor or sub-licensor but under separate licensing agreements to any trading agreements.

Tax Liability

Under the English agreement, the Liberian Corporation would be deemed by the courts to be trading in the United Kingdom[7]. The profits arising from trading, say as set out in the 'financial details' of the model, would thus be subject to assessment by the Revenue as being within the charge to corporation tax.

Accordingly, Corporations *A* and *B* would be better advised to take a substantial part of the Liberian Corporation's profits arising outside the United Kingdom, for example in a predetermined standard or 'list' price payable by the Agents or the English company so that the English agreement is one for the sale of goods or in an agency agreement concluded outside the United Kingdom, whereby the principal contracts and makes delivery outside the United Kingdom. The balance of income might be derived at low tax rates by way of royalty income if channelled through a subsidiary Netherlands N.V. company and a Netherlands Antilles N.V. investment holding company (tax at 2.4 to 3 per cent annually).

Under the sales contract, the price being predetermined and delivery being effected in Liberia, the contract between Corporations *A* and *B* and the Liberian Corporation is concluded wholly outside the United Kingdom. There would only be tax liability if the Liberian Corporation were deemed the Corporations' agent for the purpose of trading within the United Kingdom.

The question which arises out of the patent and nature of payment arrangements under the English agreement is whether, as a question of fact, the Liberian Corporation is exercising a trade in the United Kingdom. The following facts are relevant. Both the English Company and the Agents 'receive' the profits arising in England. There is no predetermined standard or 'list' price at which they purchase the goods: they simply retain a percentage commission '... of all sales', the selling price being determined by the English Company which '... sold each model at a price equal to $10,000.' Such sale(s) would have to be accounted for to the agents (to determine the commissions) and to (the Liberian Corporation but not to the Corporations and the respective remittances would be made in England, in accordance with the 'financial summary'. Either jointly or as 'partners' the Agents are authorised to act as the Liberian Corporation's '... representatives in *all* matters related to the

Superior Units...'; and, whether as agent or sub-agent, by virtue of the patent arrangement, the English Company has exclusive rights and, in addition, is exclusively bound to purchase component parts from the Liberian Corporation.

As regards the Liberian Corporation, on the basis of such 'facts' and notwithstanding that it is not resident in the United Kingdom, the argument would be that it will have been trading within the United Kingdom, because that is where, as a merchant, it is exercising its trade: that is, a business of selling goods at a profit which is carried on where the contracts of sale are made through a 'branch or agency' (see sections 246(1) and (2) and 527(1), Income and Corporation Taxes Act 1970).

The exemption or 'saving' under section 82(1) of the Taxes Management Act 1970 (in respect of a non-resident's '... profits or gains from sales or transactions carried out through such a broker or agent' and broker includes a '*general* commission merchant') has been held to have application '*except* in cases where the agent... receives the profits'.

Thus, the respective tax consequences foreseen under the model are as follows. The Corporations will not be chargeable to United Kingdom Corporation tax on the profits arising as set out in the 'financial details'. The Liberian Corporation will be so assessable on the profits arising through or from the Agent/or the English Company in the name of its 'branch or agency'. The Agents are thus assessable to corporation tax on the amounts transferred which relate to profits arising on their foreign principal's account (the Liberian Corporation), and their own profits arising on their commission, but not on any allowable costs or expenses transferred to the Liberian Corporation which so relate. The English Company will be chargeable to corporation tax solely on its profits arising unless the Liberian Corporation is its principal when it will be assessable as the 'branch or agency' (see sections 79 and 85) Tax Management Act 1970). The above statutory rules as to corporation tax (or income tax), are subject to any applicable double taxation treaty with the country of residence of the non-English party. There is no United Kingdom/Liberia treaty. (*Quaere* if the United Kingdom/United States treaty would affect the Corporations).

Product Liability

Here the manufacturer's liability in tort is briefly examined[8]. Note that the malfunction of the Superior Unit was apparently not the fault of the English Company (or by inference or implication therefore of the Agents or the Liberian Corporation). (Since it was '... a malfunction which, despite the best quality control on the part of the Foreign-Market Company, could not have been detected beforehand.'

The Corporations' liability in tort depends on what degree of negligence or breach of duty of care can be proved. Negligence must be proved in the sense of showing that on the balance of probabilities the defects arose in the course of manufacture.

Res ipsa loquitur does not apply technically to shift the onus or burden of proof of negligence from the plaintiff to the defendant where, for example, there was an unexplained explosion or overheating, as in the model. The problem facing the Corporations as defendants is whether to provide rebuttal evidence which disproves negligence or, while not extending to such disproof, to provide a reasonable explanation. Evidence in rebuttal may be difficult to provide in the circumstances of the model. The Corporations' liability would be in damages as joint tortfeasors, to the executors of the child's estate, to the 'consumer' plaintiff, and to his neighbor for the death caused, under the Fatal Accidents Acts 1946–1959, and for physical injury to the property and the neighbor (but not for non-physical or purely pecuniary loss of which the damage is deemed too remote and not the direct and foreseeable consequence of the negligence)[9].

Neither the Liberian Corporation nor the Agents would be liable in tort. The English Company as an intermediate assembler and distributor would be liable in tort if, on discovering a defect (or having responsibility to examine or test, and failing to do so), it did not remedy or give warning of the defect. If such were the case, both the Corporations and the English Company would be liable[10].

Another possibility for tortious liability would arise if the Corporations' original instructions, for example for installing the Superior Unit, contained negligent mis-statements for which the courts would award damages for pecuniary loss as not being too remote[11] (the English Company '... performed all other functions (translated instructions) without fault...'). Possible defenses are that when the Corporations, as manufacturer, parted with the goods, they were not dangerous and that they had *no* reason to expect they would become so; and evidence of a 'foolproof process' of manufacture.

The Proper Law

Although the consumer can choose his remedy, a claim founded on tort might raise a defense based on contract, and there might be a conflict of laws, in which case the courts would apply the proper law (that is the proper law of the issue)[12]. The proper law of tort is '... the law of the country with which the parties and the acts done have the most significant connection'[13]. The proper law of contract is, in the absence of express choice by the parties or as may be inferred from the circumstances the system of law 'by reference to which the contract was made' or 'with which the transaction has its closest and most real connection' (the *Bonython*[14] test or formula).

The proper law of the issue is applied to avoid the application of two systems of law, for example, one of the tort in the plaintiff's claim and the other of the contract in the defense. In general, in construing the contract, the courts look at 'the setting of the transaction' as a whole[15]. In the absence of express agreement and when the intention of the parties cannot be inferred from the circumstances, no one factor is necessarily decisive. The relevant factors are weighed without the aid of any of the presumptions which were formerly relied upon[16].

Service of a writ, or notice of a writ, out of the jurisdiction is at the discretion of the court (see RSCO 11, r1(1)). The court may take jurisdiction 'if the action begun by the writ is brought against a defendant... to recover damages or obtain other relief in respect of the breach of contract,... which... is by its terms, or by implication, governed by English law;... (or) if the action begun by writ is founded on a tort committed within the jurisdiction....' It follows that leave will be given to sue Corporations *A* and *B* in the English courts on the manufacturers' liability in tort, the tort having been committed in England. Also, if the Corporations' sales contract with the Liberian Corporation is one for the sale of goods, then they cannot be sued on that contract[17] in England (other than by reason of an express choice of law clause), because such sale of goods contract would have been made and concluded wholly outside England. The risk of an action, such as it is, would be or arise if there was *prima facie* evidence, as to an extent in the model, of agency being the contractual relationship between Corporations *A* and *B* and the Liberian Corporation.

In relation to the Agents and the English company, since there is such *prima facie* evidence of agency in the agreements with the Liberian Corporation, on the facts set out in the Model, it can be concluded that service of a writ out of the jurisdiction on the Liberian Corporation and based on a claim in contract would be regarded by the courts as within their discretion. The English Company in its turn would be the party primarily liable on the sale of goods in England, but as an agent would have the agents right of indemnity and re-imbursement from its principal, the Liberian Corporation, or, if the Agents are principals, in an English action by way of joinder of parties, through their application from the Liberian Corporation as their principal.

Agency or Sale of Goods

The courts would look at the transactions as a whole, on their facts, to determine whether there was a contract for agency or sale of goods between the parties. The model is akin to a proof of evidence and in terms provides the *modus operandi* of the parties. It must be assumed that it is available to the courts and can be supported by evidence on discovery. Since, prior to the formation of the Liberian Corporation, Corporations *A* and *B* 'separately' exported their products to the Foreign-Market Country (England) through independent foreign-market agents, the main facts will be known to the Agents and (possibly) to the Foreign-Market Company (the English company) as regards the Liberian Corporation.

As set out in the Model, the essential facts disclosing the nature of the contracts and the course of dealing between the parties is as follows.

The Corporations '... decide to co-operate in the Foreign-Market Country' (England). The Liberian Corporation is to be '... properly formed, organised and functioning...' and each of the Corporations takes a fifty per cent capital interest in the Liberian Corporation and appoints one director to the board. The Liberian Corporation, on formation, purchases for a nominal price the know-how and rights to the component parts from the Corporations and negotiates exclusive sales and purchase agreements with the Agents (*quaere*, at the introduction of the Corporations) who '... will be authorized to act as [its] representatives in all matters related to the Superior Units...', and the English Company, which must '... promise to purchase all of the Superior Components from (*quaere*, the Liberian Corporation *or* the Agents)...' and patent, assemble and sell the Superior Unit in England. The '... two basic component parts: a Solar Collector and a Solar Generator...' (the goods) are to be transferred physically from the Corporations via the Liberian Corporation to England '... at a price of cost plus shipping plus overhead and shipping expenses...', the payment of which price by the Liberian Corporation being the final payments transaction in the scheme of events. The price negotiated by the Liberian Corporation for the goods sold through the Agents to the English Company is seventy per cent of all sales in England, the Agents commission being five per cent and the English Company retaining twenty five per cent of all sales. The price is based on the English Company's promise to pay and the Agents' and Liberian Corporation's similar undertakings in turn.

It follows, therefore, that the accounts of the proceeds of sale will be made up and the remittances made in England by the English Company in the order of the English company to the Agents (less their twenty five per cent); the Agents to the Liberian Corporation (less their five per cent) (a) cost plus overhead and shipping expenses (including the Corporations' proportion) and (b) the remainder being the anonymous Swiss bank deposit; and the Liberian Corporation to the Corporations being their proportion of cost plus overhead and shipping expenses.

Where a supplier buys goods from a manufacturer and resells them, in the absence of other indications, the supplier is liable in English law to the ultimate buyer for the quality of the goods, the manufacturer being liable in tort only[18]. However, where the supplier is a 'commission merchant' and the manufacturer's agent, the supplier will remain liable to the ultimate buyer, as seller as before, but he will have his agents rights of re-imbursement and indemnity on his contract with his principal as agent. Thus, a seller is answerable for defects in description and quality whereas an agent or 'commission agent' (which the Agents may or may not be) would not be so liable, not being a party to the contract for which he acts on behalf of a disclosed principal.

Nevertheless a buyer may be paid 'commission'[19], even if pre-arranged, without thereby being an agent. It is evidence of a sale of goods that he is entitled to sell at whatever price he thinks fit, especially if he accounts to his supplier only for a pre-determined standard or 'list' price[20]. Where, as set out above and in the model, the buyer is to assemble or improve the goods, an interpretation of a sale of goods has further support, as with the English company.

The point which concerns all the parties that carries a strong inference of agency is the duty implicit on the English Company and the agents to account for the proceeds of sale[21]. Other than between the Liberian Corporation and the Corporations, there is no predetermined standard or 'list' price. How are the due proceeds of sale and the sale commissions to be calculated and deducted under the Model? It can be concluded, therefore, that the English Company is constituted as 'mercantile agent' to the Liberian Corporation or to the Agents, whether as assembler or distributor. The Agents as 'authorized', are 'commission agents' or 'commission merchants' depending on whether they are acting for a disclosed or undisclosed principal.

In addition, the English Company is to have the right to patent the 'device' without any separate payment or royalty agreement. The Agents' contract with the English Company is to be an exclusive trading agreement, as is their agreement with the Liberian Corporation. Together with the patent arrangement (which is apparently also to be sub-licensed or sub-assigned via the Agents), the transactions with the English Company are suggestive largely of agency and distributorship rather than sale of goods. Particularly if acting on behalf of the Liberian Corporation as a disclosed principal, the English Company has all the characteristics of a 'mercantile agent' or factor.

The point in favor of the agreement between the Liberian Corporation and the Corporations being one for sale of goods is that the price (promised) to be paid to the Corporations is fixed, as outlined above. The question which arises, in view of the Corporations' past dealings separately with the Agents, is as to the true status of the new Liberian Corporation when it commenced trading. The physical transfer of the component parts of the Superior Unit and the parts as goods to the Liberian Corporation in Liberia and its proper functioning there as a separate entity rather than as the cypher of the Corporations are all further contrary indications to agency as compared with an inference of sale of goods. Such difficulty as might arise turns on the degree or not to which the Liberian Corporation has a separate corporate identity or personality from the Corporations.

The so-called 'corporate veil' decisions in the English courts have been founded substantially on agency principles: that is, within a group of companies to ignore the separate legal personalities of the holding company and its subsidiaries and see through to the real economic link between them[22]. The earlier cases where the courts have been willing to 'lift the corporate veil' were mainly tax cases, partly for which reasons one may regard consideration of 'corporate veil' agency principles as relevant to the model (if only to dismiss the tax risk so far as the relationship between the Corporations and the Liberian Corporation is concerned: the cases turn on 'control' and neither of the Corporations alone will control the Liberian Corporation, *quaere* the position if it is their cypher)[23].

Since the decisions are not entirely consistent, it is not possible to formulate any single principle as to when the separate corporate personality of a company or corporation will be respected and when it will be disregarded by the courts. In this instance, the courts would be inclined to view English law as the proper law of the contract, that is if viewed as an agency contract as a whole (the sales contract and the English agreement) and in favor of claims by third parties to the agreement between the Corporations[24] and the Liberian Corporation (for example, an indemnity action by the Agents or the English company after a claim by a consumer). Despite the apparent lack of control in shareholding terms (*quaere, de facto* management control), what is established is that, in a proper case, the courts will not allow the corporate form to be used for fraud, or as a means whereby contractual or other legal obligations may be avoided[25].

The purpose here is not to point a way to an extension of English law: the principle of separate corporate personality was clearly decided in *Salomon v Salomon & Co.*, 1897, AC 22 and, particularly where the shareholders are natural persons[26], still requires strict application[27]. It remains fundamental to several aspects of English company law. Nevertheless, there have been legislative changes in recent years in the direction of extension (see sections 31 and 332, and, in group accounts, sections 150–154 CA 1948 and section 8 CA 1976). In another case, the group and its subsidiaries were treated as 'partners' in order to achieve proper compensation on the acquisition of land[28]. The courts have thus shown reluctance to accept 'technical' arguments in favor of the separate corporate personality of group companies.

Provided that the Liberian Corporation is thus managed in fact as a separate corporation from the Corporations, so as to avoid any inference of control or agency no difficulties are foreseen between them. But as regards contractual product and tax liability, it is important to the Corporations to ensure that the contract with the Liberian Corporation is one made wholly outside the United Kingdom.

Alternative Contractual Arrangements

Parts I and II of the Unfair Contract Terms Act 1977 are expressly subject to Part III and to the exceptions in Schedule I (which excludes 'international supply contracts' and contracts relating to patents from the controls of the 1977 Act) (see section 1(2) *ibid*). Thus, neither the Corporations nor the Liberian Corporation need be controlled under the Act (other then under section 27(2) in Part III *ibid*).

As to the Agents and the English Company, notwithstanding any choice of law clause, where the proper law would *otherwise* be governed by English law, the parties to a contract cannot contract out of the provisions of the 1977 Act (see section 27(2) *ibid*; and section 5(2), Supply of Goods (Implied Terms) Act 1973, which restricts the use of the Uniform Law on International Sales to govern domestic contracts). The statutory obligations imported into the sale of goods contract which arises when the English Company sells a Superior Unit to another or third party to the English agreement will now be dealt with briefly.

If the other (third) party deals with the English Company and both do so in the course of business, the contract will be governed by the mandatory rules of Sections 12–15 Sale of Goods Act 1893 (sellers' implied undertakings as to title, conformity of goods with description or sample, or as to their quality of fitness for a particular purpose). In addition, any exclusion or indemnity terms or notices imported into the transaction by the English Company would have to pass a test of 'reasonableness' in the Courts: whether they are fair and reasonable '... having regard to the circumstances which were, or ought reasonably to have been known to or in the contemplation of the parties when the contract was made' (Sections 11(1), 2(2), 3, 4, 6(3), 7(3) and (4), and 8 of the 1977 Act)[29]. Evasion by means of secondary contracts is also blocked (see section 10 *ibid*).

In this context, note that the English Company is to '... package and translate instructions for installation in appropriate foreign languages; ...': its terms and conditions of sale would have to be framed accordingly with the 1977 Act in mind, considering possible liability for misrepresentation and on tort on the principles of *Hedley Byrne & Partners* v *Heller*[30] as to negligent mis-statement (see section 8, *ibid*, which provides a new section 3 for Misrepresentation Act 1967).

Where the other (third) party deals as a 'consumer' or dealing in the course of business sells to a 'consumer' in the United Kingdom as would be the case if the English Company sold direct to a consumer, the controls of sections 2–7 of the 1977 Act apply (by which relevant contract terms of exclusion or restriction of liability are made void, where the substantive claim is for personal death or injury; or, not given legal effect unless they pass the test of 'reasonableness', where the claim is for something else such as property damage, pure economic loss or the recovery of debt) (see section 27(2)(b) *ibid*). It follows that the controls placed on the English Company by the 1977 Act enable the consumer to claim more readily under a 'consumer contract' than formerly. However, the 'international supply contract' is not so controlled which provides the Corporations and the Liberian Corporation with the opportunity mentioned to restrict or exclude their contractual liability, subject though to the doctrine of fundamental breach which, whether as a rule of construction[31] or law[32], (section 27, *ibid*) provides that:

> Notwithstanding any contract term which applies or purports to apply the law of some other country outside the United Kingdom, where (either or both)—(a) the term appears to the Court... to have been imposed wholly or mainly for the purpose of enabling the party imposing it to evade the operation of this Act; or (b) in the making of the contract one of the parties dealt as consumer, and he was then habitually resident in the United Kingdom, and the essential steps necessary for the making of the contract were taken there, whether by him or others on his behalf.

Therefore, the better alternative contractual arrangement is for Corporations *A* and *B* and the Liberian Corporation to sell the goods under a contract of which the proper law would be the law of some country outside the United Kingdom, one which would exclude the controls of sections 2 to 7 of the 1977 Act even if the parties expressly chose United Kingdom law as the proper law (see section 27(1) *ibid*).

Whether the alternative contractual arrangements under the model are agency or sale of goods, the essential requirements of the contract, so as to avoid agency inferences of trading within the United Kingdom, are that negotiation and conclusion of offer and acceptance occur outside the United Kingdom (Agents and Liberian corporation); that there be a predetermined standard or 'list' price for goods; and that there exist a normal commercial relationship, whereby an agent acts as broker for commission and a buyer is free to sell the goods in the United Kingdom at prices and profits which he is to receive, that is, no receipt on behalf of a foreign principal.

Mention should be made of the potential benefits of the Netherlands double taxation agreements; however, as between the United Kingdom and the Netherlands Antilles, direct relief does not apply in the case of dividends, interest or royalties which enjoy any of the special tax benefits available there to certain holding and investment companies (see Article 30, Netherlands Antilles, Convention of 31 October 1967, SI 1968/577). Similar provisions apply between the United States and the Netherlands (see article 1 (1), Protocol of 1963 modifying United States-Netherlands Double Tax Treaty 1948).

There are two important aspects which may assist the Corporations.

If title to the goods were to pass in the Netherlands Antilles where the profit were substantially to be taken, then such trading income would not be taxable in either the country of origin or destination, provided the income were taken in a Netherlands Antilles off-shore or free-zone[33] company which had the benefit of the concessionary tax rates of six or thirteen per cent, respectively. However, it is important that there is properly constituted local management and personnel and that documents of title and even transshipment of goods takes place in or through the Netherlands Antilles to establish that there is more than a front company there, if only to avoid the agency arguments relating to profits arising in the United Kingdom. Furthermore, if the patent rights were assigned to a wholly-owned Netherlands subsidiary company, which sub-licensed the English Company, royalties from the sub-license would be payable from the United Kingdom to the Netherlands, but with the benefit of the United Kingdom/Netherlands double taxation agreement, the rate of tax on any royalties paid from the United Kingdom thus effectively being reduced to nil (see article 13 (1), Netherlands, Convention of 31 October 1967, SI 1968/577, which is unaffected by the protocol of 22 March 1977, SI No 1300, which relates only to dividends).

If royalty income remitted from outside the Netherlands is paid to a Netherlands Antilles holding company by a Netherlands subsidiary by way of dividends, as between the Netherlands and the Netherlands Antilles, the rate of withholding tax on dividend payments of twenty five per cent is reduced to nil by virtue of their double taxation agreement. The Netherlands Antilles company, subject to payment of total tax at the concessionary rate of 2.4 to 3 per cent on investment income from abroad, could remit such income free of tax back to the Corporations (see Netherlands/Netherlands Antilles Double Tax Treaty 1965, article 11/3). However, there are two caveats to be made. The Netherlands apparently is allowing its tax code to be used to avoid taxes in other countries. Although there is as yet no indication of any change in the attitude of the Dutch tax authorities, the specific exclusions in the direct extensions of their treaties of the concessionary Netherlands Antilles companies indicates that pressure may be applied in due course, as happened in the case of Switzerland and the Netherlands in 1962 and as seems to be happening now with regard to Liechtenstein again at the instance of Switzerland (see report in *The Times of London*, 24/25 April 1978—proposal to start income tax and change company law in Liechtenstein, due to recent banking scandals in Switzerland connected with Leichtenstein)[34].

The significance of such moves in relation to the Netherlands Antilles is that the United Kingdom extension of 24 July 1970, SI 1970, number 1949, may be determined at one year's notice and the Netherlands/Netherlands Antilles double taxation treaty at two years notice. However, the latter treaty was renewed as recently as 13 April 1977 and the Netherlands Antilles Guarantee Ordinance Profits Tax 1979, *Official Gazette number* 282/1976, was renewed on 31 December 1976 (see II–20 of 1977; and I–28 of 1977, *Tax News Service of the International Bureau of Fiscal Documentation*). The Ordinance renews the concessionary tax arrangements and guarantees them for at least twenty years until 30 June 1999, or financial years terminating two years thereafter.

Finally, it should be noted that both the Netherlands and Netherlands Antilles exempt capital gains on qualifying participations which should facilitate any necessary capital re-organisations.

Alternative Locations[35]

The only comparable location to Liberia which also provides anonymity (other than as regards the founder of an *Anstalt*, which is not an insuperable problem) is Liechtenstein. There is complete banking, tax, director and shareholder secrecy and no requirements for audit or statutory returns. Such far away places as the New Hebrides or Narau have been disregarded primarily because, if the anonymity requirements are essential, by contrast to them Liechtenstein has well-established professional services.

Although Swiss exchange controls apply to the inflow of foreign capital as regards negative rates of interest on bank deposits (at ten per cent per quarter on the portion in excess of SFr. 100,000 at any one Swiss bank), there are no exchange controls on the outflow of capital from Liechtenstein. The *Anstalt* (a form of permanent establishment with its own assets but '. . . not being in the nature of a public body or other form of legal person') is the preferred form for a foreign holding company. However, there are disadvantages. As an entity peculiar to Liechtenstein, there may be no judicial reciprocity or recognition in other countries; for example, in Italy there was a recent challenge in Venice Appellate Court. Other disadvantages include the fact that the minimum paid up capital is SFr. 30,000 and there is a net-worth tax of one per cent (payable annually in advance), provided the *Anstalt* is not active in Liechtenstein (two per cent, if it is). Finally, there are no double taxation agreements with any country other than Austria.

Attention is drawn to the Netherlands Antilles because it has double-taxation agreements with the Netherlands, and, through an extension to the Dutch treaties, also with Denmark, Norway, the United Kingdom and the United States. While its Commercial Code does not provide for the full anonymity required in the Model (it requires at least one resident Director and filing of annual financial statements in the Commercial Register, that is, if corporate business consists of borrowing from third parties), there are no legal requirements regarding minimum capitalisation and no exchange control restrictions. Steps to establish limited-liability Netherlands/Netherlands Antilles companies are set out in Schedule II of the footnotes. The significant advantage of using such companies is, as stated, the use to be made of the double taxation agreements to resolve some of the negative taxation aspects outlined above. In addition, since the presumed intention of the Corporations is to 'penetrate... [the] European Community Market...', the formation of a Netherlands licensing company would facilitate patent licensing agreements with those countries which do not have double taxation agreements with Netherlands Antilles. The procedure, as with the United Kingdom example, is to remit royalties through the Netherlands company to the Netherlands Antilles by way of dividend.

Formation of an English joint-stock company by the Corporation would place its profits arising within the charge to corporation tax at present rates of fifty two per cent per annum (forty two per cent per annum special rate for companies with small profits). Disclosure requirements under Companies Act 1948–1976 are strict. There is an obligation on all limited companies to annex to their annual returns to the Registrar of Companies their accounts, by reference to accounting reference periods, an auditors' report and 'a report by the directors on the company's affairs' (section 157(1) CA 1948, as amended by section 1 CA 1976; and sections 16–20 CA 1967). Such information is publicly available.

As regards trading 'in' or 'with' the United Kingdom and United Kingdom/United States double-taxation agreements, a 'permanent establishment' includes a branch (see article 5, United Kingdom/United States Convention, 31 December 1975). According to the normal principle, profits of a trade or business are not taxed in the country where the corporations are nonresident unless arising from a permanent establishment.

Reservations

Note that Corporations *A* and *B* have sold their technological know-how in the component parts on formation: whether such rights are patentable or not is unclear from the model. The model by implication excludes consideration of the proper registration and protection of know-how and patents. Note that the Corporations have 'separately exported models through independent-market Agents Y and Z, respectively'. If so and if the components are 'known and used' in the United Kingdom they may not be patentable inventions (see section 2(1), Patents Act 1977; and section 14(1-(d), Patents Act 1949).

Also, although the monopoly of a patent may be extended beyond its life by, for example, an agreement to purchase components, the Patents Act 1977 provides for termination by either party on three months notice where such condition relates to a product which is the subject of an expired patent (see section 45(1), *ibid*). If the component parts are to be the subject of exclusive patent licensing or trading agreements (royalty payments are an alternative solution), it should be noted that the courts would apply the provisions of European Economic Community law, especially articles 85 and 86 of the Treaty of Rome and the executory directives of the Commission, particularly as regards registration of exclusive licensing or trading agreements, where applicable. This aspect is not examined because the Model expressly excludes consideration of '. . . relevant antitrust laws'. But in this context, note that the said company must promise to purchase all of the Superior Components from the Liberian Corporation'.

Since the Model also expressly excludes consideration of foreign-exchange laws, United Kingdom exchange controls have not been examined, other than to make reference to the Exchange Control notice EC 53, issued by the Bank of England, which supplements the 'Notice to Importers', issued by H.M. Treasury. This notice sets out the circumstances in which banks may authorize payments for imports and the requirements for making payments on which the banks should be satisfied. Most goods, such as the component parts can be imported freely under an open general license from the Department of Trade and Industry. The general principle of exchange control practice being that the right to import carries with it the right to pay for the goods, it can be anticipated that foreign exchange in Swiss francs would be made readily available to the Agents if their bankers can be so satisfied (*quaere*, payments to whom in Swiss francs and for what: royalties, commission or sale of goods).

Notes

1. The author expresses no opinion on other than English law (for example, not Scots law) nor on the application of European Economic Community law outside the United Kingdom. Reservations as to the exclusions in the model, which explicitly excludes foreign-exchange and antitrust law and implicitly excludes patent law other than in relation to contract, are summarized under *Alternative Contractual Arrangements* because such modifications as may be necessary to the model are themselves illustrative of the working of English law in England and Wales.
2. The result otherwise will generally be that no contract exists until the price is agreed, judgment of Denning, L.J., *Nicolene Ltd* v *Simmons*, 1953, 1 QB 543.
3. *Infra*, notes 7 and 20.
4. Agency, in relation to tax liability: reference to F (No.2) A 1915 section 31(7) which is replaced by section 82(1) Tax Management Act *1970* '. . . Its intention and effect is to exempt from taxation in the name of a resident agent. . . all sales and transactions between non-residents, even though effected through the medium of that agent. . . *except in cases where the agent receives the profits* per Viscount Cave L C *Maclaine & Co* v *Eccott*, 1926, AC 424, 435; contract and delivery made abroad—*Grainger & Son* v *H. Gough*, 1896, AC 325, 335; *Greenwood* v *Smidth (FL) & Co*, 1922, 8 TC 193, 205 HL.
5. Agency, in relation to agency contracts: 'commission agent': viz. agent with special responsibility *J.N. Lyon & Co Ltd* v *N. Fuchs*, 1920, 2 L1.L. Rep.333; 'commission merchant': viz. understanding that he will, when dealing with third parties, do so in his own name and not create

any privity of contract, i.e. between the third party and his principal; *Ireland v Livingston*, 1872, LR 5HL 395 at 408; *Armstrong* v *Stokes*, 1872, LR 5QB 598; *Anglo-African Shipping Co. of New York Inc* v *J. Mortner Ltd*, 1962, 1 Lloyds Rep 610.

6. 'Mercantile agent': [see Sections 1(1) and 2(1), Factors Act 1889; cf, also, Uniform Commercial Code section 2–403(2)]; *Oppenheimer* v *Attenborough & Son*, 1908, 1KB 221 CA; and generally: 'If I, residing in England, send down my agent to Scotland and he makes contracts for me there, it is the same as if I myself went there and made them' *Pattison* v *Mills*, 1828, 1 Dow & Cl. 342, 363.

7. Contracts and profits made in United Kingdom—*Watson* v *Sandie and Hull*, 1898, 3 TC 611; *Weiss, Biheller and Brooks Ltd* v *Fauner*, 1923, 8 TC 381, 401, 407; *Turner (Thomas) (Leicester) Ltd* v *Rickman*, 1898, 4TC 25; and *MacPherson & Co* v *Moore*, 6 TC 107.

8. Manufacturer's liability in tort—*Donoghue* v *Stevenson*, 1932, AC 562, at 599; *res ipsor loquitur—Henderson* v *Henry E. Jenkins & Sons* 1970 AC 282; *Moore* v *R. Fox & Sons*, 1956, 1QB 596.

9. *Obiter dicta—Pattendon* v *Beney*, 1934, 50 TLR 204 per Scrutton, L.J.; neighbor: consumer in proximity—*Stennett* v *Hancock*, 1939, 2 All ER 578; *Power* v *Bedford Motor Co and Harris*, 1959, 1R 391; reasonably foreseeable consequences—*O'Dwyer* v *Leo Buring Ltd*, 1966, WAR 67; *Deyong* v *Shenburn*, 1946, KB 227, 237; *Dorset Yacht Co. Ltd* v *Home Office*, 1969, 2 QB 412, 476 (affirmed, 1970, AC 1004); *Spartan Steel and Alloys Ltd* v *Martin & Co. (Contractors) Ltd*, 1973, 1QB 27.

10. *Grant* v *Australian Knitting Mills Ltd*, 1936, AC 85, at 96–97; *Lockhart* v *Barr*, 1943, SC1; *Daniels and Daniels* v *White & Sons Ltd*, 1938, 4 All ER 258; *Griffiths* v *Arch Engineering Co.*, 1968, 2 All ER 217, 222; *Paine* v *Colne Valley Electricity Supply Co.*, 1938, 4 All ER 803, 808 per Goddard, L.J.

11. *Hedley Byrne & Co. Ltd* v *Heller and Partners Ltd*, 1964, AC 465.

12. *Sayers* v *International Drilling Co.*, 1971, 1WLR 1176, at 1181 A–B.

13. *Boys* v *Chaplin*, 1968, 2 QB1, at 20; *Szalatnay-Stacho* v *Fink*, 1947, KB 1.

14. *Coast Lines* v *Hudig Chartering CA*, 1972, 2 *QB* 34, at 46; *Bonython* v *Commonwealth of Australia*, 1951, AC 201; In Re *United Railways of Havana and Regla Wharehouses*, 1961, AC 1007, at 1068.

15. *Goldsborough Mort & Co. Ltd* v *Hall*, 1949, 78 CLR 1, 18, 45; *Alan (W J) & Co. Ltd* v *El Nasr Export and Import Co.*, 1972, 2QB 189, 206 CA.

16. *Coast Lines* v *Hudig Chartering CA*, *supra* note 14, at 44A, 47G–H and 50 E; and see note 40 at page 743, Dicey and Morris, THE CONFLICT OF LAWS 9th ed.).

17. Privity of contract: a third party or stranger to a contract acquires no rights nor incurs obligations *arising under* the contract; his cause of action in a claim founded on tort, for example against a manufacturer who supplied the seller of goods, is quite 'different'; *Rookes* v *Barnard*, 1964, AC 1129, 1208.

18. *Sproule* v *Triumph Motor Cycle Co.*, 1927, NI 83; *International Harvester Co. of Australia Pty* v *Carrigans Hazeldene Pastoral Co.*, 1958, 100 CLR 644, see also *supra, note* 8.

19. *Kelly* v *Enderton*, 1913, AC 191.

20. *Re Nevill, ex parte White*, 1871, 6 Ch.App.387, affirmed sub.nom. *John Towle & Co.* v *White*, 1873, 29 LT 78.

21. *Michelin Tyre Co. Ltd* v *Macfarlane (Glasgow) Ltd*, 1917, 55 Sc. L. Rep. 55.

22. Group subsidiaries as cyphers—*Harold Houldsworth & Co. (Wakefield) Ltd* v *Caddies*, 1955, 1 All ER 725; *Littlewoods Mail Order Stores Ltd* v *McGregor*, 1969, All. ER 855, 860.

23. *Smith, Stone and Knight* v *Birmingham Corporation*, 1939, 4 All ER 116, at 121; *Firestone Tyre & Rubber Co.* v *Llewellin*, 1957, All ER 561; *Re Salaberry Realities* v *Minister of National Revenue*, 1974, 46 DLR (3d) 100.

24. Foreign corporate entities as puppets—*Wallersteiner* v *Moir* (No. 1), 1974, 1 WLR 987 CA, at 1013 F–G; conflicting decisions; Court of Appeal 'entitled and bound to decide... which it will follow', *Young* v *Bristol Aeroplane Co. Ltd.*, 1944, KB 718, 729 (CA): and Agency, third parties and the proper law-preference expressed page 874 Dicey and Morris, THE CONFLICT OF LAWS (9th ed.) for *Masopons* v *Mildred*, 1882, 9 QBD 530; and *Chatenay* v *Brazilian Submarine Telegraph Co.*, 1891, 1 QB 79; and *not Ruby S.S. Corp. Ltd* v *Commercial Union Assurance Co. Ltd*, 1933, 150 LT 38.

25. 'Corporate veil' and agency: *Re Darby*, 1911, IKB 95; *Wallersteiner* v *Moir, supra*, note 24, at 1013 F–G; *Gilford Motor Co. Ltd* v *Horne*, 1933, Ch. 935, 943, 957; *reference to 'partnership' within a group*: *D.H.N. Food Distributors Ltd* v *London Borough of Tower Hamlets*, 1976, 1 WLR 852 at 860 C–D.
26. Recent application—*E.J. Neale (Glasgow) Ltd.* v *Vickery*, 1974, S.L.T. 88.
27. *Obiter dicta—The Albezero*, 1975, 3 All ER 21, 28 F–J.
28. *D.H.N. Food Distributors Ltd* v *London Borough of Tower Hamlets, supra* note 25, at 860 C–D.
29. Application of 'reasonableness' test: summary of terms and notices –

Section 2(2): terms or notices that exclude or restrict liability for negligence, the claim being in respect of loss or damage other than death or personal injury;

Section 3: terms in standard form contracts (or contracts made with businessmen by consumers) which seek to exclude or restrict liability for breach or to allow non-performance or a performance substantially different from that which was expected;

Section 4: indemnity clauses of certain kinds in contracts made by businessmen with consumers;

Section 6(3): terms in contracts of sale or hire-purchase excluding or restricting the usual implied terms (save as to title) where the customer does not deal as consumer;

Section 7(3) and (4): terms in contracts for the supply of goods (otherwise than by sale or hire-purchase) which exclude or restrict terms as to title or, where the customer does not deal as consumer, which exclude or restrict any of the other terms that would otherwise be implied in the customer's favour;

Section 8: terms which exclude or restrict liability for misrepresentation.

30. *Supra*, note 11.
31. *Suisse Atlantique Société d'Armement Maritime SA* v *NV Rotterdamsche Kolen Centrale*, 1967, 1 AC 361.
32. *Harbutt's Plasticine Ltd* v *Wayne Tank & Pump Co. Ltd*, 1970, 1QB 447.
33. Netherlands Antilles (NA): An off-shore trading company based in NA must not have any other trade or business with the islands. Upon application and ruling by the tax authorities that eighty per cent of its income be exempted from NA tax, twenty per cent is subject to rates of thirty per cent in the Guaranty Ordinance: the effective rate is around six per cent per annum. Free-Zone trading companies which are only involved in importing and re-exporting goods not for sale in NA are taxed at one-third of basic rates of twenty-seven to thirty-four per cent plus the municipal surcharge of fifteen per cent: the effective rate is around thirteen per cent. Investment companies are chargeable to NA basic rates of tax twenty-four to thirty per cent, which is reduced to one tenth of the rate on foreign investment income: the effective rate is then 2.4 to three per cent.
34. The direct use of a Liechtenstein *Anstalt* is less certain: in view of their reputation with tax authorities, care should be taken to ensure that as far as possible the royalties represent no more than ordinary payment that would be made to a third party, viz. the royalty or other income has commercial substance.
35. The references required by the model to alternative foreign locations and the comparisons as to their advantages and disadvantages are derived from the following sources, without expressing an opinion on the matter. See Spitz, *Tax Havens Encyclopaedia, Directory of Tax Havens* (1977); and Saunders, *Tax Planning for Businesses in Europe* (1977).

Corporation formation: (b) '... steps to establish such corporation...': alternative locations -

(a) *Liechtenstein*; *Anstalt* – form of permanent establishment, not a company as such.

(i) Incorporation: The mandatory requirements of *Personen und Gesellschaftsrecht* (PGR) relate to-

– Founder(s)	Art. 535
– Articles of	
– Association	536
– published in	
– the Civil Register	537

In addition to the Articles, what are necessary steps to complete the preliminaries are a deed of incorporation, a declaration as to the firm's signature and the appointment of a representative. An inquiry stage follows entry into the Civil Register when the authorities check that the mandatory requirements are fulfilled. The Anstalt is incorporated on entry into the Civil Register.

Founder(s) may be one, individual or organizations, even corporate bodies. The Articles of Association have to be signed by the Founder(s) and its mandatory contents are -

(1) name or trade mark, registered office and description of the *Anstalt*;
(2) objects and if necessary to clarify the objects, particulars of the enterprise;
(3) if not in money, estimated value of funds (minimum 30,000 Swiss Francs capital);
(4) manner of passing resolutions;
(5) principle on which balance sheet is prepared and surplus is to be appropriated;
(6) management, and, if applicable, auditing body;
(7) form in which notices will be prepared and issued by *Anstalt*.

The Articles may provide the internal rules and regulations of the *Anstalt*'s management and its beneficiaries, whether natural or legal persons. The Articles must specify how they are to be ascertained and whether and how those concerned will participate in the organisation of the *Anstalt*.

(ii) Capital: Shares may be divided or undivided (PGR–Article 535). In practice, since 4 per cent withholding tax attaches to dividends on divided share capital, shares hardly ever are divided. Minimum capital is thirty-thousand Swiss Francs (PGR–Article 122). Liability is limited to the amount of the assets.

(iii) Organization: The Board of management may consist of one or more natural or legal persons appointed by the founder(s). However, one member of the Board must be resident in Liechtenstein.

(b) *Netherlands*: *Naamloze Vennootschap* NV) are Dutch company equivalents to French/Belgian/Luxembourg *Société Anonyme.* Two shareholders are required on incorporation, though thereafter the shares may be transferred to one non-resident company. Bearer shares may be issued. There is an annual requirement for a full financial statement to be filed and verified by an independent auditor.

(c) *Netherlands Antilles*: (*N. V.*)

(a) *Incorporation* is in accordance with the Commercial Code. After shares have all been issued, there is no published information available to the public as to the shareholders. At formation, founders can be provided by the local resident trust companies; there is no requirement for resident shareholders.

The instrument of incorporation (in Dutch) is executed before a civil notary and the N.V. is incorporated after receiving a Declaration of No-Objection, issued by the Ministry of Justice. The Articles set forth the name, registered office and corporate objectives of the N.V., together with the names of the initial and general manager(s), the amount of shares authorised and their par value. The number of shares to be issued and subscribed by the founders of the company must be specified.

The corporate objectives are important as regards favourable tax treatment, tax elections and foreign exchange restrictions. Licenses are required (1) to conduct corporate business, from the Department of Social and Economic Affairs which also authorises the Managing Director(s) to act as such and (2) from the Central Bank of Netherlands Antilles.

While there is no minimum capital requirement the Declaration of No-Objection may not be forthcoming if the capital is thought inadequate. N.A. Guilders 10,000 is regarded as appropriate for a holding company, and may consist of other assets than cash, tangible or intangible, if so provided for in the Articles. Partly paid shares must remain registered and the management of the N.V. must maintain the register under the Penal Code. Bearer shares, fully paid, may be issued.

(b) *Shareholders*: liability is limited to the par value of the shares issued and control of the N.V. is vested in shareholders in general meeting. While general meetings must be held in Netherlands Antilles, proxies may be used. Annual General Meetings must be held within nine months of the close of corporate financial years.

(c) *Management*: the N.V. must have at least one general manager, an individual or corporate person, and one must be resident in Netherlands Antilles.

The French Analysis

DENIS DEBOST

Corporation Formation

At the outset it should be noted that this discussion will deal only with French law, including treaties to which France is a party. It is assumed that advice on the United States tax and other legal aspects of the proposal has been sought from United States and that counsel on matters involving the law of countries other than the United States and France will be consulted. Nevertheless, the following comments concerning the non-French aspects of the proposed scheme can be made.

The share capital of the Liberian Corporation is to be owned half by Corporation *A* and half by Corporation *B*, and it will have two directors, one from Corporation *A* and one from Corporation *B*. This being so, how can there be 'no record of their involvement in this corporation' and how are 'the names of the directors to be anonymous'? Although the overall purpose of the scheme is apparently to generate minimally taxed income outside the United States, ultimately owned by Corporations *A* and *B*, one must assume that Corporations *A* and *B* are prepared to disclose the existence and ownership of the Liberian Corporation to the United States tax authorities, as is most probably required under United States law, and that they are prepared to pay United States taxes on the foreign income in question, either when it is ultimately repatriated to the United States, or if necessary before then, to the extent that United States tax laws may provide for taxation of such income before distribution or repatriation. It also must be assumed that funds to be paid to the Liberian Corporation's anonymous Swiss bank account will be recorded in the Liberian Corporation's books.

Since, as indicated, this discussion is limited to French law, no alternative locations for the formation of the offshore corporation will be suggested. It can be noted, however that certain large law firms maintain offices outside their jurisdiction and give advice on laws other than their own. Furthermore, since corporations *A* and *B*'s choice of location will be based mainly on tax considerations, it is suggested that they consult one of the leading firms of independent auditors who have a network of offices in most foreign countries, which can provide up-to-date tax and other information and practical advice.

France is hardly thought of as a tax haven country, which is an advantage in itself, since the mere names of Liberia, Liechtenstein, the Cayman Islands and, to a lesser degree, Luxembourg and the Netherlands Antilles, to name but a few of the more popular supposed havens, are enough to arouse the suspicion of most French tax inspectors and to cause them to investigate the scheme, with glee or resentment depending on how well the scheme is not only conceived but implemented. (The importance of implementation is stressed, for the best looking scheme on paper will often fail because the operators tend to forget about the paper structure and to deal in accordance with the realities of the situation. It is from these slip-ups that the tax inspectors obtain their greatest satisfactions).

Yet France, although its tax rates on income subject to French taxes are substantial (fifty per cent except on certain capital gains), does not tax income from extraterritorial business operations at all, when such operations are carried out either through an autonomous establishment such as a subsidiary or branch, or through non-independent employees or representatives or, even without such an establishment or representative, when the operations carried out abroad form a 'complete cycle of operations' such as when both the purchase and resale of the same goods takes place outside of France.

It may, therefore, be envisioned that a French company be used as an offshore company, in lieu of the Liberian Corporation, since the French company's proceeds from sales of components outside of France purchased from Corporation *A* and Corporation *B* also outside of France would be exempt from French company income tax. As a corollary, all costs relating to such sales, including both the cost of goods sold and a portion of overhead attributable to such extraterritorial activities, would be non-deductible from income taxable in France, if any. In the following comments, however, it will be assumed that the proposal involving a Liberian Corporation is maintained.

Contractual Considerations

Agents *Y* and *Z* are to be authorized to act as the representatives of Corporation *A* and *B* in all matters related to the Superior Units and funds to be paid by the French Company are to be collected and remitted by the Agents. Under French exchange control regulations, the Liberian Corporation can either (1) invoice the French Company directly and receive the proceeds abroad through a French bank in foreign currency, or (2) set up a French branch, which under French law would be treated for most purposes as a separate entity and which would import the components, sell them to the French Company for French francs and pay the Liberian Company for the units through a French bank in foreign currency, or (3) sell the goods to an independent distributor who would take title from the Liberian Company, sell the units for French francs and pay the Liberian Company for the units through a French bank in foreign currency. Let us examine how Agents *Y* and *Z* could fit into one of these patterns, numbered One, Two or Three as above.

Under Pattern One—direct sales to the French Company—the Liberian Corporation could have a foreign currency account in a French bank, for the operation of which the Agents would have signature powers on behalf of the Liberian Corporation. Their compensation ($500 per unit) could be paid to them out of this account in the form of a commission. As the commission would be paid by the Liberian Corporation, it would have to be expressed as a percentage of the sales of the Liberian Corporation:

$$\frac{\text{Agents' commission}}{\text{price to French company}} = \frac{\$500}{\$7{,}500} = 6\text{-}2/3\%$$

Under Pattern Two (sales through a French branch of the Liberian Corporation), the Agents would handle the funds as managers of the branch. Their compensation would be computed, as in Pattern One, as a percentage of sales (6-2/3 per cent), but would be in the nature of salary if they are employees of the branch, or of fees if they manage the branch under a contract for management services.

Under Pattern Three (sale through an independent distributor), Agents *Y* and *Z* would presumably act as owners and/or managers of the distributing enterprise, to enable Agents *Y* and *Z* to handle the funds as planned. The compensation of the distributor would again be computed as under Pattern One: 6-2/3 per cent of the price to the French Company, but would be received by the distributor in the form of a discount on the purchase of goods from the Liberian Corporation and passed on to Agents *Y* and *Z* by the distributor in the form of compensation or dividends.

For the reasons explained hereafter, it is advised that Pattern Three be adopted, with Agents *Y* and *Z* as owners and/or managers of the proposed French Company. The reasons are the following.

Pattern One creates the risk that the Liberian Corporation would be deemed to have a permanent establishment in France, due to the powers granted to the Agents. There is no treaty for the avoidance of double taxation between France and Liberia, so that we do not have the benefit, as under most such treaties, of a clear definition of what will constitute a permanent establishment of the Liberian Company in France. In the absence of a treaty, the French tax authorities generally apply the criteria usually found in the treaties, such as the existence in France of a person or persons having authority to conclude contracts on behalf of the Liberian Corporation, but with even more administrative discretion which could take account, for example, of the Agent's authority to handle the Liberian Corporation's funds.

Pattern Two automatically would subject the Liberian Corporation to French taxation and, since the French tax authorities reserve the right to allocate profits between related parties such as the Liberian Corporation and its French branch, a portion of the Liberian Corporation's profit would be taxable in France. In practice, the Liberian Corporation would have to invoice the components to the branch at a price lower than that charged to the French Company, so that the French branch could show a taxable profit on its sales.

Under Pattern Three, the discount of 6-2/3 per cent allowed to the distributor appears low and it does not seem worthwhile for the Agents to set up an intermediate distributorship between the Liberian Company and the French Company. Since the Agents are charged with finding the French Company, it would appear natural that they form it themselves, thereby increasing the efficiency of the operation and the share of profits to them.

To summarize, therefore, it is recommended that the pattern adopted be as follows (per unit):

Sale price by French Company owned or managed by Agents *Y* and *Z*	$10,000
Purchase price by French Company	7,000
Gross income covering	$ 3,000
—Compensation of *Y* and *Z*	$ 500
—French Company other costs	1,000
—French Company profit	1,500

The $7,000 purchase price is paid, as directed by the Liberian Corporation, to the extent of $2,000 to Liberia or wherever and $5,000 to the Swiss bank account. The $500 intended as compensation for the Agents could either be retained by their French Company and paid to them in the form of dividends or paid half to each as personal compensation for sales and/or management services.

It is indicated that the French Company will not only assemble the components and sell the resulting units in France but also will patent the components and the unit in France. The product resulting from the mere assembly of the Superior Collector and the Superior Generator with eight bolts, even if a bit of wiring is added between the two, is unlikely to be accepted as an invention, so it must be assumed that it is the Superior Collector or the Superior Generator that has some patentable aspect to it. However, the product already has been sold in France by Corporation *A* and Corporation *B*, each using its own components. This disclosure of the invention will prevent effective patent protection in France, unless application for a French patent is made within the one-year period of grace allowed from the date of filing for patent in the United States, pursuant to the Convention of Paris of 20 March 1883, as amended, to which the United States and France are both parties.

If this grace period has not expired, timely application for a French patent must be made in the name of the applicants for the United States patent, presumably Corporation *A* and/or Corporation *B*, instead of in the name of the French Company, as proposed. This would be done, presumably, at the patent holder's expense, a point which should be made clear. The sale of patented products by the holder or licensee of the patents would, at least under French and Common Market law concepts, 'exhaust the patent holders' rights' over those products. Therefore, although the patent rights will be held ultimately by Corporation *A* and/or *B* or by the Liberian Corporation, it does not appear necessary that a patent license be granted to the French Company, which will in effect be merely reselling the Solar Collectors and Solar Generators after connecting the two together.

Alternative Contractual Arrangements

As indicated above, it is suggested that the Liberian Company make sales directly to the French Company acting as an independent distributor, and that Agents *Y* and *Z* act as principals of the French Company. This will satisfy not only the exchange control regulations but also serve to insulate the Liberian Company from tax liability and product liability to the greatest extent possible. It also will indirectly insulate Corporation *A* and Corporation *B*, for the possibility exists under French law of 'looking through the corporate veil' of the Liberian Company, if the veil is thin enough. Neither of the alternatives mentioned in the previous section (Pattern One and Pattern Two) would provide all these advantages.

Tax Liability

If the structure proposed above is adopted, that is to say if the French Company is formed by Agents *Y* and *Z* and acts as an independent distributor for the Liberian Company, and if neither Corporation *A* nor Corporation *B* nor the Liberian Company has any other operations or dealings with France, French taxation will be as follows.

Neither Corporation *A* nor Corporation *B* will have taxable income in France, provided the French tax authorities cannot question the arm's length nature of the dealings between the group composed of Corporations *A* and *B* and their Liberian Corporation, on the one hand, and the group composed of Agents *Y* and *Z* and their French Company on the other hand.

Income of the Liberian Corporation will not be subject to French tax, whether proceeds of sales in France are paid to Liberia or to Switzerland, subject to the same proviso as above.

Assuming the Agents *Y* and *Z* to be individuals, their share can be paid to them by the French Company as total or partial compensation for their services as employees of the company. The French Company will obtain an equivalent deduction, so that this $500 item will not be taxable in the hands of the French Company. The latter will, however, pay social charges and payroll taxes on the amounts paid to Agents *Y* and *Z*. These charges, like the compensation itself, will be deductible by the French Company.

In the hands of the recipients, Agents *Y* and *Z*, their share of $500 per unit sold will be treated as salary income, which is taxed more favorably in France than most other forms of income, due to the fact that employees have standard deductions which reduce their taxable salary to seventy two per cent of actual salary. If Agents *Y* and *Z* qualify as traveling salesmen (*Voyageurs, Représentants, Placiers*, or VRPs), an additional thirty per cent of the seventy two per cent or 21.6 per cent of actual salary may be deducted, reducing taxable salary to 50.4 per cent of actual salary, subject to ceilings recently placed on these various deductions.

To the extent that Agents *Y* and *Z* do not draw down their $500 per unit share of the proceeds of sale in the form of commissions, the unpaid portion will add to the gross income and to the net income of the French Company. Dividends distributed to Agents *Y* and *Z* as shareholders of the French Company will benefit from favorable French tax provisions pursuant to which the recipients obtain a tax credit equal to fifty per cent of the dividend distributed, subject to certain conditions such as the requirement that the dividends be distributed out of profits that have borne the company income tax at the full fifty per cent rate. Despite this advantage, however, the overall tax burden on the $500 per unit share of Agents *Y* and *Z* will be considerably lower if they take out such share in the form of VRP commissions, even if income tax rates applicable to Agents *Y* and *Z* are up to the sixty per cent maximum under French law, and even taking into account the added burden of social charges.

The French Company will pay company income tax at the rate of fifty per cent on its net profits. Gross taxable income will include the $500 per unit reserved to Agents *Y* and *Z*. This item will be included in taxable income if retained by the company and paid out in the form of dividends to Agents *Y* and *Z* and will be deductible from taxable income if paid out to the Agents in the form of salaries or commissions. The French Company also will pay tax on value-added (TVA) upon the import of components, charge TVA to its customers upon the sale of the products and remit the difference to the French tax authorities. The TVA rate on most products is 17.6 per cent of the price excluding TVA, or around fifteen per cent of the price including TVA. The burden of the TVA thus falls only on the ultimate customer and not on the French Company, except of course to the extent that the TVA must be taken into account in determining pricing policy. If, for example, the maximum price chargeable for Solar Units is $10,000 including TVA and the TVA rate is 17.6 per cent, the French Company's proceeds will be only $8,500. If its costs are $1,000, plus $500 for Agents *Y* and *Z*, and it retains its profit of $1,500, it can remit only $5,500 to the Liberian Corporation.

Product Liability

A question is raised as to who would be liable under French law for personal injury and property damages due to a defective Superior Unit causing a fire in a purchaser's home.

It will be assumed that the product could be proved to be of unmerchantable quality (*vice redhibitoire*) and that the purchaser was in no way at fault for lack of maintenance or the like. On a contractual basis, the purchaser would have a right of action against the French Company for replacement or for the purchase price of the unit, plus foreseeable damages. These would appear to include all the damages suffered by the purchaser in the form of property damage as well as medical and other expenses and 'moral prejudice' resulting from injury to the owner's spouse and from the death of his child.

The French Company, which is assumed not to be at fault, due to having provided quality control, would have a right of action against the Liberian Corporation, as seller of the Superior Units, to have the latter indemnify and hold it harmless from the French Company's liability to the owner. The Liberian Corporation would in turn have the same right of action against Corporation *A* and Corporation *B*, as sellers of the components, but with the burden of proving which of the components and therefore which of the Corporations was at fault.

The third parties, including the spouse, the neighbor, and the heirs of the child, as well as the French Social Security Administration to the extent it paid medical expenses, disability benefits and the like for the injured parties, would have a direct action in tort against any party guilty of negligence (*faute*). From the facts there seems to have been no negligence on the part of the owner, the French Company, Agents *Y* and *Z* or the Liberian Corporation, but only on the part of Corporation *A* or Corporation *B*. Again, the third parties will have the burden of proving which is at fault.

Whatever the applicable law, French courts have jurisdiction over actions in contract or in tort brought by a French individual or legal entity against foreign defendants, as well as over actions related to such actions, such as the action of the Liberian Company against Corporations *A* and *B* to have the latter hold it harmless from liability to the French parties.

Under French concepts of conflicts of laws, the law applicable to the contracts involved in the actions would be that expressly chosen by the parties or, in the absence of any express choice of law, that which the parties are deemed to have chosen, as evidenced by various factors such as place of performance. As regards torts, the applicable law is that of the place where the event causing the injuries occurred. It appears likely therefore that French courts would apply French law to all actions arising from the fire caused in France by the Superior Unit bought by a French purchaser from a French seller.

The German Analysis

BODO HAGGENEY

SIGWART HÜBNER

Introduction

The two United States domestic-market corporations (corporations A and B), one producing the Superior Solar Collector and the other the Superior Solar Generator, both duly formed and registered, are attempting to enter the German market. It is to be assumed that all the technical know-how and patents have been properly registered or protected and, further, that the joint Liberian corporation has been properly licensed, is authorized to grant sub-licenses and is the sole and and exclusive distributor for these products. This article will analyze the hypothetical situation by assuming that the different corporations, companies or agents are entering German jurisdiction. It, therefore, will not deal, apart from some indications, with any contractual relationship between corporations A and B or their agreements with the Liberian corporation or the alternatively-located corporation in Liechtenstein, Switzerland or elsewhere. Consideration is limited to the German point of view and all contracts relating to Germany and, in the case of tax or product liability, to possible litigation before German courts.

Corporation Formation

Alternative Locations

Corporations A and B have chosen Liberia as the location for their joint venture company because, among other things, their participation in the Liberian corporation will not be made public and the names of the directors are to remain confidential. In addition, taxation in the country of location is to be low; for this reason the so-called high-tax countries are excluded as an alternative. For this reason, the establishment of a joint venture company in Germany will not be examined, as the secrecy requirements cannot be fulfilled if the company has a minimal capitalization. Above all, the profits of the joint venture company of the corporations would be subject in Germany to tax on earnings of approximately sixty per cent (see Introductory essay). Finally, it would not be possible for the German joint venture company to maintain a 'numbered account' (i.e. an account to be kept secret with regard to the German Finance Department and currency-control authorities).

Besides Liberia, most of the 'classic' tax oases, such as Liechtenstein, could, under the given circumstances, be considered as an alternative location for the joint-venture company. The original stock of a Liechtenstein corporation must be at least fifty-thousand Swiss Francs, of which twenty per cent is to be paid in.

Liechtenstein has numerous trust companies which have specialized in establishing companies for foreigners who wish to remain anonymous and in undertaking the function of administrative board. This is important because the majority of the board members have to be Liechtenstein citizens, i.e. at least one. The board members are entered in the so-called Public Register. As in the hypothetical case the names of the directors are not to be made public, their official appointment as administrative board members of the Liechtenstein corporation is not possible. On the contrary, it is necessary to have Liechtenstein citizens as trustees, with whom a so-called mandatory contract will be concluded. The anonymous shareholders may then operate 'their' corporation on the basis of these mandatory contracts. The formation of a Liechtenstein corporation would involve approximately fifty-thousand Swiss Francs. The annual administrative costs would be about the same.

Switzerland also may be considered as the country of location. Switzerland long since has ceased being a tax oasis. However, the corporations may, in the case at hand, consider establishing a so-called domicile company which still offers considerable tax advantages. A requirement is that the company does not do any business of its own or have an office or staff of its own in Switzerland. This does, however, hamper, as will be explained later, fiscal recognition of business with the German foreign-market company (the German company). A corporation in Switzerland must have a minimum amount of capital of fifty-thousand Swiss Francs, of which at least twenty per cent is to be paid in. The majority of the board members also must be Swiss nationals. If the directors wish to remain anonymous, the only solution would be a trusteeship due to registration obligations, but this is not difficult to realize with the help of the numerous trust companies located in Switzerland. The costs of establishment and administration for a Swiss corporation are somewhat higher than in Liechtenstein.

Finally, Hong Kong could be considered as a country of location. It is possible to establish a private-limited company quickly and unbureaucratically. The requirement of anonymity for the shareholders and directors may not be realized, however, without further ado in accordance with legal provisions in Hong Kong. For this reason, a trusteeship also would have to be used. Trust companies, lawyers and banks are available to undertake such tasks. This also is necessary as registration of the private limited company requires an authorized person resident in Hong Kong to be named, a private-limited company to maintain an office in Hong Kong, and a director resident in Hong Kong to be appointed. In this respect, the trustees mentioned will offer their services. The costs of establishment amount to approximately Hong Kong two-thousand to three-thousand dollars. As a general rule, the annual administrative costs will be the same. The tax on earnings of a Hong Kong limited company will be, for example, 17.5 per cent.

Advantages and Disadvantages

This fiscal commentary is based upon the premise that the agents, the German company and the German Finance Department are not aware of the corporations' participation in the joint venture company and that they do not infringe the tax laws of the countries in which they are active.

One advantage is that the countries named are politically stable and their currency policies liberal. However, caution is recommended when considering long-term investments, as the disturbances on the world currency market in recent years have shown. A further advantage, besides the possibility of being very flexible in organizing relations under company law between the company, its directors and shareholders, could be that these states do not yet have any obligation to publish balance sheets, as is, for example, being generally introduced for the Common Market countries beginning in 1982. The most decisive advantage for choosing one of these countries is their low level of taxation. As long as the Liberian, Swiss, Liechtenstein or Hong Kong companies do not distribute their profits but retain them, the corporations indirectly obtain in this way cheap or even untaxed equity, which they may use in their enterprise in a great variety of ways, such as by granting credits or financing investments.

If the profits accumulated by the base company at a favorable rate of taxation are, for example, distributed by the corporations, even if this occurs at a later date, the tax advantage, of course, will be lost as the dividends or rather the profits accumulated are liable to taxation to be paid by the recipients. The profits, therefore, are burdened with a latent tax which will be incurred at the latest when the company is dissolved. This narrows the tax advantage and reduces it to the advantages of a tax deferral which may be, in certain circumstances, very long-term. The 'grey area' of 'repatriating' the untaxed profits of the Liberian Corporation by means other than a distribution of dividends will not be touched upon.

A pre-requisite for realization of the tax advantages which are theoretically possible is, however, that the laws of the countries with which the joint venture company has legal relations, in particular under tax law, recognize the company as being a corporation and do not view its establishment as being that of a sham business or as a legal abuse (see, e.g., Section 42, German General Tax Law). This may be the case if the company is a so-called 'base' of 'letter-box' company, i.e. an empty cover without its own economic function. Whereas private international law in most countries recognizes a foreign corporation under civil law if it is duly established under the laws of the country of location (so-called location or establishment theory), international tax law—due to the fiscal objective of the legal subject matter—does not automatically follow this ruling. This problem has to be looked into in particular in accordance with the laws of the countries with which the Liberian corporation has legal connections, i.e. the United States and Federal Republic of Germany.

With regard to recognition of foreign corporations under tax law, German and United States tax law are focused on a 'business activity' of the corporation and 'the carrying on of business'. They refuse recognition if the corporation is a 'sham or unreal'. To be recognized for tax purposes, a corporation must display its own industrial or commercial or other activity in addition to the endeavor to avoid taxation, as this alone is not sufficient. The United States Domestic-Market Corporations therefore, must see to it that the joint-venture company develops this sort of business activity as its own business activity, roughly characterized by the minimum requirements of 'one man, one room, one telephone', if they wish to avoid the profits of the Liberian Corporation, even if these are not distributed, being attributed by the United States Internal Revenue Service directly to them, with the result that they have to pay taxes on these profits.

It also must be borne in mind that the German foreign-market agents (the agents) and the German company, who are all subject to unlimited taxation in Germany, enter into delivery and service transactions with the Liberian corporation and may claim for deduction of operating expenditure in this connection. Of the sales returns of ten-thousand dollars per unit obtained by the German company seven-thousand five-hundred will be paid to the Liberian corporation as payment for delivery and seven-thousand of this amount will go abroad (five-thousand dollars to Switzerland and two-thousand dollars to Liberia).

The German company and the agents must expect the German Finance Department to accept this deduction of operating expenditure without further ado because the recipient of payments is a company in a low-tax country (Liberia). The Finance Department may assume that German taxpayers have a share in the company in this low-tax country, for example the German agents or the shareholders of the German company.

This applies in particular if service and consideration are not in a reasonable ratio to each other. The German company and the agents must satisfactorily disperse these misgivings. They have an intensified obligation to clarify and cooperate which ends only where the German taxpayers, when clarifying the foreign situation, reach the legal limits set on them in a foreign country and they cannot be expected to continue clarification of the situation (Section 90, General Tax Law; Section 16, 17 International Transactions Tax Act). The German company and the agents must prove—by disclosing all agreements made and by making available all existing documents—that they do not participate in the Liberian Corporation either directly or indirectly. At the request of the Finance Department, they must substantiate by means of an affidavit the details they give and, if necessary, their allegation that they are unacquainted with certain facts, such as the corporate relationships in the Liberian Corporation.

The legal position in Germany makes delivery and service transactions with the company in a low-tax country extra-ordinarily difficult for German taxpayers in practise, even if they are not, as in the case here, either directly or indirectly involved in the company. This does not, however, mean that it will not be recognized if the obligation to cooperate mentioned above is completely fulfilled. In the case at hand, the practical difficulty is that it is not known who the shareholders of the Liberian Corporation are and via whom they act. The minimum requirement is, therefore, that the rates of payment are agreed to 'at arm's length' conditions. The German company at least will have to substantiate the fact that the gross-profit margin of twenty-five per cent is customary and reasonable. The Agents at least will have to prove satisfactorily that the commission of five per cent which they keep is customary for the market.

Corporations *A* and *B* must be aware that they have a further, more difficult hurdle to overcome, that being recognition by the United States Internal Revenue Service of their sales prices to the Liberian Corporation. This would appear to be improbable if not out of the question as the corporations sell their products at cost price, without any profit margin. The corporations, therefore, must reckon with a surplus adjustment (profit assessment). These disadvantages are incalculable.

Contractual Considerations

Upon its formation the Liberian Corporation has to contact the agents. The agents should represent the Liberian corporation in locating a German company to buy the Solar Collector and the Solar Generator from the Liberian Corporation, assemble the units and sell the Solar Energy Electrical Units within Germany.

What the Liberian Corporation is asking the Agents is the typical task of a commercial agent governed by Sections 84 to 92c of the German Commercial Code. No particular form is required for the agency agreement. An oral agreement, therefore, would be sufficient. The parties can agree generally that the provisions of agency law in the German Commercial Code do not apply to specific contracts. Certain provisions, however, are compulsory, and individual agreements contradicting these are considered to be null and void. For instance, the Agent is entitled to a reasonable compensation upon termination of the agreement.

As the Liberian Corporation is located outside Germany and the agents' activity is based in this country, problems may arise as to which courts have jurisdiction and which law is applicable. German courts have decided this question on the basic principle that the law applicable is the law of the country with which the agreement has its closest connection. Concerning agency agreements, this is in general the location of the agent.

The agent has to collect the price of seven-thousand five-hundred dollars, can keep the five-hundred dollars commission under the agency agreement, and has to pay on the instruction of the Liberian Corporation two-thousand dollars into the Liberian bank account and five-thousand dollars into the Swiss bank account, both of the Liberian Corporation. A written agreement containing the following provisions is recommended:

– The agents are appointed to represent the Liberian Corporation in all matters related to the Solar Collectors and Solar Generators.

– The agents must locate a German distribution company which is prepared to take over all the functions mentioned above.

– The agents must supervise the activities of the German company under the license and distribution agreements and to collect the purchase price.

– The Liberian Corporation must pay five per cent commission on the purchase price for each unit sold in Germany.

– A non-competition clause will prohibit any competitive activity for the duration of the agency agreement. (A non-competition clause for the time after termination of the contract is possible for up to two years, subject to an indemnity payment for the agreed time in the amount of at least half the commission the agents have received before termination of the contract. However, such a clause is not recommended because once the agents have found a distribution company in Germany, the distribution agreement has been concluded between the Liberian Corporation and the German company and the agents have supervised the distribution within Germany for a certain length of time, the agents could, upon termination of the contract, work for a competitive business without causing so much damage that an indemnity payment would be justified.)

– A secrecy clause.

– Duration of the agreement, termination upon notice in writing.

– Applicable law and competent court of jurisdiction.

The Liberian Corporation is prepared to enter into an agreement with the German company only if this company agrees to patent the Superior Generator, the Superior Collector and the Solar Energy Electrical Unit as a whole in its own name in Germany, purchase all spare units from the Liberian Corporation, assemble the units, package them, translate installation instructions into the German language, transfer to the agents seventy-five per cent of all sales, and charge the customers a retail price for the Superior Unit equivalent to ten-thousand dollars.

(a) If the agents have only to find a German company as a distributor, it is suggested that this company should not purchase the Superior Units from the agents but rather directly from the Liberian Corporation. Therefore, a distribution agreement between the Liberian Corporation and the German company is recommended.

(b) The intention is to require the German company to purchase all spare units from the Liberian corporation and not from any competitor. In this case, it is assumed that the German company would agree only if exclusivity for Germany is granted. The parties, therefore, intend to conclude an exclusive distribution agreement. The German company would retain two-thousand five-hundred dollars (or the equivalent) of the retail price and would pay seven-thousand five-hundred dollars to the agents on the basis of the distribution contract as the purchase price for the units delivered. For that, it would not be necessary for the secret know-how to be patented in Germany in the name of the German company; it could be registered in the name of corporations *A* and *B* or the Liberian Corporation.

(c) The German company is supposed to assemble the units, package them, translate instructions into German, and distribute the Solar Energy Electrical Units in Germany. With regard to the fact that the units are patented, the question of a license agreement arises. Should this be with exclusivity or without; should the patent be registered in Germany in the name of the corporations, the Liberian Corporation or in the name of the German company with the obligation to reassign these rights upon termination of the license agreement?

(d) Considering the intention of the parties, is a license or distribution agreement more appropriate? This conclusion is important in deciding the question of whether the Liberian Corporation is entitled to obligate the German company to maintain specific resale prices and to purchase exclusively from it. Only within a license agreement are commitments of the licensee regarding price fixing permissible and valid under German law. On the other hand, in the case of a license agreement, it is doubtful whether the German company's obligation to purchase all spare units from the Liberian Corporation would be valid. The licensor may restrain the licensee in this respect only insofar as it is justified by an interest of the licensor in the sound technical utilization of the subject matter of the protected right. This means only if the two Superior Units are patented each as a whole. If only one spare part of it is patented, the licensee cannot be restrained from buying the other parts somewhere else. Supposing that the Solar Collector as a whole and the Solar Generator as a whole already are patented in the United States and will be patented in Germany, as well, then the licensee may be obligated to purchase these two units exclusively from the Liberian Corporation. It should be pointed out that it does not matter whether the parties call the agreement a distribution or license agreement. In the light of German cartel law (Act against Restraints on Competition), it depends on what the main purpose of the contract is. It cannot be argued that this is a mixed contract and the resale price maintenance would be justified under the license part and the obligation to purchase exclusively from the Liberian Corporation under the distribution part.

(e) Since West Germany is a member of the Common Market, the Treaty of Rome should be referred to briefly. Article 85 prohibits all agreements between corporations which may affect trade between Member States and which have as their objective or effect the prevention, restriction or distortion of competition within the Common Market. Any agreement prohibited under this Article is null and void and may be subject to fines. It is the basic principle of Community law that an exclusive distributorship agreement falls within the prohibition of Article 85 when it impedes either re-export of the contract products by the distributor to other Member States or import of such products by third parties from other Member States. The Common Market Commission has exempted exclusive distributorship agreements by Regulation 67/67. This means that, as long as the provision of an agreement comes within this regulation, Article 85 does not apply to this agreement. However, it is necessary to decide in each case, in the light of all circumstances, whether the agreement significantly restricts competition in the Common Market and affects trade between member states. As far as a license agreement is concerned, it has to be pointed out that any exclusive license is regarded as being contrary to Article 85 of the Treaty of Rome. An exemption may be granted by the Common Market Commission under Article 85, paragraph 3, when they contribute to improving the production or distribution of goods, provided that they also allow consumers a fair share of the resulting benefit, only impose restrictions indispensable to achieving these objectives, and do not permit the elimination of competition.

(f) According to these considerations, the Liberian Corporation and the German company should conclude either a license or a distribution agreement with the following provisions:

- Exclusive license or distribution agreement, by which the Liberian Corporation agrees not to appoint any other licensee or distributor in Germany and the German company agrees to purchase the Solar Collector and the Solar Generator exclusively from the Liberian Corporation and to assemble and distribute them within Germany. The agreement must be in writing (Sections 18, 20, 34, act against restraints of competition).
- Depending on what contract has been chosen, assignment of know-how and patent rights to the German company and registration as German patent in their name or license.
- Obligation of the German company to buy a minimum number of Superior Units per year and the corresponding obligation of the Liberian Corporation to deliver any number of units required with reasonable notice. Possibly, the obligation of the German company to hold a certain number in stock.
- Spare parts. Repair and after-sales service.
- Sales conditions. Passing of risk, terms of payment, retention of title, liability for defects.
- Pricing conditions for resale.
- Publicity. Documents, advertising material, instruction manuals delivered by the Liberian Corporation and translated by the German licensee or distributor.
- Non-competition clause during the term of the agreement.
- Trade secrecy.
- Return of information, advertising material and instruction manuals upon termination of the contract without keeping any copies.
- Assistance in unfair competition litigation and infringements of industrial property.
- Sub-license clause.
- Duration of the agreement. Fixed period, termination upon notice.
- Liquidation of stock.
- Fulfillment of delivery contracts concluded before termination but to be delivered afterwards.
- Applicable law, competent court of jurisdiction (arbitration).
- Prohibition to sell outside Germany would be null and void under the Treaty of Rome. Once a patented product has been legally distributed within the Common Market this unit can be sold from one country to another (Article 30, et seq., Treaty of Rome).

(g) The given facts are based on the assumption that all contractual calculations would be in United States dollars. It has to be considered that the German customer would generally pay in West German marks to the German company. Considering the fact that the exchange rates are fluctuating constantly, the parties must agree upon who would bear the risk and in what currency the contractual obligations have to be fulfilled.

Alternative Contractual Arrangements

There does not seem to be any alternative contractual arrangement which would more adequately protect the parties against product liability and tax liability. The Liberian corporation will exclude its product liability in the distribution or license agreement as far as possible. This also could be done between a United States subsidiary of the corporations and the German company. As far as product liability in tort is concerned, which is of particular interest because it is the consumer who is injured and who has no contractual relations with the manufacturer, this will be discussed under the heading 'Product Liability'. There is no doubt that the arrangement planned by the corporations is the best possible solution from a tax point of view as fifty per cent of the consumer price, a total of five-thousand dollars per unit, will be accumulated (commercially or indirectly) as 'profit' by the corporations either tax-free or at least at a low rate of taxation. A further question is whether tax authorities in Germany and, above all, the United States recognize the intervention of the base company. As mentioned, there are considerable uncertainties. It will be only partly possible, if at all, to realize the tax advantages aimed at.

From a German point of view, it is, as is to be shown, in principle irrelevant in what foreign country the intermediate company has its location. The legal relations between the corporations and the intermediate company, on the one hand, and the Agents and German company, on the other, may be arranged so that neither the corporations nor the intermediate company are subject to taxation in Germany, as German taxpayers do not have a share in the intermediate company. From a German point of view, there is no advantage in the intervention of foreign companies, whether they are base companies or not.

Tax Liability

Corporations *A* and *B* do not have either their location or their corporate management in Germany. They, therefore, are liable only to limited taxation on their income in Germany (Section 2, Corporation Tax Law; Section 49, Income Tax Law). They are the manufacturers of the Superior Generator and the Superior Collector but do not deliver the equipment direct to Germany. From the point of view of taxation, they do not appear at all on the German market; they do not establish any delivery or service connections to the German company, the Agents or the ultimate consumer; they receive no license or know-how fees; they have (directly) no permanent representative in Germany and do not maintain a permanent establishment. There is no tie-in to German tax sovereignty. The corporations, therefore, have no taxable income in Germany.

The Liberian corporation, on the other hand, acts permanently as direct contract partner to the German company and the agents; it carries on business in Germany. Liberia and the Federal Republic of Germany concluded a Double Taxation Convention on 25 Nobember 1970. Under

Article 7, paragraph 1, the profits of the Liberian corporation will be taxed in Germany if the Liberian corporation carries on business through a permanent establishment situated in Germany. Under Article 5, paragraph 2, the term 'permanent establishment' includes especially a place of management, a branch, an office, a factory and a workshop; in short, a fixed place of business in which the Liberian corporation wholly or partly carries on its business. The Liberian corporation has no such fixed place of business in Germany. The mere fact that the Liberian corporation sells equipment to the German company does not constitute a permanent establishment. German taxes will not be levied on the profits for deliveries made by the Liberian corporation. The Liberian corporation and the agents, however, have concluded a representative agreement, according to which the agents act on behalf of the Liberian corporation in all matters related to the products delivered, perform certain services (finding the German company and negotiating business connections between this and the Liberian corporation), procure payment in respect of the German company and forward the sales price. The agents, therefore, work for the Liberian corporation. Under Article 5, paragraph 4, a permanent establishment of the Liberian corporation in Germany is deemed to exist if the agents have and habitually exercise in that state an authority to conclude contracts in the name of the Liberian corporation, unless their activities are limited to the purchase of goods or merchandise for the enterprise. The corporations, therefore, must take care that the Liberian corporation does not establish any employment relationship with the agents, assuring that the agents work as independent commercial agents. This will not constitute a permanent establishment, as expressly laid down in Article 5, paragraph 5 of the Double Taxation Convention.

It also is important that the agents do not receive any power of sale from the Liberian corporation, which is not required by the hypothetical case, as vendor and purchaser of the Superior Units is the German company itself. According to Number 4 of the Protocol to the Double Taxation Convention Liberia/Germany Liberian companies, which are controlled by foreigners and enjoy special tax benefits in Liberia, may not lay claim to the protection of the Double Taxation Convention. This restriction, however, does not apply to Article 5 and, consequently, not to the term 'permanent establishment' so that the solution would be the same if the German Inland Revenue is aware (e.g. within the scope of the interstate exchange of information agreed in article 26) that the Liberian corporation is a United States-controlled holding company.

The hypothetical case admits the interpretation that the Liberian corporation maintains a warehouse at the German company and that the German company does not buy Superior Units from the Liberian corporation—and remove them from the warehouse—until it has sold them. Even this arrangement does not constitute a permanent establishment of the Liberian corporation, as the stock of goods is maintained solely for the purpose of storage or delivery (Article 5, paragraph 3b). The fact that the German company assembles the Superior Units, packages them and attaches directions for use does not constitute a permanent establishment of the Liberian corporation if the German company does this work on its own behalf. It is recommended that this be taken into account when drafting contracts.

If the German company does this work on behalf of the Liberian corporation, in addition to warehousing, this does not constitute a permanent establishment of the Liberian corporation if the assembling and packaging of the units have a preparatory or auxiliary character (see Article 5, paragraph 3e). This is the case here.

It also is important that the German company is not authorized to execute orders from these stocks in the name of the Liberian corporation. Otherwise, a permanent establishment of the Liberian corporation would be deemed to exist in accordance with Article 5, paragraph 4b, and its tax liability in Germany established.

According to the hypothetical case, the German company is to have the patent registered in its own name. This does not establish any tax liability of the Liberian corporation in Germany, irrespective of whether a sales price is expressly agreed for the patent or whether payment will be made in such a way that the sales price for the products will be fixed correspondingly higher. This can result in a problem only for the German company.

If corporations *A* and *B* establish—as an alternative—a corporation in Switzerland, the legal position will be more or less identical. The Double Taxation Convention Switzerland/Germany of 11 August 1971 contains the same ruling (Articles 7 and 5) as far as the authority to tax the profits of an enterprise is concerned. In this case, however, the Swiss corporation—in contrast to Liberia—would not run the risk of establishing the existence of a permanent establishment if the German company were authorized to execute orders on behalf of the Swiss corporation out of the stocks of goods and merchandise maintained by the Swiss corporation in Germany because the Double Taxation Convention Switzerland/Germany does not contain such a restriction.

The Federal Republic of Germany has not concluded any double taxation convention with Liechtenstein or Hong Kong. West Germany taxes the income of these companies from business if a permanent establishment is maintained in Germany for this business or if a permanent representative is appointed (see Section 2, Corporation Tax Law; Section 49, Income Tax Law). The term "permanent establishment" (Section 12, General Tax Law) is broader in German tax law than in the two double taxation conventions mentioned. A warehouse maintained by the Liechtenstein or Hong Kong corporation at the German company would constitute a permanent establishment, this resulting in tax liability.

The definition of the 'permanent representative' (Section 13, General Tax Law) also is broader than in the Double Taxation Conventions. The agents would be permanent representatives if they permanently attended to the business of the Hong Kong or Liechtenstein corporation and were thereby subject to the corporation's instructions, irrespective of whether or not the agents would have the power to contract (a permanent representative is, for example, someone who permanently supervises the incoming and outgoing goods and merchandise in the warehouses of others or procures payment). In these cases, care should be taken that the agency or representative agreements between the agents and the Hong Kong or Liechtenstein corporation do not subject the representative to directions from the corporation. This may, even if it is not expressly agreed (in writing or orally), be demonstrated also by implied conduct, such as by mere approval of previous conduct. The risk that the agents or the German company constitute a permanent establishment of the intermediate company, therefore, is greater than in the case of Liberia or Switzerland.

The agents have their habitual residence in Germany and are liable to unlimited taxation in Germany. If they are natural persons, their profits are subject to business tax and income tax. If they are corporate bodies, they pay, in addition to business tax, corporation tax which, however, will be credited against income tax if profits are distributed. The commission of five-hundred dollars per unit received by the agents is an integral part of this profit. The seven-thousand dollars which the agents receive from the German company and forward to the Liberian corporation is not counted as operating expenditure of the agents but as a transitory item as it is received and spent on behalf and for the account of the Liberian corporation. It is not part of the agents' profit. The agents may not be taxed merely because they pay, as instructed, a part of the money received (five-thousand dollars) to an account of the Liberian corporation in Switzerland.

The German company's turnover with German consumers is subject to Value-Added Tax (VAT) which is not, however, a burden on the company, as the VAT is borne by the ultimate consumer. Import excise tax, which the company pays on the import of goods from Liberia (or the alternative countries) may be deducted as pre-tax. Any customs duty paid is, in comparison, operating expenditure.

The German company also pays business or corporation tax/income tax on its profit, in which its profit margin two-thousand five-hundred dollars per unit) is included. The cost price of seven-thousand five-hundred dollars, which is to be paid to the Liberian corporation, care of the agents, is considered to be operating expenditure of the German company, which means that the taxable returns/profits already have been reduced. A tax liability does not result in this respect. The deduction of operating expenditure is recognized by the tax authorities under the conditions and restrictions mentioned.

According to the hypothetical case, the patents will be acquired by the German company. However, no purchase price will be paid for these. As the German company does not manufacture the equipment itself there is—from the point of view of the German Finance Department—no plausible reason for transferring the patents at all. The question then arises as to whether strangers with opposing economic interests would conclude such an agreement. The Finance Department also will want to know whether the purchase price for the patents is 'concealed' in the purchase price of the products. It is not out of the question that the Finance Department will determine the market value of the patents and enter these patents on the asset side of the German company's accounts with this amount if the German company does not succeed in showing satisfactorily that the purchase of the units occurred at arm's length despite the *gratis* transfer of patents. The burden of argumentation (not the burden of proof) rests again with the German company. Therefore, it is recommended that the marketing contract between the Liberian corporation and the German company include an agreement whereby the patent will be transferred free of charge. This will preclude any entry on the asset side if the profit margin of the German company is otherwise customary. This already has been pointed out.

Product Liability

In one case out of one thousand solar energy models sold, the Superior Unit was installed and after two months overheated, causing a fire which destroyed the home of the purchaser, injured the owner's spouse and a visiting neighbor and killed the child of the owner. In either the Solar Generator or the Solar Collector of the Superior Unit, there was a malfunction which, despite the best quality control on the part of the German company, could not have been detected beforehand. It is assumed that the German company performed all other functions without fault and further that the owner had purchased the unit directly from the German company.

The owner and the German company had concluded a purchase contract. The question arises as to whether the owner can sue the German company for damages out of this contract. The German company as the vendor of the Solar Unit warrants that at the time when risk passes to the purchaser:

- the unit is free from defects diminishing or destroying its value or fitness for either ordinary use or the use presupposed—even through merely by implication—in the contract. A mere insignificant diminution in value and fitness is, however, irrelevant.
- the unit has all the qualities which the vendor has promised (Section 459, West German Civil Code).

Since the solar unit was defective, the owner/purchaser has two remedies: the right to cancel the contract (called *Wandlung*) and the right to demand a reduction in price (called *Minderung*) (Section 462, German Civil Code). *Wandlung* is, in fact, the rescission of the contract. *Minderung* consists of a reduction in the price by an amount equal to the deficiency in value. If the unit does not have the qualities promised by the German company, the owner may, in addition, sue for damages for non-performance of the contract.

If the owner is a merchant and the purchase agreement a commercial transaction, he is under an obligation to examine the quality of the Superior Unit delivered and to notify the German company immediately of any defect. If the defect is discovered later, he has to notify the company immediately upon its discovery. These duties are not imposed on the non-commercial buyer. All remedies under the purchase agreement are subject to limitation of six months after delivery of the Superior Unit, even if the defect has been discovered after this period.

However, none of these remedies under the purchase agreement gives any right to consequential damages, for example damages for the child killed or the home destroyed. Under West German law, the owner is entitled to these damages only in tort. As far as consequential damages are concerned, the owner may sue the German company in tort. As he may wish to sue corporations *A* and *B* or the Liberian corporation in tort, as well, both will be discussed together.

Since, in the ordinary course of business in West Germany, purchase agreements generally are subject to standard terms (Conditions of Sale, Delivery and Payment), it is assumed that the German company has sold the Superior Unit according to its standard terms. Even damages in tort usually are excluded in these sales conditions. Consider the following example:

> *Liability for Defects*
> We are liable for defects in our goods as follows, all further claims being excluded:
>
> If our goods are defective and we are liable for the defects, we are only obliged to repair or replace, free of charge and at our option either at our factory or at purchaser, those parts, which are proven to be unusable as a result of circumstances, which occurred before risk was transferred. The defective goods are to be returned to us for inspection in their original form.
>
> If defects cannot be remedied by repair or replacement, the purchaser may withdraw from the contract. The same applies when we do not meet our obligations to repair or replace defective goods for reasons for which we are responsible.
>
> The purchaser may make no further claims, in particular for redhibition, abatement or indemnification, above all with regard to consequential damages or profits lost. This also applies in so far as such claims are based on inaccurate advice, unlawful acts, product liability, positive infringement of contractual duty or negligence. This does not apply in so far as the cause is to be found in any gross negligence or intention attributable to us.

Although the purchaser may sue the seller for consequential damages in tort, this very often is excluded by the standard terms.

Since West Germany has a statute governing standard business conditions as of 1 April 1977, it must be considered whether it is permitted under this act to exclude the liability to an extent as it was and is still common practice in West Germany. It is to be emphasized that this act is not merely a consumer protection as originally conceived and applies not only to standard business conditions used in contracts with the consumer but also to standard terms used in agreements between merchants although to a more limited extent. Section 11, Number 7, stipulates that, in standard terms, the following is invalid:

> The exclusion or limitation of liability for damages resulting from a grossly negligent breach of contract by the applier or from a

> deliberate or grossly negligent breach of contract by a statutory representative or a contractual representative of the applier; this applies also to damages resulting from a breach of obligation in connection with contractual negotiations.

The same applies with regard to exclusion of liability for damages in tort. Since, based on the given facts, there is no fault of the German company at all, the exclusion is valid and the company is not liable for the damages incurred.

The owner, as the purchaser of the Superior Unit, does not have any contractual relations with either the Liberian corporation or corporations *A* and *B*. This raises the question of whether the owner may sue for damages in tort. (No further reference to the German company is made as it is assumed that this company has legally excluded its liability, but this assumption cannot be applied if the owner's spouse or the visiting neighbor sue for damages as they had no contractual relations with the German company).

Possible claims may be based on Section 823, West German Civil Code, which reads:

> A person who, intentionally or negligently, injures unlawfully the life, body, health, freedom, property or any other right of another person is liable to compensate him for any damages arising therefrom.
>
> A person who infringes a statutory provision intended for the protection of others, is liable to pay compensation for any damage arising from this violation.

The manufacturer may be liable irrespective of whether he has produced the whole product or part of it. Similarly, the assembler, the distributor, the wholesaler and the retailer may all be sued for damages if they have acted negligently. Product liability in Germany is not a strict liability. The burden of proof is generally on the plaintiff. He must prove that the manufacturer, the importer or the distributor has been negligent. Unlike normal tort cases, the courts have turned the burden of proof onto the manufacturer or the importer. This has been the basic change in court action which has enabled more plaintiffs to sue manufacturers or distributors successfully. The plaintiff has only to show that, according to normal experience, the defect in the product which caused all the damage must have arisen in the manufacturer's sphere of control. Sufficient is a prima facie proof. The reason for the courts to turn the burden of proof onto the manufacturer was that he is closer to the facts as to where the defect possibly arose and, therefore, has to bear the consequences if conclusive proof is not available.

The manufacturer, as defendant, then may prove that he has not been negligent. He has to prove that he has organized his business in such a way that defects in design, manufacture and the like were avoided and that up-to-date science and technology had been applied; he also must show that the purchaser or user had been instructed and warned by adequate instructions. He also must prove that he had a proper quality-control service to avoid any defective unit leaving his sphere of control. If he can prove that he complied with all these obligations, the risk for damage caused by such a "runaway" product (*Ausreisser*) rests with the purchaser.

The extent to which the defendant is asked to prove that he had done everything possible to avoid risk varies as to whether he is the manufacturer, the assembler, the importer, or the distributor. The extent to which quality control is required also varies from product to product. Generally speaking, it may be said that the manufacturer has to make sure that his product, when leaving his plant, is without defect. He has to disclose all relevant facts. The assembler must prove that he purchased the spare parts from a manufacturer of good standing with quality control and, depending on the circumstances, that he has a proper incoming and outgoing quality control. If any doubt arises as to whether the spare parts' manufacturer has done everything possible to avoid risk, the assembler must strengthen his own control. The distributor does not have to control each part or unit in the same way as the manufacturer must, but whenever any doubt arises, he has to make sure that everything possible has been done before selling this unit. In any case, he has to prove in a tort action that he has done everything possible to avoid any defective goods being delivered to the final consumer.

On this basis, the owner may sue corporations *A* and *B* or the Liberian corporation for damages because his home was destroyed by fire. The injured spouse also may sue these corporations for her damages and, in addition, for a certain sum compensating her for pain suffered. The visiting neighbor may do the same, and the parents may sue these corporations because their child was killed. The visiting neighbor and the owner's spouse also may sue the German company. As we have to assume, according to the given facts, that this company performed all functions without fault and had a good quality control a court action is unlikely to be successful. Attention may be drawn to the fact that the limitation period in the case of product liability in tort is three years, commencing on 1 January following the year in which the victim discovered the damage and the party which caused the damage. If there is any contributory negligence on the part of the victim, the court may, depending on the extent of negligence, reduce the damages according to Section 254, West German Civil Code.

The Italian Analysis

FEDERICO BIANCHI

Corporation Formation

A premise to the present as well as to following issues is that Italian law accepts the general principle of recognition of the existence of foreign corporations or companies regardless of their type of structure. They may or may not correspond to the type of Italian corporations which acquire legal personality upon registration (see Section 2331, paragraph 1, of the Civil Code for joint-stock corporations and Civil Code Section 2475, paragraph 2 for limited-liability companies). Thus, no authorization from Italian government authorities is required.

Said principle is sometimes held to derive from the general conflict of law provisions on the legal treatment of aliens and capacity of persons set forth in Sections 16 and 17 of the Preliminary Provisions to the Civil Code. It is reflected in the provisions of Civil Code Sections 2505 et. seq., under the Chapter 'Companies Formed or Operating Abroad'. The following Sections, which are relevant for an evaluation of the problem are set out below in their English translation.

> *Section* 2505—*Companies formed abroad with headquarters within the territory of the State.* Companies formed abroad, having their management, headquarters, or the principal object of their business within the territory of the State, are subject to all provisions of Italian law, including those with respect to the requisites for the validity of the articles of association.
>
> *Section* 2506—*Foreign companies with branch offices within the territory of the State.* Companies formed abroad, which establish one or more branch offices with permanent representation within the territory of the State, are subject, for each of such branch offices, to the provisions of Italian law concerning the filing and registration of the articles of association in the register of enterprises and publication of the balance sheet and shall, in the same manner, publish the surnames and names of the persons who represent the company permanently within the State and deposit their respective handwritten signatures.
>
> Such companies are also subject, insofar as their branch offices are concerned, to the provisions which govern the operation of enterprises or subject them to the observance of particular conditions.
>
> *Section* 2507—*Foreign companies of a type different from domestic companies.* Companies organized abroad which are of a type

different from those regulated by this code are subject to the rules on joint stock companies with respect to the duties relating to registration of the company's documents and resolutions in the register of enterprises and the liability of directors.

Section 2508—*Liability in case of non-observance of formalities.* Until the above mentioned formalities have been fulfilled, those who act in the name of the company are liable without limit, jointly and severally, for company obligations.

The rules of law contemplated in Civil Code Sections 2505–2507, presuppose that a foreign company was validly formed abroad and, according to the extent of its contacts with the Italian law system, impose compliance with all or at least some of the legal requirements conditioning the formation and operation of an Italian company. Maximum compliance is required for companies contemplated in Civil Code Section 2505 for the purpose of 'avoiding that the establishing of companies abroad becomes an easy device for by-passing our laws'. (This quotation is from the Ministerial Report on the text of the Civil Code of 1942, which is the one presently in force with some amendments). In the case of Civil Code Section 2506, when only part of the activities of a foreign company are carried out in Italy through a branch or a permanent establishment, that is an operational unit forming part of the foreign company's organization, legal requirements to be met by that foreign company basically refer to giving public notice. Non-compliance with all these filing and notification steps will bring about the consequences described in Section 2508 without, however, questioning the existence of the foreign company. It also is generally accepted that the place of establishment determines which law will apply to a foreign company.

The preceding observations may suffice for holding that the matter concerning the steps to be taken by Corporations *A* and *B* to form a Liberian Corporation is not directly relevant to Italian law. Such steps will be those required by United States and Liberian laws (Common Law) for the purpose of a valid establishment of the Liberian Corporation. Proper resolutions or deeds from the pertinent corporate bodies or officers of Corporations *A* and *B* respectively, which supposedly are qualified to do business abroad, will have to be taken or executed for investing capital into the company to be formed, participating in its deed of incorporation, appointing corporate officers, and so on. According to general principles of conflict of laws and jurisdiction, it is assumed that United States corporate laws will be applicable to the above. The remaining matters will be governed by Liberian law, that is the form of incorporation, its structure, possible governmental authorizations to export, and so on.

As stated above, the structure of the Liberian corporation is not *per se* determinant of its recognition in Italy. It must, however, fall within the general concept of companies and corporations in Italian law, that is the contribution by two or more subjects of property or services for the exercise in common of an economic activity for the purpose of sharing the profits thereof (Civil Code, Section 2247). It should also not present connotations conflicting with some fundamental provisions of Italian law pertaining to the so-called public order.

A variety of factors, not only of a legal nature but also political and economic, might play a significant role in suggesting that this jointly owned corporation be formed in another country. First, there could be reasons connected with United States tax laws and international trade regulations. One country might be more attractive than another because, according to its laws, no special problems arise concerning minimum capitalization, the possibility of participation of foreign shareholders, controls and authorizations from local authorities especially as regards the operations of that corporation and so forth. Some countries may even contemplate fiscal easements. In the present case, the company's possession of valid, transferable rights to technological know-how and patents would be relevant.

Although from the standpoint of Italian civil law the location of the foreign company is basically unimportant, evidence of its valid constitution and existence, when required, will have to be produced in Italy. This will be easier in respect to those countries where official certifications from the pertinent registries or authorities are available. Legalization of these documents by Italian Consular authorities is not required when an international treaty applies, such as the Hague Treaty signed on 5 October 1961.

If one looks at the substance rather than at the formal aspects of the matter, the following hypothetical choices could be made from the Italian point of view: a European Economic Community (EEC) country or an Organization for Economic Cooperation and Development (OECD) country because of certain applicable financial and foreign exchange facilitations; a country with which a treaty to avoid double taxation exists or in respect of which there are other preferential treatments resulting from international agreements and no special limitations are imposed on the import–export trade. It would be fair to acknowledge, however, that the generalities of these observations are not much of a guide for presenting an acceptable alternative location in this case. Tentatively Switzerland, whose laws are designed to allow for the establishment of corporations of this kind, might be indicated as preferential on the assumption that a treaty to avoid double taxation which was signed between Switzerland and Italy on 9 March 1976 becomes enforceable in this country. Otherwise, a location such as Bermuda would be more acceptable than Liberia as it is known that even large United States corporations have subsidiaries there.

Concerning the steps for establishing the corporation in a location other than Liberia, the observations above mentioned will apply. The problem is basically the same, as it will be a matter of compliance with the laws of the United States and of the selected country respectively.

The formation of a corporation jointly owned by Corporations *A* and *B* in Italy would not present specific problems as far as steps to be taken and the participation of foreign subjects both in the capital and in the management are concerned. The twenty-thousand Italian lira minimum capital required by Law 904 of 16 December 1977 to establish a limited-liability company is not unreasonable.

A legal entity would thereby be created under the systems of Italian and EEC laws. The following general advantages could be cited, among others: Italian Law 43 of 7 February 1956 governing foreign investments; the United States–Italy treaty to avoid double taxation signed in Washington on 30 March 1955 which by Law 233 of 6 April 1977 was made expressly applicable to new income tax laws in force as of 1 January 1974; the protection of patents for industrial inventions afforded by Italian law whereby a foreigner may obtain patents upon the same conditions as an Italian citizen (Article 21 of R. D. 29 June 1939, number 1127, which is the Special Law on patents) as well as by International Conventions to which Italy is a party, such as the Paris Union Treaty of 20 March 1883, as subsequently amended. Some of these guarantees are substantially equivalent to those available to other countries of the EEC, except for different rules applying in the various states especially on investments and taxes.

A noteworthy remark relates to the rather scarce possibilities under Italian law of disregarding the corporate body or piercing the corporate veil when this is used for fraudulent purposes or against the law. A one man corporation is possible, as is indirectly confirmed by the provision of Section 2362 reading: 'For obligations of the company which arose during the period in which the shares are shown to have belonged to one person only, such person is liable without limitation in the case of insolvency of the company.' Attempts made thus far to extend the reach of that provision in order to make a parent company liable for the obligations of an Italian subsidiary, which unquestionably belongs to the same group, have been rather unsuccessful.

Conversely, the formation of a corporation in a country which is known to be a tax haven or used to avoid other burdens which would derive from Italian law, might induce local authorities to challenge its operations in Italy. This was the case with the *Anstalten* of Liechtenstein, whose capacity to act in Italy as companies with limited-liability was challenged in some decisions of lower courts. It was held that they conflict with the principle that an individual enterprise must unlimitedly be liable for its obligations. However, by a judgment rendered on 27 July 1977, number 3352, the Supreme Court (*Cassazione*), although referring to another type of Liechtenstein company (*Treuunternehmen*) seems to have reversed that trend.

Along the same line, the formation of a Liberian Corporation destined to operate in Italy through Agents *Y* and *Z*, without making known the names of the company's directors, might violate another basic principle of Italian law. Italian law provisions requiring that the names of the directors who legally represent the company must be indicated in the deed of incorporation are of a mandatory nature (Civil Code, Section 2328). The same may be held to apply as regards publicity of the founding shareholders, although disclosure of Corporations *A* and *B* in this case could be avoided through nominees.

A decisive consideration, however, nullifies all possible advantages of forming this corporation in Italy. According to the plan of action envisaged by Corporations *A* and *B*, one of its main purposes is that of minimizing taxation by means of accumulating maximum profits in an anonymous Swiss account. The general assumption of said plan of action, that the international transactions herein contemplated do not violate foreign exchange control laws, could not stand if the corporation were formed in Italy because of Law 159 of 30 April 1976, which qualifies as a criminal offense the unlawful export of money abroad. Article 1 of this law states that anybody who, without the prior authorization provided by the currency regulations or with authorization obtained by improper means, exports out of the territory of the Italian State national or foreign currency, or 'sets up outside of the territory of the State, in his own favor or in favor of others, availability of currency or assets of any nature whatsoever' will be punished by a fine and, above a certain mininum, by imprisonment. Both the Italian corporation, as holder of the anonymous Swiss bank account, and agents *Y* and *Z*, for remitting money into it, could be prosecuted under the above law.

Contractual Considerations

The position of the Agents as representatives of the Liberian Corporation in their contract or contracts with the Italian foreign-market Company (the Italian company) deserves some preliminary clarification. The plan of action contemplates that the Agents are entrusted with the task of acting in the name and on behalf of the Liberian Corporation in regard to all matters concerning the Superior Units. Consequently, according to Italian law, the relationship between the Liberian Corporation and the Agents would qualify as a *mandato*, an institution which does not coincide with the common law concept of agency. Civil Code, Section 1703, defines *mandato* as 'the contract whereby one party binds himself to accomplish one or more legal transactions for the account of another.' Civil Code, Section 1704, further specifies that 'if the mandatory has been given the power to act in the name of the principal, the provisions of Chapter VI of Title II of this Book [Book IV] also apply.' These provisions are embodied in Civil Code, Sections 1387–1400, dealing with 'the power of representation', whereby 'contract made by a representative in the name and in the interest of the principal, within the limits of the powers conferred on the representative, produces effects directly as to the principal.' (Civil Code, Section 1388).

The internal relationship between the Liberian Corporation and the Agents need not necessarily be governed by Italian law. The general conflict of laws rule in matters of obligation, which is set forth in Section 25, paragraph 1, of the Preliminary Provisions to the Civil Code, states that 'obligations arising from contract are governed by the national law of the contracting parties, if common to them; otherwise by that of the place in which the contract was made. In any case a different intention of the parties controls'.

The crucial issue, however, will be that of determining whether the Agents, in dealing with the Italian Company, will act as full representatives of the Liberian Corporation or in their own name on behalf of the Liberian Corporation. This may depend on the existence of a possible proxy from the Liberian Corporation exhibited by the Agents or a possible ratification by the Liberian Corporation of the Agents' acts. In deciding such issue, courts may not limit themselves to an evaluation of the formal side of the proxy but could take into account the nature of the tasks performed and the functions carried out by the agents on behalf of their principal (Judgment of the United Sections of *Cassazione* on 15 November 1960, number 3041).

It may be added that these agents do not seem to qualify as *agenti* pursuant to Civil Code, Sections 1742–1752, that is those who permanently undertake, for remuneration, to promote the making of contracts for the account of another person within a specified territory (Civil Code, Section 1742). Also these *agenti* may be given powers for representing the principal in the conclusion of contracts (Civil Code, Section 1752). However, due to the complexity of the duties assigned to agents *Y* and *Z* on one side, and to their being entrusted to deal only with the Italian Company on the other side, their appointment appears to differ from the ordinary scope contemplated by Civil Code, Section 1742.

If the Agents are given full power of representation of the Liberian Corporation, the following consequences should be taken into account. A general proxy granted to the Agents which does not specifically exclude the power for them to appear in court on behalf of the principal would allow a plaintiff to sue the Liberian Corporation through the Agents in Italy. Italian jurisdiction over the foreign defendant would be based on the presence in Italy of an authorized representative (article 77, paragraph 2, and article 4.1, of the Code of Civil Procedure). A general proxy to the agents could lead to the assumption that a branch of the Liberian corporation was established in Italy without compliance with the requirements set forth in Civil Code, Section 2506. The application of Civil Code, Section 2508, would ensue, whereby the Agents would be held responsible jointly and severally, without limitation, for the obligations undertaken on behalf of the Liberian Corporation. The above considerations would make it advisable to avoid, to the extent possible, granting the Agents a general proxy to act in the name and on behalf of the Liberian Corporation. They might nevertheless be qualified as representatives in a loose sense, as is accepted by local practice.

The content of the contract with the Italian Company, as results from the plan of action, does not allow for the classification into one of the types of contracts contemplated by the Civil Code. This, however, does not violate the law since, according to Section 1322, the 'parties can freely determine the contents of the contract within the limits imposed by law. The parties can also make contracts that are not of the types that are specifically regulated provided that they are directed to the realization of interests worthy of protection according to the legal order'. Further, Civil Code, Section 1323, sets forth that 'all contracts, even though they are not of the types that are specifically regulated, are subject to the general rules contained in this Title.' This also means that an atypical contract, such as the one in question, should meet basic legal requirements for all contracts which are: the agreement of the parties, that is the meeting of the minds; the *causa* (somehow comparable to consideration under Common Law); the object and a specific form when prescribed by law under penalty of nullity (Civil Code, Sections 1325 and following). Lack of any of these and of some other requisites, such as that concerning non-violation of mandatory rules, would make the contract void.

It could also be annulled for lack of capacity of the parties or defects in consent (Civil Code, Sections 1425 and 1427).

In evaluating the content of an atypical contract, courts are led to apply, by way of analogy, the provisions applicable to similar types of contracts. This is the case, for instance, with license agreements which are not specifically contemplated by the Civil Code and for which there is a trend to apply provisions of a lease contract (Civil Code Section 1571). In other cases, the provisions of more than one type of contract are taken into consideration by courts in their analogical interpretation of atypical contracts, which are therefore called complex or mixed contracts. Commercial contracts dealing with the distribution of goods and the rendering of services may fall into this category. For example, distribution agreements which are not contemplated, as such, by the Civil Code may call for the combined application of provisions covering the sales-purchase contract, the supply contract or the *agenti* contract. Reference is often made to the provisions of the supply contract (*somministrazione*) which is the one whereby 'a party binds himself to supply another with things continuously or periodically, in return for a price' (Civil Code, Section 1559) and for which exclusivity either in favor of supplier or customer is contemplated (Civil Code, Sections 1567, 1568).

The contractual arrangements between the Liberian Corporation, acting through its Agents, and the Italian Company could be construed as follows. The Agents make available to the Italian Company the technology relative to the two Components and to the Units including the right to patent the invention covering the Units as a whole, on the assumption that requirements for covering the Unit as a whole, on the assumption that requirements for obtaining the patent are met. This is permissible according to Italian law. Civil Code, Sections 2588 and 2589, read respectively: 'A patent right belongs to the author of an invention and to his successors in interest'; 'The rights deriving from industrial inventions, except the right to be acknowledged as their author, are transferable.' (see also Article 7, paragraph 1, and Article 27 of R.D. 29 June 1939, number 1127). The Italian Company's obligation to purchase the Components from the Agents, to build and distribute the Unit and to pay a price corresponding to a percentage of sales also do not violate the mandatory provisions of Italian law or the EEC rules on competition, as no restrictions are imposed on exports to EEC countries. Lacking specific provisions in the contract to this effect, its duration may be held to coincide with that of the patent.

Using the analogical approach above mentioned, this contract, as regards the mechanics, has features which can be compared to those of the independent contract or contractor's agreement as defined by Civil Code, Section 1655: 'The contractor's agreement is a contract by which a party undertakes to perform a piece of work or render services, organizing the necessary means and operating at his own risk, in return for compensation in money'. By this contract the Italian Company undertakes to produce a result, that is, the manufacture of the Unit and its commercial exploitation on an independent basis. The Liberian Corporation or the Agents are the suppliers of the Components, that is, of 'the materials necessary to perform the work'

(Civil Code, Section 1658). The fixing of price on a percentage basis is also in line with the contractor's agreement scheme (Civil Code, Section 1657).

If one looks instead more at the economic nature of the contract, the basic provisions of association in participation are evoked. 'In a contract of association in participation, the associating party grants the associated party a participation in the profits of his enterprise or of one or more transactions, in return for a specified contribution' (Civil Code, Section 2549). In return for the Liberian Corporation's contribution, through its Agents, to the Italian Company's business in the way of technology grants and the supply of the components, the Italian Company agrees to assign a portion of its profits to the first party. The lack of control by the first party of second party's business is not an essential requirement of this contract, which may have a rather flexible scheme (Civil Code, Sections 2552–2554).

Because of the complexity of its contents, one could hardly forecast how courts might interpret single provisions of this contract. As a whole, since it does not have aspects which violate Italian law, it could be held to be enforceable as one whereby the parties have sufficiently determined the object and have achieved an economic balance between respective performances, which would entitle it to the protection of law. Further, it could hardly be qualified as a partnership agreement involving an unlimited exposure of the Liberian Corporation or its Agents. Under the profile of an analogical application of the provisions of the Civil Code governing contractors' agreements, the Liberian Corporation or its Agents would be more exposed to an indemnity action by the Italian Company based on defects of the Components. In all cases, the Italian Company would act towards purchasers of the Units as an autonomous subject.

To enable the Italian Company to manufacture and distribute the Units, other contractual arrangements would be possible.

Patent registration of the Components or both Components and Units might be obtained by the Liberian Corporation through its Agents either in Italy or at the Geneva International Bureau (BIRPI), according to the Union Treaty above quoted. If patents are registered by the Liberian Corporation for Components only, this Corporation should agree in the contract or by a separate contract to let the Italian Company patent the Unit. In this case, the patent could be construed as an improvement of, or as dependent on, the patented inventions relative to the Components and therefore its registration presupposes the consent of the owner of the patents covering the Components (Civil Code, Section 2587, and Article 5 of the Special Law on Patents). In both cases, payments made by the Italian Company net of the costs for supply of the Components, would be treated as royalties and, as such, would be subject to taxation as will be seen below. Besides, the Liberian Corporation would be more exposed to product liability.

Since, as per this plan of action, Corporations *A* and *B* are more concerned with taxes and product liability than with the risk that the Italian Company would exploit the patent on the Unit for its exclusive benefit beyond the scope of the contract, the license arrangement scheme does not seem attractive. On the other side, if no distinction is made at all between that portion of the Italian Company's payment which could be imputed to the use and grants of technology and patent rights, and that portion which could be considered as a price for the resale of components from the Liberian Corporation or its Agents, there is the risk that all payments would be considered just as the price for the latter. The point will be dealt with later with reference to taxation.

All considered, it does not appear that there is a much better alternative than entering into a general contract with the Italian Company, describing the whole content of the agreement and emphasizing as much as possible the independent role of the Italian Company and its desire to exploit the Unit. This contract would be between the Italian Company and the Liberian Corporation itself or, if the plan of action were to be entirely followed, by its Agents. A special proxy would be delivered to the Agents for this purpose, not a general one. The contract should state, among other things, that the Italian Company undertakes to build the Unit and sell it at its own risk and commits itself to pay the total twenty five per cent on sales as per instructions that will be given by the Agents from time to time. A clause of the contract would set forth the duty for the Italian Company to transfer its patent as per the Agents' instructions in any case of termination of the contract, the duration of which could be left indefinite, subject to reasonable notice of termination.

As far as the implementation of this contract is concerned, it would be to the Liberian Corporation's advantage if the Agents were to sell the Components and act for the transfer of technology to the Italian Company as concessionaires of the Liberian Corporation. However, all money that they will collect from the Italian Company in that capacity will be treated as earnings of their local enterprise, subject to Italian taxation.

Tax Liability

It may be preliminarily observed that with the income tax reform which became effective on 1 January 1974, the principle of a worldwide basis for assessing taxable income of residents was introduced into the Italian system of law with some limitations and without prejudice to international treaties to avoid double taxation. Income taxes applicable to corporations are the corporate income tax and the local income tax respectively instituted by Presidential Decrees 598 (DPR 598 and 599 (DPR 599) of 29 September 1973. Their present rates are respectively twenty-five per cent and fifteen per cent.

An application of the above principle is found as regards the corporate income tax for foreign corporations which have their administrative headquarters or principal business activity within the territory of the Italian State (Article 2a), Article 3 of DPR 598). Note that this definition almost corresponds to that of Civil Code, Section 2505. Foreign corporations which do not fall within this category, but have a branch or another permanent establishment or source of income in Italy, are taxed only on income earned in the Italian territory (Article 22 of DPR 598 which refers to Article 19 of DPR 597 for the classification of taxable income of non-residents. Presidential

Decree 597 instituted the personal income tax and contains provisions defining the different sources of income to which reference is made in the provisions on the corporate income tax and other tax laws).

The local income tax, instead, is levied only on income earned by companies in the Italian State (DPR 599, Article 1). Exceptions to this rule are made for companies falling into the category of Civil Code, Section 2505, and for certain incomes deriving from foreign operations but not connected with a permanent establishment or a fixed base. These incomes are treated as income earned in Italy (DPR 599, article 3). In view of the above, if the Liberian Corporation is validly constituted as an independent corporation and its main activity is carried on outside Italy; or it does not have a permanent establishment in Italy, it should be exempt from Italian taxation. If the Agents' activity, as true representatives of the Liberian Corporation, is held to be equivalent to a permanent establishment of that Corporation, the latter's Italian business income would be taxed. In the extreme hypothesis that the Liberian corporation is found to have its main activity in Italy, it should be taxed on all income, including that earned abroad. In practice, however, these two hypothetical cases of taxation in Italy will result in taxes for the Agents based on income attributable to their Italian organization, as will be seen below.

Corporations *A* and *B*, in all cases, should not be taxed for income presumably earned in Italy. For one thing, they are foreign corporations, legally existing and doing business abroad. On the other hand, income earned in Italy by the Liberian Corporation through the Agents will be attributed to the Agents activity in Italy.

If the Liberian Corporation were to establish a branch in Italy in compliance with Civil Code, Section 2506, it would be taxed for corporate and local income taxes as above noted. Otherwise, the following alternative cases could be envisioned.

The Agents could do business as independent enterpreneurs, in which case payments made to them by the Italian Company would contribute as business income to the formation of their total taxable income (article 51 and following of DPR 597). This point will be dealt with later.

Another possibility is that the tax authorities might assume that there is a permanent establishment in Italy of the Liberian Corporation notwithstanding the fact that requirements set forth in Civil Code, Section 2506, have not been met. A clear definition of permanent establishment of foreign companies is not given by tax laws, although reference to it is made in scattered provisions (see, for instance, Article 3, paragraph 2 of Law 904 of 16 December 1977). The definitions embodied in international treaties to avoid double taxation concluded by Italy and perhaps also the OECD Draft Treaty may be of help. In the present case, considering also the lack of treaties between Italy and Liberia and the evanescent nature of the Liberian Corporation, not to mention the impossibility of assessing possible foreign income of that corporation if the case were that contemplated in Civil Code, Section 2505, Italian tax authorities will only have the possibility of taxing the Agents for income assumedly earned by the Liberian Corporation in Italy.

A distinction may be drawn between the case of Agents acting as true representatives, that is as managers of the Liberian Corporation branch in Italy and the Agents doing business as independent entrepreneurs. Only the second hypothesis will be dealt with here, since the first already has been considered above.

According to the plan of action, the Agents will engage in a commercial activity since they will import goods from abroad, sell or resell them to the Italian Company and collect payments from the latter. In order to do this, they will have an official status which implies registration with an Italian Chamber of Commerce, possessing a fiscal code number and being listed in the Roster of Operators Abroad. As a matter of fact, since the Agents have in the past already imported components from Corporations *A* and *B* into Italy, they should already be qualified to do business in Italy. They are or will be taxable subjects here. Since the fact pattern contemplates that the Agents will sell the imported components to the Italian Company, these transactions will be subject to value-added tax (VAT). In conclusion, the Agents cannot avoid being taxed on their incomes, whether or not their activity is carried out by them individually or in the form of a company. In the first case, however, the existence of a *de facto* unlimited partnership would be assumed by tax authorities (as per Article 5, paragraph 3b, and Article 51 of DPR 597).

Reverting now to this operation in action, the five-hundred dollars share that the Agents will retain for each Superior Unit will contribute to form their taxable income. Because of the kind of transactions that the Agents are supposed to execute, their earnings could not be treated as income from an independent, personal working activity pursuant to Article 49 of DPR 597 with a consequent rebate for the purposes of local income tax. Their income will be that of a business enterprise as defined by Article 51 of DPR 597 and will be assessed on the basis of required accounting books and records kept by the Agents. The basic question is then to determine whether the seven-thousand dollars total expenses of the Agents per Unit will be considered as a tax-deductible cost.

Let us suppose that five-thousand dollars is transferred to the Swiss account, which is only an academic question for the reasons explained above, and also because under the general authorization relative to foreign-exchange control, banks would hardly be allowed to remit an amount of this magnitude abroad in respect to each Unit. Such payment could be treated as compensation for the rendering of services or transferring or granting the use of industrial property rights and similar transactions from abroad, subject to a twenty per cent tax to be withheld by the Agents according to Article 25, paragraph 2, DPR 600 of 29 September 1973. Application of this provision is debatable in some cases but fiscal offices request that withholdings be made in all cases. Consequently, the foreign recipient of such payments should file income tax returns in Italy and pay the local income tax.

Another possible assumption is that all or part of the five-thousand dollars would be imputed to the cost of the acquisition of the Components. If so, however, the excess value in respect to the normal value of these goods would not be accepted as costs as is provided for by Article 56, paragraph 2 of DPR 597 in the event that an enterprise undertakes the business of selling or placing raw materials or goods or manufacturing or processing its products on behalf of companies which do not have their administrative offices nor their principal activity within the territory of the Italian State. All considered, a relevant portion if not all of the five-thousand dollars will likely be treated as income for the Agents.

The Italian Company will be subject to corporate and local income taxes on its business activity as this is developed in Italy. The point is whether the seventy five per cent of invoiced sales paid to the Agents will be entirely accepted as costs. This presupposes that payments from the Italian Company covering all grants and supplies be made to Agents as managers of a branch of the Liberian Corporation or as independent enterpreneurs against proper invoices. VAT will have to be added to the invoiced price and the Italian Company will in turn charge VAT to customers on its sales. If one wants to comply with the plan of action proposed, no other solution appears to be available except perhaps that of isolating the five-hundred dollars as a commission paid by the Italian Company to Agents, subject to withholding tax. If, instead, one were to involve the Italian Company in making payments other than against the Agents invoices or bills, the Italian Company would be exposed to the kind of risks of excess taxation referred to above.

Product Liability

Italian law does not yet have rules dealing with product liability as such. They are expected to come into force in the future following initiatives taken at the international level. Under present laws, product liability may be considered a contractual responsibility of the supplier of products to customers. This especially happens in matters of sale-purchase, where the law sets forth seller's warranties regarding flaws or defects which render the goods sold unsuitable for their use or not corresponding to the legitimate expectations of the purchaser (Civil Code, Sections 1490–1497). However, the right of action of a purchaser is barred by a rather short statute of limitation periods (Civil Code, Section 1495) and is enforced only against the seller, who often is not the manufacturer of the products. The seller, in turn, may have recourse against the supplier, and so on, so that the manufacturer is ultimately involved, but the need to comply with the statute of limitation periods applicable to each single relationship and procedural considerations make these remedies not too effective.

Aside from contracts, an autonomous source of product liability is available and has been found by courts in the general tort rule of Civil Code, Section 2043, which reads as follows: 'Any fraudulent, malicious or negligent act that causes an unjustified injury to another obliges the person who has committed the act to pay damages'. The manufacturer's exposure to this non-contractual liability in carrying out certain risky industrial activities is further qualified by Civil Code, Section 2050, whereby 'Whoever causes injury to another in the performance of an activity dangerous by its nature or by reason of the instrumentalities employed, is liable for damages, unless he proves that he has taken all suitable measures to avoid the injury'.

Commentators generally favor the idea of a general assumption of responsibility by manufacturers of products, destined for widespread consumer use, which are found to be defective. This view is also reflected by court decisions, such as that rendered by the Supreme Court (*Cassazione*) on 25 May 1964, number 1270, in a suit relative to personal injuries caused by faulty food products which were purchased from a retailer in their original packaging. In this interesting precedent the court, while excluding liability of retailer when deterioration of the products cannot be imputed to poor conservation or sale after the time limit of the guarantee given by the manufacturer, held that a fault of the manufacturer in such a case might be presumed.

Under general principles of law governing the burden of evidence, the party claiming responsibility for negligence must prove the existence of a cause and effect connection between the alleged defect and the damaging event. The manufacturer who has complied with all public license requirements for the exercise of his activity and taken all security measures deriving from regulations and the criteria of prudence, including compliance with special provisions dealing with packaging and labeling of dangerous products, has a chance of defending himself against these claims. This is also in accordance with the general law principles whereby the party who has used its best diligence as is required by the nature of its activity cannot be held liable for fortuitous events exceeding the foreseeable risks inherent to that activity.

The manufacturer and, under some circumstances, the seller of the defective product causing injury or death to persons may be held criminally liable. Criminal prosecution, which is entrusted to public authorities, does not encounter limitations of evidence existing in civil suits. It might be added that in the present socio-political climate, public attorneys and judges are rather interested in pursuing these penal matters. When the alleged criminal offense arises out of the operation of a company, the problem is that of indicting the physical person or persons who may be responsible. There is a tendency in such cases to involve also the company's higher executives who, in order to defend themselves, must demonstrate that they have exercised the utmost care in issuing proper instructions, appointing the right persons in charge of industrial departments or sectors and supervising them. Foreigners not residing in Italy who are accused of involuntary homicide and involuntary injuries could be prosecuted here if these events occurred in Italy (see Section 6 of the Penal Code).

Herebelow, however, the possible exposure of the parties of these international transactions to civil suits based either on contracts or on negligence or both will be considered. A suit based on contracts would be available to the owner of the house and, by way of recourse to the other parties who are transferees of the Components. The negligence action would be a remedy both for the consumer, that is the owner of the house and for the bystanders, that is the owner's spouse and the visiting neighbor. When the fact, as is the case here, constitutes a criminal offense, the injured subjects are entitled, in addition to material damages, also to the *pretium doloris*, that is moral damages. These last damages could also be claimed by the parents because of the loss of their child. According to circumstances, both manufacturer and supplier could be held liable.

An action based on contract against Corporations *A* and *B* is not admissable since the owner of the house bought the Unit as a whole from the Italian Company. Actions based on contract in the way of recourse would be available against those Corporations to the Agents and/or the Liberian Corporation if these were summoned as defendants in a suit lodged before an Italian court. An action based on negligence would be possible against Corporations *A* and *B*.

Italian jurisdiction over these foreign defendants would derive from the provisions of Section 4 of the Code of Civil Procedure, because of the connection with a suit already pending before an Italian court and/or because the case against those Corporations would refer to obligations which arose or which were to be fulfilled in Italy. Pursuant to Section 25 of the Preliminary Provisions to the Civil Code, 'non-contractual obligations are governed by the law of the place where the facts from which they arise took place'.

The liability of Corporations *A* and *B* as manufacturers of the components could only be upheld if claimants were able to prove that the malfunction was attributable to one of the components and that it was manufactured by either Corporation *A* or *B*. This should not be an impossible task in a suit brought against the Italian Company which would then act in recourse. Evidence of the origin of the Components could be obtained also through orders from the judge to the parties to produce documents or at the judge's request for information from public agencies or offices such as customs offices.

It would not be easy for Corporations *A* and *B* to take exception by alleging that the Italian Company is exclusively responsible since, in fact, the Italian Company is exempt from any fault. A defense based on the fact that, in the light of technological-scientific knowledge presently available, the malfunction could not have been discovered when the Components were delivered to the Liberian Corporation, would likely be unsuccessful. The novelty of this apparatus itself increases manufacturer's risks.

The same comments made above regarding a possible law suit based on contract against Corporations *A* and *B* would apply to the Liberian Corporation. A recourse action could be brought against it either if the Agents had acted in the capacity of true representatives of the Liberian Corporation, or by the Agents themselves. Since, as above noted, the relationship between the Liberian Corporation and the Agents will qualify as a mandate, the latter could invoke the rule set forth in Civil Code, Section 1720, paragraph 2, which makes it a duty for a principal to compensate the mandatory for damages incurred by him by reason of his undertaking.

Also, an action not based on contract might be possible against the Liberian Corporation if claimants were able to allege contributory negligence inasmuch as this Corporation served as a device for the realization of the plan of action which was instituted by Corporations *A* and *B* for their benefit. If, instead, it would prove difficult for claimants to establish these facts the Liberian Corporation, as supplier of the components, might find itself in the difficult position of having to rebut the assumption that the supplier of the goods who does not disclose the identity of manufacturer undertakes the product liability of the latter. This appears to be rather speculative as Italian law presently stands, but finds grounds in the text of a proposed EEC Directive on product liability.

If the Agents have acted in their own name, a recourse action by the Italian Company would be possible against them. In the above capacity they would also be exposed to liability for negligence and this, in substance, for the same reasons mentioned above with reference to the Liberian Corporation. The Agents liability could specifically be connected with the fact of having imported products of unknown manufacture from the Liberian Corporation and not having tested them before resale. The above mentioned proposed EEC Directive (Article 2, last paragraph) states that 'Anybody who imports goods to the EEC Territory for resale or for a similar scope is considered to be the manufacturer'. The Italian Company could be liable both as seller of the Unit and under the general negligence principle. As seller, however, the Italian Company would have a chance of defending itself because it was not at fault in assembling the Components, in packaging them and in supplying proper instructions concerning their use. It could therefore maintain that, through no fault of its own, it had no knowledge of the malfunction of the component (Civil Code, Section 1494).

From the standpoint of an action based on negligence, a discrepancy between the present status of Italian law and the proposed EEC legislation is again noted. The absence of fault by the Italian Company in carrying out the rather limited operations assigned to it and its extraneousness to the devious intents of the plan of action designed by Corporations *A* and *B* could be sufficient protection for the Italian Company. It would not be so if, as is not unlikely, the principle of product liability, independent of fault, will extend also to the assembler as a result of expected new laws in this field.

The Swiss Analysis

KARL ARNOLD

Alternative Corporate Locations

As an alternative, one might consider forming a joint-stock company in Liechtenstein. The Liechtenstein joint-stock company can be structured rather flexibly. The costs of incorporation amount to approximately four-thousand Swiss francs. At least one of the board members must be a Liechtenstein citizen. Name, legal domicile, capital and board members are registered in a register which is open to public inspection. The annual running costs including taxes, will amount to about four-thousand Swiss francs. A Liechtenstein joint-stock company provides as much anonymity as may be desirable. It is common practice for anonymous shareholders of such a company to enter into a mandate agreement with the members of the board of directors under which the directors agree to act exclusively upon instruction of the principals.

Corporations *A* and *B* might further consider establishing a corporation in Switzerland. The minimum capital for establishing a Swiss company is fifty-thousand Swiss francs of which at least twenty-thousand Swiss francs must be paid in. The majority of the directors must be Swiss citizens residing in Switzerland. The formation costs include: a professional fee for preparation of formation, deed and articles, two-thousand to three-thousand Swiss francs; notary's fees for incorporation, about five-hundred Swiss francs; registration fee (commercial register) about four-hundred Swiss francs; and federal stamp duty of three per cent of the nominal capital. The cost of forming a corporation having a share capital of one-hundred-thousand Swiss francs is likely to be about six-thousand Swiss francs. The annual tax depends to a certain extent on the location where the company is domiciled and operating.

We also might consider using a Swiss domiciliary company, that is a company which has no income from inside of Switzerland.

Advantages and Disadvantages

Liberia has a reputation of being a tax haven. Any payments going to a Liberian company have a tendency of being examined thoroughly by the tax inspectors of the country from which the payment comes. There is a risk that the profit generated in the Liberian Corporation will be allocated to its stockholders. On the other hand the taxes in Liberia seem to be low, the costs of establishing the corporation are low, the anonymity of the beneficial owner of the stock may be secured and it is a simple matter to have Liberian officers appointed who act exclusively upon instruction of the actual or beneficial owner of the corporation.

In this case, Corporations *A* and *B* do not want to have their stock ownership disclosed. It is assumed that the need for secrecy is not based on the intention to use the Liberian Corporation for improper or illegal purposes but is commercially motivated. Assuming further that Corporations *A* and *B* are located in the United States, the question comes up how and where the profit of the Liberian Corporation will be used ultimately? Either Corporations *A* and *B* will wish to have the profit distributed as dividends or the Liberian Corporation will be used as a finance company, financing other operations of Corporations *A* and *B*. Since the Liberian Corporation will actually not be managed in Liberia there will always be the risk that it will be taxed at the place of its actual management.

Liechtenstein has likewise a reputation of being a tax haven and calling the tax inspectors' attention to any transaction made with the Liechtenstein company. However, the liberal commercial laws of Liechtenstein have induced many foreign enterprises to establish business entities of substance in Liechtenstein. The official currency of Liechtenstein is the Swiss franc. With a Liechtenstein company the risk is likewise high that its profits will be allocated to its foreign stockholders or that it will be taxed at the place of its actual management. It must further be said that the Swiss Foreign-Market Company (the Swiss company) as well as the Swiss agents are likely to be most reluctant to enter into long-term contracts with a Liberian or Liechtenstein legal entity. In case of a dispute it will be time-consuming and frustrating to have a Liberian or Liechtenstein court render a final judgment or to have a foreign judgment enforced in Liberia or Liechtenstein. Experience has shown that Liberian and Liechtenstein companies often are liquidated and their assets distributed to unknown stockholders before a judgment against them can be enforced.

The taxes in Switzerland exceed the taxes in Liberia or Liechtenstein. Nevertheless, Switzerland may be considered as a favorable tax location without suffering from the disadvantages of a pure tax haven. The anonymity of any kind of commercial transaction appears to be as well protected in Switzerland as in Liberia or Liechtenstein. Swiss custom barriers are low. However, the high rate of exchange, labor shortages, and severe permit restrictions on bringing in foreign staff from home locations have contributed to making it more difficult to locate a new operation in Switzerland. If the profit generated in the Swiss company is distributed, then the profit distributed is subject to a thirty-five per cent Swiss withholding tax. However, at least a portion of this amount is usually refunded under the applicable double taxation treaties, for example the treaty with the United States.

Contractual Considerations

Under Swiss law, the person or company filing a patent application may be the inventor or his assignee. The inventor must be named. If his name is not to be published, he must sign a renunciation. In our case, the Swiss Company will register the patents in its own name and submit the inventor's renunciation. It might be advisable for the Liberian Corporation to agree with the Swiss Company that in case of termination of the distribution contract the patents must be reassigned to the Liberian Corporation.

Based on the facts presented it is advisable for the Swiss Company to enter into a distribution contract with the Liberian Corporation. This agreement would provide for the Swiss Company to transfer for each unit seven-thousand-five-hundred dollars to the Agents. The contract is likely to include provisions on:

- Legal situation of the Swiss Company (distributor sells in his own name and for his own account);
- Assignment of know-how and patent rights;
- Obligation to assemble the units (quality control);
- Obligation to register patents;
- Price and conditions of resale (currency);
- Obligation to buy a minimum quantity of Superior Components;
- Publicity;
- Non-competition during the term of the agreement;
- Trade secrets;
- Sub-agents;
- Prohibition to sell outside Switzerland;
- Fair competition;
- Assistance against unfair competition and infringements of industrial property;
- Minimum stock;
- Repair and after sales service;
- Documents, advertising material, instruction manuals;
- Obligation for the Liberian Corporation to supply a minimum quantity;
- Obligation for the Liberian Corporation not to appoint another distributor for Switzerland and not to sell directly in Switzerland;
- Prohibition of other distributors to sell in Switzerland;
- Spare parts;
- Maturity and payment;
- Taxes;
- Expiration of the contract;
- Premature termination;
- Return of information, advertising material, instruction manuals;
- Liquidation of the stock and execution of orders on expiration of the contract;
- Indemnity on termination of the contract;
- Applicable law;
- Arbitration, jurisdiction;
- Modifications of contract, and
- Prohibition to assign contract.

The payments made under this distribution contract constitute the purchase price for each unit paid by the Swiss Company. The total amount may be paid to the Agents or it may be agreed that one portion of the price must be paid to a Swiss bank account (five-thousand dollars), one portion to the Agents (one-thousand dollars) and one portion to the Liberian Corporation in Libera (one-thousand-five-hundred dollars) or for the Liberian Corporation to the Corporations *A* and *B*. In these calculations it must be considered that the customers of the Swiss Company will expect the purchase price to be quoted in Swiss francs and that the exchange rate of the Swiss franc and United States dollar is fluctuating constantly and substantially.

It is further suggested that the Liberian Corporation enter into an agency contract with the Agents. This contract might provide that:

The Agents are to supervise the activities of the Swiss Company under the distribution contract;

The Swiss Agents are to give advice to the Liberian Corporation on the requirements of the Swiss market and on possible technical improvements of the Superior Unit;

The Agents are to render such other service to the Liberian Corporation as will be reasonably required in the ordinary course of business;

The Liberian Corporation is to pay the Agents United States $1,000 for each unit sold in Switzerland.

It has been noted that the Liberian Corporation will try to include in the distribution contract wording whereby its product liability is restricted to the minimum legally permitted. The Swiss Company will likewise include in its terms and conditions a clause which will limit its liability to the full extent possible. The following wording might be included:

> The Swiss Company's liability for direct physical damage to persons or property caused by the Superior Unit or the Swiss Company's employees shall be limited to the purchase price of the products involved. Under no circumstances shall the Swiss Company be liable for consequential damage to the customer. The Swiss Company shall be liable exclusively in case of gross negligence.

From a purely Swiss point of view it is hard to see any advantage in establishing the Liberian Corporation. The Liberian Corporation is likely to add problems, for example, the tax situation of Corporations *A* and *B*, without giving additional protection with respect to product or tax liability. Depending on where Corporations *A* and *B* wish to use the profit, other schemes might be explored, such as the use of a patent holding company, or a worldwide marketing company in the United States or other countries.

Tax Liability

In this case, it is assumed that Corporations *A* and *B* are established under the laws of and engage in business in the United States. It must now be examined whether they become liable to pay Swiss taxes due to the fact that goods sold by them are purchased in Switzerland. The United States and Switzerland have signed on 24 May 1951, a double taxation treaty. Under this treaty, a United

States enterprise is not subject to taxation in Switzerland in respect to its industrial and commercial profits except as to profits allocable to its permanent establishment situated in Switzerland (Article III, Section 1, lit. b). Under the treaty, 'permanent establishment' means a branch, office, factory, workshop, warehouse or other fixed place of business. It does not include the temporary use of storage facilities nor does it include an agency unless the agent has exercised a general authority to negotiate and conclude contracts on behalf of the United States enterprise or has a stock of merchandise from which he fills orders on behalf of the United States enterprise. This language shows that the Corporations *A* and *B* have no permanent establishment in Switzerland and are therefore not subject to Swiss taxes. They would also be exempt from Swiss taxation if they were to sell the Solar Collector and Solar Generator directly to the Swiss Company.

There exists no double taxation treaty between Liberia and Switzerland. However, under the rules of international double taxation applied by Switzerland, the prerequisite for levying a tax is, as a rule, a permanent establishment of the foreign corporation in Switzerland. The definition of the permanent establishment in this connection is somewhat different from the definition as set forth in the United States/Switzerland double taxation treaty. However, the fact that the Liberian Corporation holds a Swiss bank account and is paid for the goods purchased by the Swiss Company does not constitute a permanent establishment.

It is safe to assume that the Agents will not be taxed on the amounts transferred to the Liberian Corporation or the Swiss bank account, provided that the Agents are dealing at arm's length. The tax situation would be different if the Agents appeared to be closely related either to the Swiss Company or to the Liberian Corporation and the commission paid to the Agents would not be considered a compensation at a fair market price.

The Swiss Company will be required to pay the turnover tax on the Superior Unit sold to the end user. At this time the turnover tax amounts to 5.6 per cent of the value of the goods sold. A proposal to introduce the value-added tax was recently rejected in a referendum. In addition, the Swiss company is liable for the ordinary federal, cantonal and municipal taxes on net profit and capital.

Product Liability

Swiss law distinguishes between contractual and non-contractual liability. Under the concept of contractual liability, the party who does not fulfill his obligation properly is liable for damages, unless he proves that there is no fault on his part (Section 97, Swiss Code of Obligations). The Swiss Company and the purchasers of the Superior Unit enter into a purchase contract. We therefore have to examine whether the Swiss Company is liable to the purchaser under Sections 184 to 215 of the Swiss Code of Obligations.

Unless otherwise agreed, benefit and risk of the property pass to the buyer when the contract is made (Section 185, Swiss Code of Obligations). In our case the purchase contract was entered into when the Superior Unit was delivered to the purchaser by the Swiss Company. The Swiss Company is liable to the buyer both for express representations made and for the implied representation that the Superior Unit is without physical or legal defects which eliminate or substantially reduce its value or its fitness for the intended use. The Swiss Company is liable even if it does not know of the defects. If the damage is a direct consequence of a defect in the Superior Unit, there is a presumption that the Swiss Company is liable.

The purchaser of the Superior Unit does not have a contract with quality of the Superior Unit as soon as it is customary in accordance with usual business practice (Section 201, Swiss Code of Obligations). The buyer has to immediately notify the Swiss Company of any defects. If defects are discovered at a later date, notification must be given immediately upon their discovery.

Since, in our case, the defect was hidden and could not have been detected, the action based on a warranty for defects is barred at the end of one year after delivery to the purchaser even if the defect was only discovered by the purchaser at a later date, unless the Swiss Company has assumed liability for a longer period (Section 210, Swiss Code of Obligations).

The Swiss Company is liable unless there is no fault at all attributable to it. In our case the Swiss Company would allege in a court case that 999 units were without defect. In addition the Swiss Company would emphasize that it applied the best possible quality control and that the defects could not have been detected. It is safe to assume that in this case the Swiss Company can produce enough evidence to prove that there is no liability on its part.

The purchaser of the Superior Unit does not have a contract with Corporations *A* and *B*, the Liberian Corporation or the Agents. The basis for non-contractual or tort liability in Switzerland is Section 41 of the Swiss Code of Obligations: whoever unlawfully causes damage to another, whether willfully or negligently, is liable for damages. It seems unlikely that Corporations *A* and *B*, the Liberian Corporation or the Agents acted with fault in the sense of Section 41. If there is no fault on their part, there is no liability.

The United States Analysis

DONALD PRINZ

CLAUDE ROHWER

Jurisdiction

The European-Liberian enterprise purportedly was structured to afford it maximum insulation against the jurisdictional assertions and judgments of American courts. Whether such insulation was attained or is attainable is dependent upon various unstated factors and upon resolution of unresolved constitutional questions.

The pages to follow are directed to those who are concerned with the structuring of foreign businesses. They are designed to furnish an analytical framework which will assist the business structurer who is attempting to insulate his business from United States court actions. If maximum insulation is to be achieved, *today's* structurer must anticipate both the ingenuity of tomorrow's plaintiffs' attorneys, and the constitutional interpretations of tomorrow's Supreme Court. This anticipatory effort requires some understanding of United States Constitutional decision-making. Moreover, it requires an understanding of the various theories and concepts utilized by plaintiffs' attorneys in their efforts to expand United States court jurisdictional reach over non-resident manufacturers[1].

The due process clause of the United States Constitution has been interpreted to impose limitations on the jurisdictional reach of courts situated in the United States. These interpretations purport to place certain non-resident defendants beyond a court's jurisdiction, and thereby effectively insulated the qualifying non-resident from lawsuits filed in the United States.

These constitutional interpretations are not yet definitive. They do, however, state that a court cannot assert 'in personam' jurisdiction[2] over a defendant unless the defendant has some 'minimum contact' with the state and has derived benefit from the state. 'Minimum contact' means different things to different people. It lends itself to ingenious expansion. It permits someone else's 'minimum contact' to be attributed to the defendant non-resident via alter ego, agency or joint enterprise theories. Under these theories, jurisdiction is asserted over the non-resident despite the fact that the defendant has never set foot in the United States. The physical presence or 'minimum contact' of someone else, that is, of some agent, or alter ego, or joint enterpriser, is ascribed to the foreign defendant, thereby subjecting the 'absent' foreigner to the court's jurisdiction and judgment. While these theories are being utilized ever more frequently by the state courts, there is little United States Supreme Court guidance or limitation upon their use. The

European and Liberian corporations are clearly vulnerable under these theories and concepts, which will be separately discussed. Preliminary to that discussion it is essential to understand the underlying 'minimum contact' aspect of due process.

The due process 'minimum contact' limitation is subject to interpretation by the United States Supreme Court which is the final interpreter of the United States Constitution. Its rulings are supreme. State courts are subject to these rulings to the extent that they are definitive, or to the extent that the facts of a subsequent case are indistinguishable. Unfortunately, the Supreme Court has not made many rulings in this due process-jurisdiction area. The few rulings they have made are not definitive, and they are easily circumvented or distinguished by a plaintiff's attorney. It may be years before a definitive ruling is issued by the Supreme Court. Indeed, it is within the power of the United States Supreme Court to delay or avoid ruling on these issues forever. There is no absolute right to Supreme Court review. Four of the nine Supreme Court justices must vote to review a case. In the absence of such vote, the lower court decision is final. When, over a period of time, the Supreme Court has failed to review or give guidance in a certain area (such as alter ego), state courts and lower federal courts are invariably tempted to expand the area to excess. As these excesses become widespread, the Supreme Court usually selects a case for review. While the Supreme Court's ruling in the reviewed case is usually limited to the precise facts of that case, lower courts do receive guidance for resolution of future cases.

The Supreme Court has evidenced a recent interest in the general due process-jurisdictional area, and has reviewed three state court decisions which involved the adequacy of defendants' 'minimum contact.' The review of these cases came after a lapse of many years, during which some state courts expanded their jurisdiction to a degree which the Supreme Court viewed as excessive. The Supreme Court ruled against the states' expansive jurisdictional assertion in each of the three decisions. In these cases the Supreme Court was careful to limit its decisions to the precise facts of each case, and cautioned against drawing any broad conclusions. The court itself is unsure of future application of the due process limitation as evidenced by one of the opinions:

> Like any standard that requires a determination of 'reasonableness', the 'minimum contacts' test of *International Shoe* is not susceptible of mechanical application; rather, the facts of each case must be weighed to determine whether the requisite 'affiliating circumstances' are present. *Hansen v. Denckla*, 357 U.S. 235, 246 (1958). We recognize that this determination is one in which few answers will be written 'in black and white. The greys are dominant and even among them the shades are innumerable'[3].

When the court itself admits that there are few black and white answers in this area of constitutional interpretation, one should use caution when advising the foreign business structurer who seeks risk-free assurances. Nevertheless, an essential function of the lawyer is to anticipate constitutional interpretations so as to enable clients to structure their business in the safer shades of that vast grey area.

The solar hypothetical is appropos for analysis. The foreign manufacturers have no direct United States contact or presence (contrary to given facts, we assume that the United States parties are neither agent, alter ego, or joint venturers), yet it is their foreign restraint of trade, and their foreign product, which has an injurious *effect* upon citizens in the state of the forum. We assume that the state's product liability law has been violated and that everyone connected with the production and distribution of the defective product would be liable if jurisdiction is attainable.

It is the trial court which makes the initial determination as to its jurisdiction under the due process clause. It is realistic to assume that trial courts will be predisposed to interpret the due process limitations narrowly. This attitude springs from several sources: their desire to prevent defective products from entering the state; sentiment for the injured citizen and concern that he obtain redress; a desire to insure that domestic manufacturers (who are subject to damage awards) are not placed in the unfair or uncompetitive position which would result were foreign based businesses insulated from similar damage suits. Moreover, these courts will be influenced by the fact that the prestigious American Law Institute's *Restatement (Second) of Conflicts* (1971), Section 37 purports to authorize jurisdiction over a party who causes an 'effect' within the state[4]. The Law Institute's rationale[5] would extend to foreign based designers and manufacturers of defective products. These combined influences inevitably will lead to a trial court decision finding jurisdiction for tort liability over the Liberian and European corporations. The trial court decision can be reviewed by an appellate court which would look to past Supreme Court opinions for guidance, and to appellate counsel for analysis and distinguishing factors. To the dismay of foreign defendants, plaintiffs' attorneys are quick to seize upon distinctions which lower courts tend to utilize as justification for limiting Supreme Court decisions.

In the recent *Kulko*[6] case, for example, the Supreme Court ruled that the due process clause does not permit a California court to assert jurisdiction over a non-resident on the basis of the *effects* of his out of state conduct. If the Liberian or European corporations were sued in the same California court the *Kulko* case might be distinguished on the grounds that *Kulko* was not a products liability case. Plaintiff would assert that the Supreme Court in *Kulko* implied that it might treat a tort effect (personal injury) differently[7]. Indeed, the court quoted Section 37 of the Restatement, *supra*, and then pointedly avoided addressing its validity or invalidity. Accordingly, one may anticipate that some lower courts will distinguish *Kulko*, and will not apply its limitation to products liability or antitrust cases where a foreigner is involved in causing an *effect* within the United States. Indeed, some courts may attempt to distinguish *Kulko* irrespective of the type of effect involved. See *Great Western United Corp. v. Kidwell*, 577 F.2d 1256 (1978), a decision issued after *Kulko*, and not easily distinguishable from *Kulko*[8]. The *Kidwell* court's analysis in distinguishing *Kulko* is certainly suspect, and may be reversed upon review by the United States Supreme Court[9]. The case does illustrate that lower courts are prone to accept any analysis offered by a plaintiff's attorney which purports to justify the court's assertion of jurisdiction over a non-resident defendant. And, of course, the plaintiff's analysis and justification for expansive jurisdiction in a products liability case can be structured in a very persuasive manner. See *Gray v. American Radiator and Standard Sanitary Corp.*, 22 Ill.2d 432, N.E.2d 761 (1961) where plaintiff was successful in persuading the court to take jurisdiction over a non-resident manufacturer of a component part of the defective product. The *Gray* decision and analysis would apply to all non-residents including European-based corporations[10].

This *Gray* reasoning and decision has a following among state courts. While the Supreme Court has not yet ruled on this reasoning, several justices of the high court have indicated their acceptance of it. If and when the high court does rule, the *Gray* reasoning may be accepted (particularly if the due process limitation is interpreted to be a simple balance of relative fairness to, and relative burden on, plaintiff, defendant, and state). Many state courts and writers perceive the due process limitation to be just that—a simple question of fairness achieved by balancing the equities.

When questioning the validity of this perceived fairness standard, defendant's attorney should vigorously assert two points. From a historical perspective, fairness has had little to do with the constitutional limitation on a state court's exercise of in personam or in rem jurisdiction. In its origin this limitation was viewed as a *territorial* limitation on the *power* of any court which sought to assert power over something beyond its territorial boundaries. In contrast, the limitation today is viewed as having evolved into a personal due process *right* of the defendant. The earlier territorial standard was premised upon the theory that the maintenance of a workable federation of states required a limitation upon the states. Without constitutional limitation on the power of individual states and their courts, it was believed that intolerable projections of power, retaliatory activities, and uncertainty would result. These considerations arguably remain valid today with respect to foreign nations and foreign nationals.

It is difficult to square the *Gray* court use of the subjective fairness standard with the terminology and rationale of Supreme Court decisions[11]. A persuasive argument can be made that the criteria and analytical threads, utilized and applied in decided Supreme Court decisions, are consistent with only one hypotheses: that the due process standard is a dual standard of power and fairness. If and when the Supreme Court addresses the issue, the dual standard is likely to prevail. Implicit in recent Supreme Court decisions is the message to state courts that the Supreme Court is monitoring the situation after a nineteen year lapse[12].

The question before us is whether the European and Liberian solar product manufacturers are subject to a state court's jurisdiction in a products liability lawsuit. The 'effects' were caused in the United States. The Restatement and *Gray* reasoning would support the state's assertion of jurisdiction. The question is whether there are limits to the application of *Gray*.

Certainly a basketweaver in central India who leaves a hidden needle in his work product doesn't have 'minimum contact' with the State of Nebraska (the situs of the pin-pricked customer). Nor does the basketweaver receive 'benefit protection' from the laws or police of Nebraska. Should it make any difference whether the weaver knows where his baskets will be utilized? Should it make any difference whether he instigated the establishment of a Nebraska market for his product as contrasted with a sale to a Nebraska tourist on the streets of New Delhi? Is it reasonable to assert that worldwide 'in personam' jurisdiction is justified because he should have priced his product to cover worldwide defense of damage suits arising under diverse and even perverse tort laws?[13] Of course, we suspect the Supreme Court would deny Nebraska jurisdiction over the seller who makes the casual sale. But the essential question is—upon what precise basis would they deny Nebraska jurisdiction? This limitation upon jurisdiction could be based upon fairness to the weaver vis-à-vis the plaintiff's interests. Alternatively, the Supreme Court could hold that there is no minimum contact, no benefit or protection provided by the state, and no basis for the state to ignore its territorial borders. This choice of rationale becomes critical to our hypothetical problem if we change but one factor, i.e., the relative danger in, or cost of, the product. Instead of a needle in a basket, suppose bolts were improperly inserted when an airplane was manufactured in India, resulting in multiple Nebraska fatalities. Under a *Gray* subjective fairness test, the outcome is changed; whereas under minimum contact-benefit-territorial thinking, the outcome should follow the basket-weaver analysis.

If the state's 'mere effect' fairness approach is subjected to Supreme Court review and the Supreme Court mandates a 'minimum contact and benefits' standard, then the European and Liberian corporations may be insulated from product liability suits. Until such a Supreme Court decision is rendered, state and federal decisions following *Gray* and *Kidwell* must be anticipated. Some states and lower federal courts will not accept the *Gray* and *Kidwell* analysis. These courts will be guided by the fact that every Supreme Court case discusses, and presupposes, 'minimum contact' as a prerequisite. Indeed, every case subsequent to *International Shoe* can be reasonably interpreted to require some direct contact with the state by the defendant himself (or his agent). In an over-simplified summary of the cases, the Court seems to have stated that while physical presence within the jurisdiction is no longer a strict requirement for in personam jurisdiction, certain minimum contacts with the jurisdiction are required. Hence, if the defendant has had no contact, tie or relation with the forum state, there can be no in personam jurisdiction. If there is some contact, tie, or relation, the determination of whether it meets the threshold *minimum* level is dependent upon an evaluation of 'the quality and nature of the [defendant's] activity [in the forum] in relation to the fair and orderly administration of the (forum's) law'[14]. 'Thus the relationship among the defendant, the forum, and the litigation'[15] are the determining factors. 'The facts of each case must be weighed to determine whether the *requisite* "affiliating circumstances" are present'[16].

The court has utilized a nearly identical 'benefits and protection' approach in a closely related, but often overlooked, line of cases[17]. The cases are closely related in that they impose due process limitations on the state legislative power to require non-resident businesses to collect the state's use tax. In every one of these cases, the relationship between the non-resident vendor and the instate consumer was a direct one; that is to say, there were no middlemen or independent contractors involved. And yet, in some of these cases the court held that the due process clause precluded the state from imposing such a duty upon the vendor. In the most recent case the court allowed the state to impose the tax collecting duty on the outstate vendor because 'protection and benefits had been conferred' upon the defendant by the state. 'Here the [defendant's] two offices, without regard to the nature of their activities, had the advantage of the same municipal services—fire and police protection and the like . . .'[18] In this line of cases dealing with legislative power, due process requires some minimum physical connection with, and/or benefit and protection provided by, the state. If these same requirements were applied by courts to jurisdiction questions, then a foreign based company could structure its operations to stay beyond the jurisdiction of domestic courts. However, unless the Supreme Court definitively imposes these requirements, we anticipate expansive trial court decisions based on the subjective fairness standard.

The concept of 'benefit and protection' is also susceptible of vast liberalization. Accordingly, any contract with United States businesses or consumers may influence a court to conclude that the foreign party to the contract has received the 'benefit' of and 'protection' of the state's contract law. Of course physical contact should be avoided. The risk would be reduced if the Liberian and European solar enterprise corporations would negotiate and execute all contracts in Europe or Liberia. Further, the contracts should be completely performed abroad with title and risk of loss passing outside the United States. While these precautions would not guarantee insulation of the foreign corporation from a *Gray* court assertion of jurisdiction, they will provide a strong test case for appeal to the United States Supreme Court.

Jurisdiction via Alter Ego, Agency, or Joint Enterprise

Past trial court decisions concerning jurisdictional reach sometimes utilize terminology such as 'alter ego', 'agency', and 'joint enterprise.' These terms are rarely defined; rather, they are fluid and expansive concepts which are sometimes used interchangeably. They arise in cases where the court seeks to acquire jurisdiction over an outstate or foreign entity which has little or no direct physical or business contact with the jurisdiction. Accordingly, it would appear that the foreign entity is beyond the court's jurisdiction. Yet, courts frequently hold that the non-present foreigner is subject to the court's jurisdiction because *someone else's* presence is ascribed to the foreigner, i.e., he is present through his agent, alter ego or partner.

These concepts are a trap for the unwary. They provide plaintiffs' lawyers and courts with vast areas in which to exercise discretion. Armed with this discretion, some trial courts have applied these fluid concepts so broadly as to ensnare all but the most carefully structured foreign exporter[19]. Until these theories and fluid concepts are understood, one cannot approach assurance of jurisdictional immunity.

In illustrating the present status of these concepts, we need only to delineate and analyze the assertions which a hypothetical plaintiff might make were he to bring suit in a United States court against the Liberian or European corporations. Of course, we here assume *subject matter* jurisdiction irrespective of whether plaintiff is alleging an antitrust cause of action[20] or products liability tort action[21].

The first assertion our hypothetical plaintiff would make is: (1) that *Y* and *Z* are agents of (or in the alternative partners of) the Liberian corporation. As such, the Liberian corporation has a presence in the state through its agents (or partners) and accordingly is subject to in personam jurisdiction; (2) that if the Liberian corporation has a presence in the United States, then its parents have a United States presence because the Liberian corporation is either an agent of the parents, a partner with the parents, or the alter ego of the parents. United States law will be utilized to determine whether an agency exists[22], whether a partnership or joint venture exists, and whether the alter ego doctrine applies. Each concept is different. In addition, the controlling substantive law is state law, and the fifty-one United States jurisdictions are not uniform.

In most jurisdictions, in order to establish the agency theory, the plaintiff would be interested in discovering facts revealing that *Y* and *Z* were subject to the ultimate control of the Liberian corporation. Perhaps *Y* and *Z* were following Liberian instructions when they sought out or negotiated with the American marketing company. From a business standpoint, it would seem the Liberian company would insist on final control over the terms of a contract under which they would transfer valuable patent and technical data[23]. If the alleged agent appears to be acting on behalf of the alleged principal, or tends to further the principal's interests, there is a possibility that the agency concept will be utilized even where there is little evidence of right of control by the principal (the Liberian corporation) and no evidence of actual exercise of control.

Of course, by its very nature, the Liberian subsidiary is subject to the parents' control vis-à-vis their status as controlling shareholders. While parent-subsidiary status alone is not enough to make an agent out of a subsidiary, it does form the foundation for asserting an agency relationship. If the subsidiary and parent share common directors and if the subsidiary appears to be performing a function beneficial to the parents' business, an agency assertion for jurisdictional purposes may prevail. The various state and federal courts use varying tests to support their findings of agency for jurisdiction purposes. One may anticipate that some day the United States Supreme Court will establish due process parameters on the use or abuse of the agency theory[24]. Until such time, extreme caution is in order.

The partnership theory is seldom used in the jurisdictional setting.

Nonetheless, it has great potential, and it may be the appropriate theory to use in this hypothetical. Partnership and joint venture are one and the same for our purposes. Jurisdiction over one member of the partnership or joint venture is jurisdiction over the partnership or venture. Section 6 of the Uniform Partnership Act defines a partnership as 'an association of two or more . . . to carry on as co-owners a business for profit.' A sharing in profits with some ostensible form of control is prima facie evidence of partnership. A partnership can be found to exist under the law irrespective of what the parties call their relationship or believe it to be[25].

Y and *Z*, former competitors, have joined forces and will share profits (commissions) after costs are deducted. The Liberian corporation will also receive profits after reimbursement for costs. The three of them have elements of control over the continuing venture which is producing shared profits. They do seem to have joined forces to promote a common endeavor. Traditionally, joint promoters are joint venturers. Without more facts, a plaintiff might assert that *Y*, *Z* and the Liberian corporation are joint venturers or partners. For a jurisdiction decision which apparently utilized this joint venture theory see *In Re Electric & Musical Ltd., Middlesex Eng.*,[26] a case which cannot be justified under the agency theory because of an absence of control and cannot be justified under the alter ego theory because the corporations were clearly separate and distinct.

It is not inconsistent for the Liberian corporation to be in a dual partnership. That relationship might be used to subject all three foreign partners to the in personam jurisdiction of an American court in suits where plaintiff's cause of action arose out of partnership activity. As stated above, this partnership theory is not often utilized by plaintiffs[27]. This under-use may be premised on the belief that jurisdiction over one partner is not jurisdiction over all individual partners. That belief may be ill-founded, however. Clearly, the acts of the one partner can bind the partnership entity[28]. Some states have laws which provide that a judgment against one partner is collectable against the partnership itself out of partnership assets[29]. While these laws do not permit collection out of the personal assets of non-resident partners who were not joined in the action, the partnership assets and entity are subject to the impact of the court's judgment[30]. This impact would not appear to violate due process and presumably would be a valid judgment.

The most fluid and potentially expansive concept is the alter ego theory. Court decisions often confuse the alter ego concept and the agency concept, and mistakenly use them interchangeably. While they are separate and distinct, they accomplish the same result of expanding the reach of the courts' jurisdiction. Agency presupposes two separate entities, one working for the other. An agency analysis would result in holding the other party (principal) because he could have exercised control had he elected to do so, and he is the party for whom the agent was working. Agency-principal law is well established in the United States. It applies whether or not corporations are involved. The alter ego concept, sometimes aptly described as 'piercing the corporate veil,' is used to deny the existence of two entities. It pierces the corporate existence of one entity and effectively ignores its existence as a separate entity. The entity is perceived as a mere adjunct of the shareholder.

This alter ego concept is a judicial creation in equity. It was initiated to achieve an equitable result, often in contravention of the legislature's incorporation statutes, which statutes implicitly shield shareholders from corporate liability by declaring that corporations are separate entities. Two factors are generally present when shareholders are held liable by resort to this judicial device of piercing the corporate veil. Factor one requires evidence to indicate that the acting shareholder (or parent corporation) did not treat the corporation as a distinct and separate entity. Factor two merely requires a showing that some inequitable result would occur if the court were to recognize the corporate entity when the very shareholder who seeks to use it as a shield had not recognized or treated it as an entity.

Judicial use of alter ego to impose liability upon shareholders is used sparingly in most American states. California courts are among the more liberal users of the doctrines[31]. A co-mingling of corporate funds with the shareholder's personal funds would qualify as evidence under factor one above. In a similar vein, when shareholder funds are used to pay the salaries of corporate employees, or when such employees are controlled by the shareholder, there is strong evidence of failure to treat the corporation as an entity. See *Hoffman Motors Corporation v. Alfa Romeo S.P.A.* 244 F. Supp. 70 (1965), wherein the court stated at page 76: 'the parent completely controlled the subsidiary, setting its policies in Italy, appointing its own officers and employees and directors as officers and employees of the subsidiary and paying their salaries. Under such circumstances, the foreign corporation will not be permitted to hide behind its local instrumentality.'

Failure to treat the corporation as a distinct entity is sometimes evidenced by the contractual or business arrangement between shareholder and corporation. If the corporation is not allowed to prosper or if all the profit is siphoned off to the parent shareholder, then the corporation's separate identity arguably is not being respected[32]. If the hypothetical Liberian corporation were only receiving reimbursement for costs, it would be evidence that it is a mere adjunct, or alter ego, of its parents.

If in fact the Liberian corporation receives all the profits and only reimburses its parents for costs, this becomes evidence in support of joint venture rather than agency or alter ego. An interesting task awaits the lawyer intent upon structuring a foreign business so as to avoid being ensnared by these concepts. Under the present state of the law, with foresight and planning, it is theoretically possible to insulate a foreign corporation from these pitfalls. A United States corporation with ninety wholly owned subsidiaries all operating in the United States believed that it could insulate itself from the venue requirement of a United States federal court. (See *Xerox Corp. v. Litton Industries*, 353 F. Supp. 412 (1973).) The case is a trial court decision which concludes more evidence must be taken and thus is not definitive. However, the opinion contains an interesting analysis of alter ego factual assertions by plaintiff and separate entity factual assertions by defendant.

Factor two of the alter ego theory should not be difficult to meet in a jurisdictional dispute. Of course, if that dispute arises in a plaintiff's suit based on contract, then it may be equitable to limit plaintiff to suing the party with whom he contracted. If he knowingly contracted with a single corporate entity and reasonably anticipated that he would look to that entity alone for redress, then the court in the exercise of its equitable discretion might not conclude that justice requires it to pierce the corporate veil. On the other hand, when tort or antitrust laws are being frustrated from abroad, the court may be compelled to utilize expanded concepts in order to justify jurisdiction over the perpetrators of the wrong. The United States Supreme Court has not addressed itself to these expanding concepts in recent years.

It is unlikely that the Supreme Court would permit the agency or alter ego theories to be utilized in such sham fashion as to undermine and circumvent the basic due process 'minimum contact' cases discussed above. In the few instances where the Supreme Court has addressed these issues, it has generally recognized the separate identities of parent and subsidiary for jurisdictional and venue purposes[33]. While the *United States v. Scophony Corporation* case[34] is capable of being interpreted as limiting these earlier cases, the better view is that the *Scophony* holding is not based upon agency or alter ego analysis. If anything, Scophony Ltd. (British) was found to be *personally* engaged in supervising a partnership business in The United States[35]. If the parent is personally present, there is no need to find a presence by way of subsidiary agents or alter ego subsidiaries. The Ninth Circuit of the United States Court of Appeals recently issued an opinion in which it concluded that a subsidiary's presence should not be attributable to the parent where they were found to be separate entities[36].

To carefully structure the hypothetical plan, one should attempt to fashion as wide a gap between the Liberian corporation and *Y* and *Z* as is realistically possible. Alter ego is of no concern because Liberian is not a shareholder of *Y* and *Z*, but the joint venture and agency concepts are potential concerns. Liberian should make a clean sale and transfer to *Y* and *Z*. *Y* and *Z* should not be required or authorized to collect and forward Liberian's money. *Y* and *Z* should do nothing for Liberian once they have resold the patent rights to a domestic corporation. The fact that the terms of the sale by the Liberian corporation to *Y* and *Z* require resale and negotiation of terms with the United States corporation is evidence of agency. If *Y* and *Z* police and monitor the United States corporation or collect monies for the Liberian corporation, this is further evidence of agency or joint venture. Of course Liberian should not make deliveries in the United States. Title and risk of loss should pass in Liberia. From a practical standpoint, it would be very difficult to conduct and monitor this business without the presence of an alleged agent in America. Moreover, the fact that a patent is involved creates additional difficulties to be discussed *infra*. While Liberian may be able to insulate itself from in personam contractual and antitrust judgments, insulation from product liability suits is speculative so long as the 'effects' theory, discussed *supra*, is followed. In addition, an antitrust judgment and decree against *Y*, *Z* and the United States corporation, can effectively destroy the European and Liberian corporate profit dreams.

Jurisdiction in Rem

Quasi in rem and in rem jurisdiction traditionally are based on attachment and seizure of property physically present in the jurisdiction. It normally is utilized when the defendant owner is not personally subject to the court's jurisdiction. Any resulting judgment affects only the property and does not become a personal obligation of the defendant. Under the ancient territorial theory of jurisdiction, it was believed that the state had jurisdiction over the persons and property within its territory and that the state was without jurisdiction if the person or property was without the territory. As we have seen, the territorial concept has been supplanted with a 'minimum contacts' fairness theory in the area of personam jurisdiction. This change to a fairness theory increased the court's in personam jurisdiction over foreign persons previously insulated. In 1977, the Supreme Court modified the in rem theory and effectively decreased state courts' jurisdiction over property previously thought subject to state court jurisdiction[37].

The *Shaffer* decision holds that the mere presence of property in the jurisdiction does not establish a basis for in rem jurisdiction in those cases where the plaintiff's cause of action is completely unrelated to the property. The court reasons that the due process clause is violated when in rem jurisdiction is asserted in such a case. The court rejected the ancient fiction that 'only the property, and not the person' is affected by in rem judgments. The court concluded that the owner's interest and title is affected by an in rem judgment. Accordingly, due process fairness requires that where the plaintiff's cause of action is completely unrelated to the defendant's property, the action cannot be maintained unless the defendant is subject to in personam jurisdiction. While the property's presence does establish some contact with the state, that contact is insufficient (absent other ties or contact) to establish in personam jurisdiction. Accordingly, the property and person may be insulated from assertions of in personam and in rem jurisdiction[38]. In rem jurisdiction as a concept is not destroyed by this decision. It remains viable in at least two areas, one of which is ill-defined. The *Shaffer* court impliedly sanctioned the utilization of in rem jurisdiction in actions which assert a claim to the property itself. Interestingly enough, however, even here the court alluded to the in personam 'protection and benefit' concept by stating, 'In such cases, the *defendant's claim to property* located in the state would normally indicate that *he* expected to benefit from the state's protection of *his* interest.' (Emphasis added.)

The ill-defined area, as we perceive it, arises by reason of this sentence in the decision:

> The presence of property may also favor jurisdiction in cases such as suits for injury suffered on the land of an absentee owner, where the defendant's ownership of the property is conceded but the cause of action is otherwise related to rights and duties growing out of that ownership.

By this reference to 'suits for injury' the court is referring to a personal injury tort suit premised on an owner's duty to persons entering upon his property. In such suits the property causes or is involved in the injury, but it is the owner's alleged duty (arising out of ownership) which is the crux of the suit. This kind of suit is somewhat similar to product liability suits. In both types of suits, property causes the injury, and liability is contingent on defendant's duty to plaintiff. If in rem jurisdiction can be utilized in one type of suit, it is likely that an attempt will be made to utilize it in the other type of suit. Therefore, an entire shipment of solar units could be subjected to in rem seizure in an antitrust or products liability suit. One distinction which can be drawn between the two types of lawsuits is that in a products liability suit, defendant's duty is not affixed to and does not arise out of the defendant's *ownership* of property within the state. That is to say, the defendant does not own, or receive state benefits relative to, the precise property which causes the products liability injury. Accordingly, the quoted sentence, which refers to related rights and duties growing out of property ownership, does not directly support an assertion of in rem jurisdiction over defendant's unrelated property in a product liability or antitrust suit.

It should be noted that the above quoted sentence was mere dicta on the part of the *Shaffer* court. Unless limited in scope this dicta would seem to be at odds with the court's basic rationale. The court clearly was attempting to limit the use of in rem jurisdiction where in personam jurisdiction is lacking. It said as much in footnote 22 of the opinion wherein it inserted the quote: 'All proceedings, like all rights, are really against persons.' (See also court footnote 23.)[39] Analytically, one must conclude that the concept of in rem is contracting in scope while the concept of in personam is expanding.

The European and Liberian corporations should be alerted to three hybrid types of in rem jurisdiction. All three are creations of federal statute.

Section 293 of the Patent Code applies to non-resident United States patentees and affords the Washington, D.C., District Court jurisdiction over the patentees as to 'any action respecting the patent or rights thereunder[40]. This statute's use against foreign based patentees should be limited to suits respecting patents or patent claims. It should not cover product liability suits. It may, however, cover patent misuse antitrust suits.

Of greater danger to the foreign based companies would be Section 6 of the Sherman Act[41] and Section 76 of the Wilson Tariff Act[42]. Both statutes authorize a type of in rem seizure and forfeiture of property. Section 6 provides:

> Any property owned under any contract or by any combination, or pursuant to any conspiracy (and being the subject thereof) mentioned in Section 1 of this title, and being in the course of transportation from one state to another, or to a foreign country, shall be forfeited to the United States, and may be seized and condemned by like proceedings as those provided by law for the forfeiture, seizure, and condemnation of property imported into the United States contrary to laws.

These statutes are rarely utilized. However, the Antitrust Division of the

Justice Department has resorted to them in cases where alleged foreign antitrust combinations or contracts were present. By seizing the imports or proceeds, the department is able to exert heavy pressure on the foreign conspirators. The Justice Department conceded some years ago that it resorts 'to this method of obtaining jurisdiction because of the fact that the principal parties to the alleged conspiracy were beyond the jurisdiction of this court and non-amenable to its processes'[43]. Invariably the alleged conspirators consent to a court decree enjoining them from continued operation of the conspiracy[44].

The Justice Department might utilize these statutes against the Liberian and European corporations in our hypothetical. Assuming they are carefully structured so as to be insulated from in personam jurisdiction, and assuming they are violating United States antitrust laws, the Justice Department might be tempted to seize the imported items *or* the proceeds destined for the Swiss account. Whether or not the Supreme Court would sanction such a seizure would be dependant upon two elements: (1) whether or not the court would apply the *Shaffer* in rem reasoning to federal courts and to federal authorization statutes; and (2) if it does apply the *Shaffer* reasoning, whether it would perceive this to be a suit arising out of ownership of the property, or—in the alternative—would liken this to an in personam suit. One can speculate on the answers to these questions. Supreme Court due process cases to date are concerned with state power and the Fourteenth Amendment's due process clause. While the Fifth Amendment contains a comparable due process clause which purports to limit federal power, the court has been known to treat the two clauses differently out of deference to the co-equal branches of federal government. Moreover, we are dealing here with specific statutes purporting to grant the court jurisdiction. In both *Kulko* and *Shaffer*, supra, the court intimated that a specific state statute granting jurisdiction might have made a difference. Because of the *Shaffer* requirement that the plaintiff's cause of action must be related to or flow from the property, one must assume that the American-held patent rights and the imported solar units are more vulnerable to seizure than is the money to be transmitted to Switzerland. The patent transfer to the United States company, and the solar units themselves are the very instruments of the antitrust conspiracy. Accordingly, the solar units seem to be vulnerable whether or not title passes to the American company in Liberia, particularly if the United States company is implicated in an antitrust violation. The United States company and *Y* and *Z* will probably be sued as parties to the antitrust combination. Accordingly, not only is any United States-situated property vulnerable, but the entire contractual agreement may be subject to an antitrust decree and injunction. In light of the antitrust discussion to follow, major restructuring of the proposed plan is essential if these problems are to be minimized.

Antitrust Implications

The hypothetical facts present an array of antitrust problems. Indeed, it can be said that the hypothetical solar enterprise is on a fatal collision course with

United States antitrust law. Antitrust law is comprehensive. There are numerous Federal statutes. Should there be an infraction of any one of these laws, the defendant may be subjected to the burden of defending multiple lawsuits. The United States Justice Department might bring criminal or civil suits or both. The United States Federal Trade Commission might initiate separate injunctive suits at the same time in different courts. Moreover, multiple separate civil suits requesting triple damages may be brought by private litigants. All of these suits might arise out of a single violation founded upon a single fact. All of these suits might require defending at the same time. He who ignores antitrust law does so at great risk.

Free and unfettered competition is deemed to be the guardian of economic liberty, and the insurer of material plenitude and individual opportunity. The various antitrust laws are designed to protect the free enterprise economy from anti-competitive practices. Competition is considered essential to the preservation of economic and political freedom[45]. Since Congress has ascribed such fundamental importance to the role of competition, it is easy to understand why it affixed extraterritorial reach to its laws by prohibiting foreign-based business activity which has an anti-competitive damaging effect in the United States. Congress concluded that foreign-based conspiracies, contracts, and mergers could have a serious impact on domestic competition. Moreover, if the location of the conspiracy were allowed to immunize it from United States law, the laws could easily be evaded and there would be business incentive to abandon United States—based operations in favor of foreign (immunized) operations. Accordingly, Congress has asserted its constitutional power over interstate and foreign commerce, and has prohibited all violations affecting trade or commerce among the states or with foreign nations irrespective of where the violation occurs.

The precise parameters of the antitrust laws' extraterritorial reach remains unclear. The Antitrust Division of the United States Justice Department recently issued an informative guide for the international businessman wherein the Department said: 'When foreign transactions have a substantial and foreseeable effect on United States commerce, they are subject to United States law regardless of where they take place'[46]. The Justice Department's use of the terminology is not definitive; hence, it leaves the basis for determining substantiality and foreseeability largely up to the discretion of the courts. Moreover, the courts and private plaintiffs are not bound by the Justice Department's pronouncement, suits may be brought on the basis of *mere* injurious *effect* on United States commerce. The Congressional statutes, as written, lend themselves to this 'mere effect' interpretation. Characteristically, in the absence of an authoritative ruling by the Supreme Court, different lower courts construe and apply a single statute differently.

A recent Ninth Circuit Court of Appeals ruling illustrates the various elements and concepts which it believes must be weighed in reaching a decision on extraterritorial reach[47]. In summary, the Ninth Circuit concluded that there are three parts to an extraterritorial reach test, namely;

(1) Does the alleged restraint affect, or was it intended to affect, the

foreign commerce of the United States? (2) Is it of such a type and magnitude so as to be cognizable as a violation of the Sherman Act? (3) As a matter of international comity and fairness, should the extraterritorial jurisdiction of the United States be asserted to cover it[48]?

It is significant that factor (1) uses 'affect' or 'intended to affect' in the alternative. An additional caveat should be noted: the 'international comity' factor under (3) is not traditionally an element which need be considered for purposes of determining subject matter jurisdiction, and it is highly unlikely that all courts will apply this factor. Consequently, the single element which will consistently be applied is whether or not the foreign activity affects American commerce in some substantial manner. When determining whether or not commerce is substantially affected, the court will focus upon the degree of interference with the goals of antitrust law rather than dollar amounts. The Justice Department guide sets forth two goals: (1) the protection of United States consumers by assuring them the benefits of foreign competition, and (2) the protection of American initiative and investment opportunity. These goals are very broad. When the two European manufacturers impliedly agree to terminate competition with each other in sales to the United States, the interference with the first goal is obvious.

Irrespective of which of the above tests is utilized, the hypothetical solar enterprise falls easily within the territorial reach of United States antitrust law. The whole purpose and intent of the enterprise is to exploit the United States market and to lessen competition therein. Accordingly, subject matter jurisdiction and territorial reach of the law are not likely to be effective avoidance-defenses. As previously suggested, it is somewhat risky to assume that the due process clause will act as an insulator from United States Court jurisdiction and judgments. Moreover, even if the clause does insulate the European corporations or the Liberian corporation or both from judgments, it will not insulate them from the damaging impact of court decrees directed against *Y*, *Z* and the American corporation if they are found to have violated antitrust law. Accordingly, we turn our attention to the specific laws which are brought into play by the solar enterprise facts.

The hypothetical plan may violate the following federal statutes:

(1) Sections 1 and 2 of the Sherman Act, prohibiting contracts, combinations or conspiracies in restraint of trade, and prohibiting acts of monopolization or attempts to monopolize any part of commerce[49];

(2) Section 7 of the Clayton Act prohibiting mergers, asset acquisitions, or joint ventures, where the effect may be to substantially lessen competition[50];

(3) Section 3 of the Clayton Act prohibiting certain conditions in the sale of goods and restricting the use of requirements contracts, territorial divisions, tying agreements, etc.[51];

(4) Section 337 of the 1930 Tariff Act regulating unfair activity respecting patents[52];

(5) Section 73 of the Wilson Tariff Act prohibiting unfair methods of competition and restraint of trade respecting imports[53]; and

(6) Section 5 of the F.T.C. Act prohibiting 'Unfair methods of competition in commerce, and unfair or deceptive acts or practices . . .'[54].

The above is an imprecise condensation of the statutory provisions. Additional laws may be applicable, depending upon the presence of facts unnoticed or unstated in the hypothetical[55].

In applying the statutes to the solar enterprise hypothetical, we note initially that two joint ventures were formed. The *very formation* of a joint venture may violate Sherman 1 or 2, or Clayton 7, and/or Section 5 of the FTC Act. In addition, specific contractual *terms* defining operational parameters of the venture may violate Sherman 1 or 2, as well as Clayton 3. Moreover, the *duration* of the joint venture and its *operational impact* are subject to scrutiny under the above acts.

While there is a paucity of joint venture cases involving extraterritorial parties, the creation of the Liberian subsidiary presents a classic situation where Clayton 7 would apply. The parents were horizontal competitors before the joint venture[56]. Both parents were engaged in commerce in the United States[57]. The effect of the joint venture will be to lessen substantially competition or to tend to create a monopoly in a line of commerce[58]. There is little doubt that Clayton 7 is applicable to the creation of the Liberian corporation. *If* jurisdiction can be obtained, the court will be likely to order dissolution of the joint venture. Sherman 1 and 2 also appear to be violated by creation of the subsidiary, since an implied agreement creating a monopoly in a line of commerce appears to exist. At the very least an attempt to monopolize appears to be present.

The activities of agents *Y* and *Z* may also violate Clayton 7. They were previous competitors. They have joined forces by jointly acquiring and transferring Liberian's patent rights and by sharing royalties or commissions. They seem to be partners or joint venturers in contractual rights acquired from the Liberian corporation[59]. United States courts will have jurisdiction over *Y*, *Z* and the American corporation to whom the Liberian corporation transfer the right to patent.

The solar business activities of the three American parties will be subjected to scrutiny under all six of the above noted statutes. Should a single violation be found—and it most assuredly will be under the hypothetical facts[60]—the judgment and decree of the court will undoubtedly affect the European and Liberian corporations. The antitrust decree may enjoin the American parties from performing their contracts with the Liberian corporation[61], or might require mandatory patent licensing or both. It may also void use or territorial restrictions. The impact on the European businesses may be disastrous. Consequently, the European attorney and business structurer should be concerned about antitrust infractions committed by his client's United States distributors or patent holders, even though the European client is not a party to the infraction or is beyond the court's jurisdiction. In addition, he should be alert to the possibility that the foreign company may be named as co-conspirator (but not joined in the suit) with an American party. It must be emphasized that if a United States citizen is found to have conspired or entered into an agreement in violation of antitrust law, a court decree may affect a foreign party's contracts and his relationships with the American violator. In summary, three distinct business relationships and zones of inquiry are involved in the solar hypothetical, each one of which constitutes an antitrust concern to the European corporations. They are:

(1) the relationship and agreements between the European companies themselves, and between them and the Liberian company;

(2) the relationship and agreements between the Liberian company and *Y* and *Z*, and between the Liberian company and the American company; and,

(3) the relationship and agreements between *Y*, *Z* and the United States company.

While the validity of a triple damage-money judgment against a foreigner is dependent upon due process jurisdiction over him (and also upon personal involvement under groups 1 and 2 above), the before-mentioned destructive court decrees are not dependent upon such jurisdiction.

Due to the pervasive antitrust problems in the plan as presented, some restructuring of the solar enterprise is essential. To minimize the impact of Clayton 7 on formation of the two joint ventures, we might revise one fact, to wit, the two European corporations forming the Liberian corporation had *not* previously marketed or competed in the United States. This revision of the facts permits the formation of the joint venture without violation of Clayton 7 for two reasons: (1) the parties to the venture are not engaged in United States commerce per the terms of Clayton 7; and (2) the creation of a joint venture does not substantially lessen competition in the United States, but may actually increase competition[62].

This fact revision should also remove the joint venture from Clayton 7 condemnation because it removes the damning fact of previously having been competitors in the handling of European solar units. A caveat is in order, however. The fact revision does not remove the European joint venture from scrutiny under Section 2 of the Sherman Act[63]. Since these two European corporations possess patented technology in a unique product or line of commerce, their joining of forces is an act of monopolization under Sherman 2. Moreover, because their joint venture is intended to have, and presumably will have, an anticompetitive effect in the United States, it will be vulnerable to Sherman 1 attack unless it is 'necessary'[64].

Assuming the formation qua formation of the joint venture does not violate antitrust law, one should next consider the terms of all agreements between the parties and the transfer and sale or licensing of the patents, and know-how. For our purposes we can only guess at the hypothetical terms and accordingly must generalize. Suffice it to say, Section 1 of the Sherman Act ostensibly covers any and all unreasonable restraints of trade, that is all unreasonable limitations, discouragements, or restrictions (contractual or ostensibly covers any and all unreasonable restraints of trade, that is, all to operate one's business. (The question of unreasonableness is determined by applying a combined alternative means and weighing test). Moreover, certain restraints are per se unreasonable. Both Sherman 1 and Clayton 3 are applicable with respect to tying arrangements, requirements contracts, and exclusive territorial restrictions upon one's distributor.

The agreement entered into between the Liberian corporation and the United States corporation is invalid per se. It can be attacked and invalidated by the United States corporation itself. The proffered agreement conditioned the sale of the patent on the purchase of all required solar units. The patent is the tying item, and the solar units are the tied product. The tying item is clearly unique and gives the seller power which he uses to extract sales in another product line, i.e., the solar units. Therefore, it is illegal per se[65]. Of course this assumes the patent rights were sold to the American company which then obtained a United States patent in its name. Because a patentee has an inherent right to manufacture the patented item, the Liberian restriction on the United States patent holder may be attacked as a patent misuse[66]. Moreover, because the patentee is completely restricted in utilization of the patent, it may be evidence that the patentee is a mere agent for the Liberian corporation. In any event, the patent-requirements contract arrangement will be invalidated if attacked, and it can be attacked by the American corporation. Equally foreboding is the threat of a suit by the Justice Department, for in such event, the court decree would be likely to require the United States company to license any manufacturer applicant who wished to procure the superior electrical units. When patents are used as a means of antitrust violation, compulsory licensing of others is increasingly employed in antitrust decrees[67].

It seems that the proposed plan needs revision in this area of patent sale. Instead of selling, the Liberian corporation would be better advised to obtain United States patent rights in its own name. Sales of the units should then be made to an independent United States distributor. Y and Z, who appear to be mere agents, should be eliminated from the operation. By keeping the patent rights in the Liberian corporation, we have avoided the tying problem, the requirements contract problem, and the patent misuse problem. This revision of the plan may result in preferential United States income tax treatment, and it prevents the patent right from being considered an asset of the United States corporation in the event of bankruptcy.

The fact revisions do not turn what was a horrible antitrust situation into a perfect one. Some problems remain even if we assume the precise terms of all agreements will be carefully drafted by a knowledgeable antitrust lawyer. The very appointment of an exclusive distributor creates possible grounds for a claim of unreasonable restraint of trade. Obviously it would be extremely dangerous to select a potential United States competitor as one's distributor[68]. Moreover, it is dangerous to restrict the distributor's market area[69]. The most significant risk resides in the very fact that two European competitors have joined to utilize one Liberian distributor, thereby involving the distributor in a three-party conspiracy to lessen competition or create a monopoly in the United States market[70].

Tax Implications

The Liberian corporation will be required to pay a United States tax on some of its income unless the hypothetical facts are changed. The rate of tax, and the portion of income taxed, is dependent upon a determination of whether Liberian is conducting a trade or business in the United States either itself or through agents (*Y* and *Z*) or a partner (the United States corporation). If found to be conducting business in the United States, the Liberian corporation's *net* income is subject to taxation at United States corporate tax rates (currently, forty-six per cent of net income above one-hundred-thousand dollars plus lower rates on initial one-hundred-thousand dollars. With careful structuring and planning the Liberian corporation can avoid this conducting-business status.

Even if the Liberian corporation is not conducting business in the United States, a portion of its United States-source gross receipts probably is going to be taxed at a thirty per cent rate. United States-source royalty payments made to foreigners are subject to a thirty per cent tax on *gross* receipts unless lower rates are provided for by treaty. Because it is a tax on gross receipts no deductions are allowed. The United States payer of the royalty must withhold the tax from his royalty payment, and forward the tax to the Treasury. The Treasury Department will probably claim that the contract arrangement between the Liberian and the United States corporations is a disguised royalty arrangement or a contingency sale of a patent. (The income from a contingency sale is treated like royalty income and taxed at the thirty per cent rate). A contingency sale of patents takes place if the *amount* of proceeds from the sale is contingent upon the volume or number of units manufactured or sold, or contingent upon use or disposition of the interest sold. In other words, a sale of a patent is not contingent if the sale price is definite and settled (for example, one-hundred-thousand dollars cash). On the other hand, the patent sale is contingent if the sale price is for example, 'one dollar per unit manufactured under the patent[71]'.

The hypothetical involves transfer to the United States corporation of the right to patent. A definite sales price is not utilized. The United States corporation will be paying for this patent transfer as it purchases the Liberian corporation's products on a continuing and required basis. This payment for the patent rights is based on the volume of products purchased and hence is contingent. The Treasury Department's Internal Revenue Service (hereafter IRS) probably will claim that a portion of each payment made by the United States corporation to the Liberian corporation is consideration attributable to the contingency sale of a patent. This portion of the gross receipts would be subject to taxation at the rate of thirty per cent. The other portion will be deemed attributable to the real purchase price of the solar units. It is conceivable the IRS will claim that other portion is derived from a trade or business conducted by the Liberian corporation through its partners or agents in the United States. To avoid this latter characterization, it would behove the Liberian corporation to avoid all indicia and attributes of agency or partnership.

In restructuring the facts, the Liberian corporation should not transfer any patent rights to the United States corporation. Instead, the Liberian corporation should acquire and hold the United States patent rights. It should then sell the patented *product* to some independent United States contractor. The sale of all products should take place in Liberia with title, risk of loss and consideration passing in Liberia. Arguably, profits from such Liberian sales of the product are derived entirely from sources and transactions without the United States. The Liberian corporation might thus avoid all United States tax. Note, however, that this arrangement might be challenged by the IRS if its primary purpose is thought to be tax avoidance. Moreover, even under this arrangement, one must be careful lest a partnership between the United States corporation and the Liberian corporation be found. Still further, the IRS may assert that part of the sales price received for the patented products is attributable to the protections and privileges afforded a United States patent holder, and accordingly the Liberian patent holder would be deemed to have income derived from a United States source.

The United States does not have a tax convention or treaty with Liberia. Since there are such treaties with numerous other countries, the selection of Liberia might be reconsidered. Under these treaties a foreign corporation which qualifies can completely immunize itself from United States income taxes upon corporate profits and royalties. Such treaty provisions are illustrated by the following selected portions of the Germany-United States treaty, operative 1 January, 1954.

ARTICLE III

1. Industrial or commercial *profits* of an enterprise of one of the contracting states shall be exempt from tax by the other State unless the enterprise is engaged in trade or business in such other State through a permanent establishment situated therein. ...

Section (1) c. of Article II defines permanent establishment in detail. For our purposes it is worth noting two portions of that detailed definition. Section (1) c(dd) states:

> Even if an enterprise of one of the contracting States does not have a permanent establishment in the other State under subparagraph (c) (aa) to (cc) of this paragraph, nevertheless it shall be deemed to have a permanent establishment in the latter State if it is engaged in trade or business in that State through an agent who has an authority to conclude contracts in the name of the enterprise and regularly exercises that authority in that State, unless the exercise of authority is limited to the purchase of goods or merchandise for the account of the enterprise.

Also (ee) states:

> An enterprise of one of the contracting States shall not be deemed to have a permanent establishment in the other State merely because it is engaged in trade or business in that other State

> through a broker, general commission agent or any other agent of an independent status, where such person is acting in the ordinary course of business.

With respect to royalties, Article VIII of the German-United States tax treaty states in relevant portion:

'(1) Royalties derived by a . . . German company shall be exempt from tax by the United States'.

The treaty defines royalties to include gains from the alienation of any right or property giving rise to such royalties. These royalty exemptions from tax do not apply if the recipient of the royalty is found to have a permanent establishment in the United States.

Similar United States treaties are operative with respect to numerous other countries including Switzerland, Sweden, Belgium and the United Kingdom. While the terminology is quite different in some of these treaties, the treatment of profits and royalties is similar. The France-United States treaty is similar in its treatment of profits, but it does not completely immunize royalty income. The Japan-United States treaty is quite different in its treatment of both profits and royalties.

Taxation of corporate income by states of the United States may be preempted by a treaty. In the absence of such preemption, state taxation of corporate income can be a significant factor.

Because there is no treaty between the United States and Liberia we anticipate that the IRS would rigorously apply United States tax law and United States source-of-income rules per the previous discussion. If United States tax implications were the sole consideration, Liberia is not the ideal location from which to exploit the United States market.

Products Liability

The basic substantive law controlling the subject of liability for defective products in the United States is state rather than Federal law. Accordingly, these laws vary from one jurisdiction to another, and it is best to begin with some general principles.

If the loss resulting from a defective product is categorized as an 'economic loss', or 'commercial loss', most states will analyze the rights of the plaintiff (claimant) by applying the law of contracts, specifically the law of sales of goods[72]. Such 'economic' or 'commercial loss' would include such things as diminished value of the goods themselves and loss of profits or benefits resulting from the loss of use of inferior performance of the goods[73]. Such loss has been held to have occurred where a seller supplied the wrong type of oil which resulted in an engine being ruined[74].

If the loss resulting from the defective product is death of or injury to a human being, whether or not it is a person who purchased the goods or was actually using the goods, the rights of the plaintiff will be determined by application of tort law in virtually all states[75].

The problem area, which has been the subject of extensive debate and conflicting positions, involves cases in which there is damage to property but no personal injury or death. From the decided cases it appears that courts are distinguishing between accidental injury to property (which would be decided under tort law) and conditions which cause loss of use or loss of potential benefits from the goods (which would be decided under the contracts law dealing with sales warranties). This is a distinction which, like obscenity, is easier to 'know' than it is to explain.

In the case of *Russell v. Ford Motor Co.*,[76] the Supreme Court of the State of Oregon held that a defective weld on an axle housing which caused a vehicle to turn over created a cause of action in tort despite the absence of any claim of personal injury. In its opinion the Court reviewed prior Oregon Supreme Court decisions rendered over the previous thirteen years, noting: in some cases the opinions had stated that the line should be drawn between losses resulting from an 'accident'; in some cases the line was drawn between products which were or were not 'unreasonably dangerous'; and, in other cases the distinction was made between defects which did or did not create a danger to human life. The opinion included the following:

> The focus in the foregoing evolution of products liability has been on the premise for (sic) the seller's responsibility beyond warranty or negligence, though the motivating concern was with injuries to personal health. ... Had it been absolute liability, making an enterprise an insurer against harm caused by its products, the focus in delimiting this remedy would have been on the characteristics of the plaintiff and his injury rather than on those of the defendant and his product. It has, however, been on the latter. ... Whether the seller has met this responsibility cannot depend on the fortuitous extent of the damage done when the danger created by the defect subsequently comes to pass.
>
> ... The loss must be a consequence of the kind of danger and occur under the kind of circumstances, 'accidental' or not, that made the condition of the product a basis or strict liability. This distinguishes such a loss from economic losses due only to the poor performance or the reduced resale value of a defective, even a dangerously defective, product[77].

(The law of the State of Oregon is not selected as an example because it makes the subject clear nor because Oregon is the leading jurisdiction in the United States. It simply demonstrates the problems which many states are experiencing).

A California court has held that a defect in a heater which caused a fire and destroyed a house gave rise to an action in tort for products liability[78]. This situation is somewhat analogous to the type of loss which might be anticipated from defective solar generators. Where there is an element of loss which will be treated as giving rise to a claim in tort, then the law of tort is applied to the entire claim even though some of the elements of damage, considered alone, would have been labeled 'economic loss' and would have been handled under contract law[79].

The decision to treat a plaintiff's loss as one arising in contract as distinguished from tort produces significant differences with respect to the law's treatment of jurisdiction, liability, procedure and damages. If a claim for loss is treated under the substantive law of contracts, the historical premise was that only the buyer of the goods was a proper plaintiff and only the immediate seller was a proper defendant. The category of persons who may have legal rights has been extended to include members of the buyer's family and household and guests in the buyer's home. Some jurisdictions have further extended the category of proper plaintiffs to include any person who may reasonably be expected to use, consume or be affected by the goods[80]. The basic rule is that liability is still limited to the immediate seller of the goods, as distinguished from manufacturers or others in the chain of distribution. Exceptions have been made where a remote party has made representations in advertisements or has otherwise expressly warranted the goods in a fashion that the buyer has been invited to rely upon those representatives[81].

Contract liability can be avoided or limited if there is a clear disclaimer of warranties or limitation of liability by the seller[82]. Limitation or exclusion of damages for injury to the person is prima facie unconscionable[83], but such losses are now governed by the law of tort as noted above. Liability can extend to any loss resulting from general or particular requirements and needs of the buyer of which the seller at the time of contracting had reason to know[84]. Notice of the defect must be given to the seller within a reasonable time after the buyer discovered or should have discovered the defect or all right of action is lost[85]. Liability is predicated upon a loss resulting from the goods being of a type or quality which does not conform to the warranties expressly made by the seller or implied by the law of sales of goods[86]. The buyer need not prove any other 'fault' on the part of the seller, and proof of the absence of 'fault' by the seller is not a defense.

Virtually all states would apply the law of tort to the losses sustained in the problem presented as each claim is partly or wholly for personal injury or wrongful death. As distinguished from a contract action, tort law permits any person who sustained a loss which was proximately (legally) caused by a defective product to maintain an action for that loss. Liability can extend to the manufacturer and to all parties who sold the product and possibly to all parties who can be termed an integral part of the enterprise that placed the defective product in the stream of commerce[87]. Tort law does not permit the disclaimer of liability or limitation of liability. Liability extends to all losses proximately caused by the defect without regard to whether they arose from circumstances of facts of which the seller had reason to know. Proof of the amount of damages is subject to the more relaxed rules as to certainty which apply in tort law as distinguished from contract law. There is no requirement that the injured party give prompt notice when the defect is or should have been discovered.

1. Jurisdiction

If the nature of the action for losses arising from a defective product were such that a state would apply the law of contracts, the plaintiff would have to establish minimum contacts of the defendant with the state in question in order to acquire jurisdiction. As the problem is presented, Corporations *A* and *B* and the Liberian corporation do not appear to have any contacts with any state in the United States, unless those contacts are attributed to them by way of their United States counterparts. (See Agency, alter ego and piercing discussion, *supra*).

The nature of the proposed activities of the Liberian corporation (sales and delivery of goods to the agents or to the United States distributor) would no doubt provide the necessary minimum contacts in at least one state in the United States, but they might not subject the foreign corporations to jurisdiction in all states. In addition, jurisdiction over the funds which are payable to the Liberian corporation could be asserted under a quasi in rem theory. (See quasi in rem and in rem discussion, *supra*). Jurisdiction over the United States corporation and the agents, *Y* and *Z*, would depend upon further facts regarding the nature of their activities in the particular state in which the action was brought, but it is obvious that these United States entities would be subject to the jurisdiction of one or more states.

Since the nature of the plaintiff's suits in the hypothetical problem involve the substantive law of torts, the jurisdiction question is very different. United States law purportedly allows a state to assert jurisdiction over any person who commits a tort in that state and most states have adopted statutes which do so[88]. The basic proposition is that the tort is committed where the last element of the tort occurred, which in this case would be injury resulting from the defect. This element occurred in the state where the plaintiffs are located and thus all of the parties, including Corporations *A*, *B*, and the Liberian corporation, are potentially subject to the jurisdiction of that state. There would probably be no jurisdiction over a European corporation which made and sold a product in Europe with no reason to know that it would be taken to the United States to be used or resold[89]. However, in the problem presented, importation into the United States for resale and use is an intended result of the marketing system utilized by Corporations *A* and *B*, and many states would hold that they are subject to the jurisdiction of the state where their defective product caused injury. (See discussion of in personam jurisdiction, *supra*).

Jurisdiction may not be defeated on the grounds that Corporations *A* and *B* are merely manufacturers of component parts. If their components constituted only a minor part of the product in question, jurisdiction would not exist unless there was a showing of sufficient economic benefit from the forum state to make it fair to require a defense in that state. But under the facts presented in the problem, this issue presumably is not presented[90]. (The fact that only one of the two component parts is defective, and thus presumably only one of the two corporations has committed a tort making it subject to jurisdiction in the forum state, creates a problem with which we will deal under 'Liability', *infra*).

2. Choice of Law

The result most frequently reached on the choice of law issue is application of the law of the jurisdiction where the injury occurred. There is some authority, however, for applying the law of the place where the defendant's wrongful conduct occurred, which in the case of Corporations *A* or *B* would be the country in which they manufactured the goods[91]. It would appear reasonable to predict that a state court in the United States would consider the protection of the rights of persons in that state to be the paramount concern. Thus it would be highly unlikely that such a court would apply the law of any jurisdiction which did not afford to the plaintiffs the same basic substantive rights that they would enjoy under the law of the forum state[92].

3. Liability

The basic questions in a tort action for products liability are whether or not the defendant manufactured or sold a defective product and whether that defect was the cause of the plaintiff's damages or injury. The plaintiff must prove that the product was defective when it left the defendant's hands or that the defect resulted from subsequent foreseeable mishandling. The defendant may not avoid liability by proving that he exercised appropriate care or was otherwise without fault.

The *American Law Institute Restatement of Torts (Second)*, Section 402 A, provides:

> (1) One who sells any product in a defective condition unreasonably dangerous to the user or consumer or to his property is subject to liability for physical harm thereby caused to the ultimate user or consumer, or to his property if
> (a) the seller is engaged in the business of selling such a product, and
> (b) it is expected to and does reach the user or consumer without substantial change in the condition in which it is sold.
> (2) The rule stated in Subsection (1) applies although
> (a) the seller has exercised all possible care in the preparation and sale of his product, and
> (b) the user or consumer has not bought the product from or entered into any contractual relation with the seller.

While it is sometimes stated by practicing attorneys that products liability is virtually absolute, for example, 'if the product caused an injury or damage, it must have been defective', in fact the plaintiff must establish that the 'malfunction' mentioned in the problem comes within the above definition. Factors which may be considered in making this determination include the state of the art, defects in design, non-conformity with specifications, inappropriate method of construction, availability of alternatives, cost of such alternatives, benefit to consumers from the availability of these goods, and absence of warning or notice of particular traits of the product. The burden of proof is on the defendant with respect to some of these factors[93].

Proof that the defect in the product concerned was the actual cause of the plaintiff's damages is often a major issue in products liability cases. In the problem presented, the facts appear to stipulate that the malfunction caused the injury, but the plaintiff would have to establish causal connection between the malfunction and the particular product defect or defects which the plaintiff was able to prove.

If the product were being used in other than in the intended fashion, this could defeat liability. The given facts indicate this is not the case.

Since the facts indicate that the malfunction occurred in *either* the generator or the collector, and since jurisdiction over Corporation A or Corporation B is predicated upon those corporations having committed a tort in the forum state, a question is presented as to whether either or both corporations are subject to jurisdiction if the plaintiff cannot present more specific facts concerning who is the alleged tortfeasor[94]. The plaintiff could be defeated on the jurisdiction question and on the substantive law question of liability if it cannot establish with reasonable certainty which component had the defect which caused the loss. However, there are circumstances in which a plaintiff need prove only that one of the defendants did tortiously cause the plaintiff's injury and thus establish the plaintiff's right to judgment against all such defendants. At this stage, each defendant has the burden of proving that it is not the responsible party[95].

As previously stated, the plaintiff's burden of proof also requires that he establish that the defect existed when the product left the hands of the defendant. There are insufficient facts given to explore this issue. If the defect involves design or materials, for example, the plaintiff has no particular problem. If the defect is one which could have been caused by improper handling during shipment or assembly after the goods left the defendant's control, then the plaintiff has the burden of proving that such mishandling is not the cause of the defect or that the defendant should have foreseen and guarded against such mishandling[96].

The remaining question is the potential liability of the agents, *Y* and *Z*, for products liability. This issue turns upon whether they are merely agents acting for a disclosed principal or are parties who acted as 'sellers.' (*See Restatement of Torts* (*Second*), Section 402 *A*, *supra*).

Contractual Considerations

As set forth in the problem, Corporations *A* and *B* are marketing in the United States through *Y* and *Z*, respectively; *Y* and *Z* are described as 'independent foreign market agents'. Without additional facts, it is not possible to determine the true status of *Y* and *Z* with the description given. Under United States law, agents act for, and on behalf of, their principals and subject to their principals' right to control. Thus, they are not independent. If, on the other hand, they are independent business entities, enjoying exclusive rights to sell the energy units of *A* and *B* on the United States market, then they are not properly described as agents. If *Y* and *Z* are in fact agents, their actions and presence produce the same legal consequences with respect to jurisdiction and antitrust laws as if *A* and *B* were conducting such activities in the United States through their own employees.

It is not apparent why the proposed plan of action contemplates the continued involvement of *Y* and *Z* as we cannot discern what benefit comes from that involvement. We see serious legal disadvantages apart from the fact that the five per cent, or five-hundred dollars per unit commission could be saved.

Because of the rather unique arrangement whereby the United States marketing corporation will take the patents in its own name, but will refrain from manufacturing and instead will purchase the component parts exclusively from the Liberian corporation, it is difficult to categorize the nature of the payments which are to be made by the United States corporation. Certainly a portion of those payments may properly be allocated to the purchase of the component parts. The right to obtain the United States patents was transferred to the United States corporation in exchange for its promise to buy the patented items exclusively from the Liberian corporation, and thus the only value which the United States corporation is giving for the patent rights transferred is a portion of the purchase price, that is, a part of the seventy per cent or seventy-five per cent of the gross sales price. For this reason, the balance of the money paid (in excess of the portion allocated to the purchase of the goods) could be described as deferred compensation for the transfer of the right to patent. However, because of the restrictions upon the rights which the United States corporation obtains with its patents, a court could adopt the view that the beneficial interest in the patents was really retained by the Liberian corporation in which case the balance of the money paid might be categorized as royalty payments. Since the United States Government might tax royalty payments without foreign tax credit (depending upon the particular treaty involved), this latter characterization of the payments might be pursued by the United States tax agencies.

While United States courts might be receptive to the argument that the United States patents should be treated as beneficially owned by the Liberian corporation for tax purposes, a different treatment should be expected in the event of the bankruptcy of the United States corporation. In that event, the assets of the United States corporation, including the patents, would pass to the trustee in bankruptcy to be used or sold for the benefit of the estate of the bankrupt and ultimately for the benefit of the bankrupt's creditors. Corporations *A* and *B* and their Liberian subsidiary would thus lose any effective control over the United States patents. The trustee of the United States corporation's bankrupt estate could (and undoubtedly would) elect to disaffirm the unperformed portions of the United States corporation's contract with the Liberian corporation, thus leaving the Liberian corporation with the sole remedy of filing an unsecured creditor's claim for its money damages resulting from the breach of contract. Since this claim would result in a distribution ranging from nothing to something less than one hundred per cent of the claim, the sad result would be that the United States patents would be lost and the Liberian corporation would have nothing but a dollar distribution from the bankruptcy proceeding. Any restructuring of the proposed plan of action should involve keeping the ownership of the United States patents in *A* and *B* or their Liberian subsidiary, or carefully constructing a security agreement which would give them a perfected security interest in the patent rights to secure full performance of the balance of the contract obligations of the United States corporation to the Liberian corporation[97].

Restructuring the Plan

The facts presented and the plan of action proposed present such clear, obvious violations of United States antitrust laws, and the results of such violations would be so disastrous that proposals for restructuring must involve fundamental alterations. The first proposal is not a true solution of the problem presented. It involves anticipating the United States problems prior to Corporations *A* and *B* entering the United States market as competitors. As discussed in the antitrust section, two separate corporations can act in concert in the development of a product which they have not previously marketed as competitors where such joint activity is reasonable. Thus if one could 'turn back the clock,' one could structure a joint marketing program utilizing any number of organizational devices. This would not cause all antitrust problems to dissolve, but it would remove the rather obvious per se violation which could be found if these two corporations, which are already competitors in the United States market, were to join forces with each other.

The second proposal for restructuring the transaction involves avoiding the monopolistic aspects which arise from Corporations *A* and *B* acting through a single marketer. This would presumably result in sacrificing some of the rather exorbitant profits which the given plan of action contemplates, which, not incidentally, is precisely what the United States antitrust laws were designed to accomplish.

Corporations A and B could each obtain United States patents on their respective devices and could cross-license each other to use those patents. Each could thus produce and market in the United States the superior units which combine the best features. They would remain in competition with each other in the United States market, but each would presumably enjoy a significant competitive edge over other sellers. In implementing this proposal, each corporation could set up and utilize such Liberian or other tax-haven organizations as they deemed appropriate.

Since this 'solution' presumably involves sacrificing a substantial part of the profits which the proposed plan of action anticipated, it might be viewed as no solution at all. However, it is a bit like advising a friend not to rob a bank. This advice does not suggest the most profitable course of action, but it has the virtue of not violating the law.

The third proposal for restructuring the transaction is risky but theoretically possible. It involves making certain that all actions which arguably would constitute a violation of the United States antitrust laws are undertaken by parties which are not subject to United States jurisdiction. A secondary aspect of this proposal is to avoid actions which would be clear violations of United States antitrust laws in order to avoid challenging the United States government and private parties in the United States to find some basis for asserting jurisdiction.

The first step in this proposal would be for Corporations *A* and *B* to independently terminate their present marketing activities in the United States and to terminate all other contact with the United States which might constutite a basis for United States jurisdiction. (This might be highly impractical if *A* or *B* have other marketing activities in the United States in addition to the sales in question.) Part of this procedure would involve the termination of relationships with *Y* and *Z*, making whatever financial settlement with these agents as may be necessary.

If *A* and *B* wish to operate through a Liberian subsidiary, then the second step would be for each to separately incorporate its own subsidiary in Liberia. Thereafter, these Liberian subsidiaries would obtain United States patents for the various components.

After the above steps have been accomplished, one of the Liberian subsidiaries could invite representatives of a United States corporation to come to Liberia to discuss the purchase of solar generating equipment. Each Liberian corporation would separately negotiate a contract with the United States corporation which would provide for sale of the appropriate units in Liberia. These sales would be for cash, payable in Liberia, and would provide for delivery of the goods in Liberia. Given the hypothetical facts respecting costs and potential market prices, the sale price for each of the basic components of the superior unit might be approximately three-thousand five hundred dollars. The United States corporation would transport the units to the United States and assemble and sell them in the United States, retaining all of the proceeds of such sales.

The United States corporation would not be guaranteed any exclusive right in the United States market. (Such a guarantee would very probably constitute a violation of United States antitrust laws for which the United States Justice Department could take action based upon jurisdiction over the United States corporation.) The United States corporation would be assured that no sales would be made to others for resale in the United States market on more favorable terms. (This provision does not violate United States antitrust laws and is probably legally required under United States law).[98] The Liberian corporations could in fact sell to more than one United States corporation for resale in the United States, and such introduction of competition should have the result of expanding the total United States market to the ultimate benefit of Corporations *A* and *B*.

Establishing the fact of violation of the United States antitrust laws would involve proof that Corporations *A* and *B* (or their respective Liberian subsidiaries) were acting in concert when they ceased selling in the United States market, created their subsidiaries, entered negotiations with the United States corporations or priced their respective components at $3,500 each. Assuming that any one of these facts is subject to proof, their insulation from the penalties of United States antitrust laws is dependent upon them not being subject to United States jurisdiction.

The action of the Liberian subsidiaries in obtaining United States patents subjects those corporations to United States jurisdiction only for the limited purpose of patent jurisdiction[99].

As previously discussed, there may be a question whether Corporations *A* and *B* and their Liberian subsidiaries would be subject to United States jurisdiction in a products liability action, but existing state court authority points to the conclusion that they might be. However, this should not subject them to jurisdiction for other actions.

This third solution involves numerous potential pitfalls. Each step in the transactions would have to be carefully monitored, and the clients would have to be apprised of the significant danger that the plan could fail with resulting serious consequences.

The authors would have serious ethical reservations about advising a client to pursue the course of action proposed under the third solution[100]. From the point of view of those practicing in other legal systems, the attempt by the United States to affect extensive extraterritorial application of its antitrust laws may appear to be the major ethical issue involved in the problem.

Notes

1. For an illustration of expansive jurisdictional reach, see *Boykin v. Lindenkranar*, 252 So.2d 467 (La. 1971). The Court found jurisdiction over a foreign manufacturer who sold cranes to an independent intermediary who resold them in the United States.

2. When a court's action and judgment are based on the court's authority over the defendant's person, the action and judgment are denominated *in personam*. The judgment imposes a personal obligation on the defendant in favor of the plaintiff. The judgment of one state court will be recognized and enforced in the courts of all sister states and in many foreign countries.

3. *Kulko v. Superior Court of California*, etc., 436 U.S. 84, at 92, 98 S.Ct. 1690, at 1697, 56 L.EdZd 132, at 141 (1978). *International Shoe Co. v. Washington*, 326 U.S. 310, 66 S.Ct. 154, 90 L.Ed. 95 (1945), which is cited in *Kulko*, is the original basic case on the subject of personal jurisdiction arising from "minimum contacts". The basic case requiring physical presence for jurisdiction is *Pennoyer v. Neff*, 95 U.S. 714, 24 L.Ed. 565 (1878).

4. Section 37: 'A state has power to exercise judicial jurisdiction over an individual who causes effects in the state by an act done elsewhere with respect to any cause of action arising from these effects unless the nature of the effects and of the individual's relationship to the state make the exercise of such jurisdiction unreasonable.'

5. The American Law Institute, Restatement of Conflicts, Section 37. Caveat (a) provides illustrations for the rationale behind the rule. In pertinent part it states: "The state may exercise judicial jurisdiction over the defendant if the effects which could have been anticipated and which actually occurred are of a sort highly dangerous to persons or things. This is so *even though the defendant has no other relationship to the state.* So one who in State *X* explodes dynamite close to the border of State *Y* is subject to *Y*'s judicial jurisdiction as to causes of action arising from injuries caused by the explosion to persons or things in *Y*. Similarly, one who *permits another* to drive his automobile into a state is subject to the judicial jurisdiction of that

state as to causes of action arising from operation of the automobile in the state.' (Emphasis added).

6. *Kulko v. Superior Court of California*, Footnote 3, *supra*. California suit to increase child support. Jurisdiction asserted over new York father who had acquiesced in sending child into California to live with mother. The *effect* occasioned by sending the child to California was inadequate contact to support a California court's assertion of jurisdiction over the absent father.

7. The *Kulko* court stated: 'There is no claim that appellant has visited physical injury... within California,' (436 U.S. 84, at 96, 97, 98 S.Ct. 1690, at 1699, 56 L.Ed. 2d 132, at 144 (1978).)

8. *Great-Western United Corp. v. Kidwell*, 577 F.2d 1256 (1978); probable jurisdiction noted, 47 U.S.L.W. 3463. The forum state was Texas. Defendant was an Idaho state official with absolutely no Texas presence or physical contact. Defendant issued an order delaying the effectiveness of a Texas based tender offer. The order was to force compliance with an Idaho law. This order caused a Texas corporation to make an effort to comply with Idaho law. This effort meant changing business plans in Texas, thereby producing an 'effect' in Texas. This 'foreseeable' effect in Texas, subjected the non-resident Idaho official to the Texas court's jurisdiction.

9. The case must be considered suspect under Supreme Court due process criteria because of its near abolition of the criteria of 'minimum contact' with, and of 'benefit and protection' afforded by, the forum state. In January of 1979 the U.S. Supreme Court elected to review the *Kidwell* decision. A ruling can be expected in mid 1979. Watch for this ruling. It has the potential of being a decision of great significance, particularily if the Supreme Court surprises us by affirming the lower courts finding of 'minimum contact.' (See note 101 for current status.)

10. For state jurisdictional purposes, the drafters of the U.S. Constitution treated residents of a sister state as though they were residents of a foreign territory. Therefore, *Gray* applies to our problem because European (alien) manufacturers and United States (non-resident of the forum state) manufacturers are accorded identical due process protection against state court jurisdictional assertions. While foreign based defendants arguably should be afforded preferred treatment, courts are not likely to accept a distinction between non-resident domestics and foreigners because it would afford more constitutional protection to a non-resident alien than to a domestic person (which is the reverse of traditional thinking). Of course, the foreign based company may have some advantage because it might more easily show burden and unfairness if it has to travel a great distance to a strange forum in order to avoid default judgment. Moreover, when foreign commerce and foreign relations are involved, occasional treaty and foreign affairs issues arise which might be asserted by an alien but not by a domestic.

11. See *Shaffer v. Heitner*, 433 U.S. 186, 97 S.Ct. 2569, 53 L.Ed.2d 683 (1977). The very terminology of 'minimum contact' with the state, and enjoying the 'benefits or protections' of the state, are suggestive of some actual personal affiliation or contact with, or of some direct participation in or penetration of the territorial borders of the state whether by the method of salesman, letter or advertising material. If component part makers located exclusively in Europe are said to have minimum contact with, and to have enjoyed the benefits or protections of an American state merely because independent contractors, several vertical marketing tiers removed, have sold the completed product to residents of that state, then either the wrong terminology is being used by the Supreme Court or the *Gray* case exceeds Supreme Court standards.

12. *Shaffer v. Heitner, supra*, marked the courts reentry into the field after *Hanson v. Denkla*, 357 U.S. 235, 78 S.Ct. 1228, 2 L.Ed.2d 1283 (1958).

13. *See National Bellas Hess, Inc. v. Dept. of Rev.*, 386 U.S. 753, 87 S.Ct. 1389; 18 L.Ed.2d 505 (1967), wherein the court concluded a state legislature under the due process clause could not impose onerous requirements on non-residents. The onerous requirement was administering and becoming familiar with the tax laws of many jurisdictions.

14. *International Shoe* as quoted in *Shaffer v. Heitner*, 433 U.S. 186, at 204, 97 S.Ct. 2569 at 2580, 53 L.Ed.2d 683 at 697. Bracketed inserts are the author's interpretation of the *Shaffer* opinion's use of the quoted material.

15. *Shaffer*, 433 U.S. 186, at 204, 97 S.Ct. 2569 at 2580, 53 L.Ed.2d 683 at 698.

16. *Kulko*, 436 U.S. 84, at 92, 98 S.Ct. 1690 at 1697, 56 L.Ed.2d 132 at 141 (1978), *supra*.

17. *Miller Bros. Co. v. Maryland*, 347 U.S. 340, 74 S.Ct. 535, 98 L.Ed. 744 (1954); *National Bellas Hess, Inc. v. Dept. of Rev.*, 386 U.S. 753, 87 S.Ct. 1389, 18 L.Ed.2d 505 (1967); *Scripto, Inc. v. Carson*, 362 U.S. 207, 80 S.Ct. 619, 4 L.Ed.2d 660 (1960).

18. *National Geographic Soc'y v. California Bd. of Equal.*, 430 U.S. 551 at 561, 97 S.Ct. 1386 at 1393, 51 L.Ed.2d 631 at 640 (1977). Non-resident mail order business had two offices in the forum state which were used to solicit advertising copy.

19. For example, see *Vergara v. Aeroflot 'Soviet Airlines'* 390 F. Supp. 1266 (1975), wherein 'agency theory' was used to give a Nebraska court jurisdiction over the Soviet airline for a tort occuring in Pakistan. Plaintiff a Nebraska citizen had purchased a series of airline tickets for an around the world trip from an Omaha, Nebraska, travel agency. The Omaha travel agency was one of many independent agencies authorized to issue tickets by the International Air Transport Assn., of which Pan Am is a member. Aeroflot had authorized Pan Am to issue Aeroflot tickets, and Pan Am through IATA authorized thousands of travel agencies to issue Aeroflot tickets. Defendent had no other contact with Nebraska.

20. 'When foreign transactions have a substantial and foreseeable effect on United States commerce, they are subject to United States law regardless of where they take place.' Statement by the United States Justice Department in 'Antitrust Guide for International Operations.' Legal basis and limitations are more fully discussed, *infra.*

21. If defective product produced injury within the territorial borders of the state, the state court has subject matter jurisdiction.

22. An analysis of some decisions leads to the conclusion that courts may imply an agency for jurisdictional purposes where they wouldn't find an agency for other purposes. For instance, in some cases the alleged agent doesn't possess the express, implied, or apparent authority to obligate the principal or subject him to tort liability, yet for *jurisdictional purposes* an agency is found to exist. The United States Supreme Court will some day have to grapple with this issue. The authors would forecast that if and when the Supreme Court addresses the issue, it will prohibit any approach which varies the elements in finding an actual agency and jurisdictional agency. Such a dual approach smacks of a sham and device designed to overcome the due process protection otherwise afforded a foreign based defendant. No such forecast is made regarding the states expanded use of the alter ego theory, particularly where states uniformly apply the theory whether for instate liability suits or for defendent jurisdictional purposes.

23. It is conceivable that *Y* and *Z* were treated as, and acted as, independent contractors. In the proposed plan, this would require facts showing they had independently purchased the patent rights and technical data which rights and data they then independently sold and transferred to the United States marketing corporation. Their future conduct would likewise have to be completely disassociated from a right of control by the Liberian corporation.

24. In the case of *NAACP v. Overstreet*, 221 Ga. 16, 142 S.E. 2d 816 (1965) cert. dismissed 384 U.S. 118, 86 S.Ct. 1306, 16 L. Ed.2d 409 (1966), reh. denied 384 U.S. 981, 86 S.Ct. 1857, 16 L. Ed.2d 692 (1966), the Supreme Court of the State of Georgia applied the sustantive law of Georgia and held the National Association for the Advancement of Colored Peoples (a civil rights organization) liable for torts committed by two members in Savannah, Georgia. The United States Supreme Court granted certiorari but then dismissed it on the grounds that certiorari was improvidently granted. (The apparent basis of this dismissal is that the law of agency is a state law matter and thus no federal question was presented.) Four justices dissented from the dismissal stating in part: 1. To equate the liability of the national organization with that of the Branch in the absence of any proof that the national authorized or ratified the misconduct in question could ultimately destroy it. The rights of political association are fragile enough without adding the additional threat of destruction by lawsuit.... 2. The present case contains no less a threat to political association.... 3. This case thus carries us into territory in which principles of state law must be accommodated with overriding federal precepts. The law of agency which a State chooses to follow functions, for the most part, free of constitutional restraint; in our federal system, each State may regulate the relations between principal, agent, and third parties according to its own standard of fairness and sound policy. But when a state policy thwarts interests which the Federal Constitution affords special protection, that state policy must yield.

As this dissenting opinion demonstrates, there are limits upon the extent to which a state can interpret or reinterpret its own law of agency. A state cannot use its substantive law to produce an effect prohibited by the United States Constitution. Thus a state finding of in personam jurisdiction based upon agency concepts is subject to Federal review under the due process clause of the United States Constitution.

25. Even if the parties to the relationship expressly agree and state that no partnership is intended courts may find a partnership. Objective facts and the law are determinative, not words or intent. *Martin v. Peyton*, 246 NY 213, 158 N.E. 77 (1927).

26. 155 F. Supp. 892 (1957). EMI, a British Co. was subject to United States court subpoena served on American subsidiaries. All three corporations were large producers of records and exchanged licenses, etc. In the opinion at 895–896, the court stated '. . . that EMI has two organizations here which it is using not as mere distributors which buy its products for resale but as reciprocating partners in (its worldwide) competition, partners who record both European and American artists and European and American music for distribution by EMI abroad, as well as distribute EMI listings here, and which are headed by men of aggressiveness, independence and prestige whose contribution to the EMI organization goes beyond that of local distributors and includes the building up of a substantial part of the total EMI repertoire . . .'

27. The partnership theory is utilized in one portion of *United States v. Watchmakers of Switzerland Inf C*, 133 F. Supp. 40 at 47 (1955); '. . . taking an overall look at the Longines–Wittnauer relationships, they are a corporate partnership with a single program.' Without careful delineation, this decision appears to ensnare one party under the partnership theory, another under the agency theory, and still another under the alter ego theory.

28. Uniform Partnership Act, Section 9.

29. W. L. Cary, Partnership Planning, An Introductory Pamphlet, page 48 (1970).

30. A number of states permit the partnership entity qua entity to be sued. Execution of the judgment may be levied on partnership property. See page 6, Partnership Planning *supra*.

31. This doctrine is normally used when corporate formalities are ignored by a small corporation with few shareholders. Corporate formalities include: conducting board meeting, keeping minutes, issuing shares, appointing officers, etc. For a listing of the many legal formalities which should be observed see *Harris v. Curtis*, 8 Cal. App.3d 837, 87 Cal Rptr. 614 (1970).

32. *In Re Siemens and Halske A. G., Berline, Germany*, 155 F. Supp. 897 (1957). The subsidiary received a flat allowance plus five per cent price differential with respect to sales or purchases made for the parent. In addition, subsidiary expenditures above budget had to be approved by the parent. The court concluded it was obligated to pierce the veil for purposes of sustaining service of process.

33. *Cannon Manufacturing Co. v. Cudahy Packing Co.*, 267 U.S. 333, 45 S.Ct. 250, 69 L.Ed. 634 (1925). The court was concerned with whether the foreign corporation was doing business within the state for jurisdictional purposes. The foreign corporation was shown to have dominated the decisions and activities of its subsidiary which was doing business in the state. 'The corporate separation though perhaps merely formal, was real. It was not pure fiction.' Id. at 337. See also *People's Tobacco Co. v. American Tobacco Co.*, 246 U.S. 79, 38 S.Ct. 233, 62 L.Ed. 587 (1918) and the dictum in *Eastman Kodak of New York v. Southern Photo Materials Co.*, 273 U.S. 359, 47 S.Ct. 400, 71 L.Ed. 684 (1927).

34. *United States v. Scophony Corporation of America*, 333 U.S. 795, 68 S.Ct. 855, 92 L.Ed. 1091 (1948).

35. *Scophony* is not a due process case. Scophony was found to be 'transacting business' within the venue statute and 'found' within the service of process statute. Scophony was 'found' because it was enmeshed in 'complex working arrangements partaking practically of the character of a common enterprise with others and requiring constant supervision and intervention beyond normal exercise of shareholders' rights by the participating companies representatives qua such.' 333 U.S. 795, at 816; the 'constant supervision' occurring in the United States was accomplished by a Scophony authorized representative who was an individual. His task was active supervision of 'What practically if not also technically was a joint venture with other companies.'

36. *O.S.C. Corporation v. Toshiba America, Inc.*, 491 F.2d (1064 (1974).

37. *Schaffer v. Heitner*, Footnote 11, *supra*.

38. This decision evidences the continued vitality of the due process clause as a means of insulating oneself from the jurisdiction of the American court system.

39. 'It is true that the potential liability of a defendant in an in rem action is limited by the value of the property, but that limitation does not affect the argument. The fairness of subjecting a defendant to state court jurisdiction does not depend on the size of the claim being litigated.' *Shaffer v. Heitner*, 433 U.S. 186 at 207, n. 23, 97 S.Ct. 2569 at 2582, n. 23, 53 L.Ed.2d 683 at 700, n. 23.

40. 35 U.S.C.A. Section 293 as amended 1975: '... the court shall have the same jurisdiction to take any action respecting the patent or rights thereunder that it would have if the patentee were personally within the jurisdiction of the court.'

41. 15 U.S.C.A., Section 6 (1978).

42. 15 U.S.C.A., Section 11 (1978).

43. From a press release by the Department of Justice (1930).

44. Oseas, Antitrust Prosecutions of International Business, 30 Cornell Law Quarterly 42 (1944).

45. 'The Sherman Act was designed to be a comprehensive charter of economic liberty aimed at preserving free and unfettered competition as the rule of trade. It rests on the promise that the unrestrained interaction of competitive forces will yield the best allocation of our economic resources, the lowest prices, the highest quality and the greatest material progress, while at the same time providing an environment conducive to the preservation of our democratic political and social institutions.' *Northern Pacific Railroad Co. v. U.S.*, 356 U.S. 1 at 4; 78 S.Ct. 514 at 517; 2 L.Ed.2d 545 at 549 (1958).

46. United States Department of Justice, Antitrust Division, Antitrust Guide for International Operations, 26 January, 1977. This guide contains hypothetical cases and is one of the few Justice Department Publications wherein their policy and analysis of extraterritorial anti-trust issues is set forth.

47. 'The elements to be weighed include the degree of conflict with foreign law or policy, the nationality or allegiance of the parties and the locations or principal places of business of corporations, the extent to which enforcement by either state can be expected to achieve compliance, the relative significance of effects on the United States as compared with those elsewhere, the extent to which there is explicit purpose to harm or affect American commerce, the foreseeability of such effect, and the relative importance to the violations charged of conduct within the United States as compared with conduct abroad. A court evaluating these factors should identify the potential degree of conflict if American authority is asserted. A difference in law or policy is one likely sore spot, though one which may not always be present. Nationality is another; though foreign governments may have some concern for the treatment of American citizens and business residing there, they primarily care about their own nationals. Having assessed the conflict, the court should then determine whether in the face of it the contacts and interests of the United States are sufficient to support the exercise of extraterritorial jurisdiction.' *Timberlane Lumber Company v. Bank of America*, 549 F.2d 597 at 614–615 (9th Cir. 1976) (footnotes deleted).

48. Id. at 615.

49. 15 U.S.C.A. Sections 1 and 2.

50. 15 U.S.C.A. Section 18 (1973).

51. 15 U.S.C.A. Section 14 (1973).

52. 19 U.S.C.A. Section 1337 (1965 & Supp. 1978).

53. 15 U.S.C.A. Section 8.

54. 15 U.S.C.A. Section 45 (1973).

55. For example, a recently enacted statute deals with 'pre-merger notification for international acquisitions of certain large joint ventures and multiple parent-subsidiary creations.' See Title II of Hart–Scott–Rodino Antitrust Improvements Act of 1976 which is the new section 7A of the Clayton Act. 15 U.S.C.A. Section 18(a) Supp. 1978.

56. The horizontal merger rules developed under Section 7 of the Clayton Act apply where the joint ventures were competitors prior to formation of the joint venture (subsidiary), and the subsidiary is thereafter to engage in the same business and market. *United States v. Penn-Olin Chemical Co.*, 378 U.S. 158, 84 S.Ct. 1693, 12 L.Ed.2d 711, (1964). For a case where a non-horizontal joint venture was justified see *U.S. v. Pan American World Airways*, 193 F. Supp. 18 (1961). Given that there is a need or necessity for the joint venture, it is justifiable to form a joint venture for the limited purpose of researching or developing a new high technology product. On the other hand a selling or marketing joint venture formed by competitors can seldom be justified. Consequently *Y* and *Z*, the marketing agents, may be subject to Clayton 7.

57. Courts have yet to determine whether Section 7 requires both joint venturers to be 'engaged in commerce', or merely one of the joint venturers. We assume here the joint venture (subsidiary) will engage in U.S. Commerce once it begins operating. The Justice Department would seem to take the position that all three might need to be engaged in commerce. See United States Department of Justice, Antitrust Division, Antitrust Guide for International Operations, Case B.

26 January 1977. Irrespective of the Section 7 standard, the broader Sherman standard, ('affecting interstate or foreign commerce') will ensnare many extraterritorial joint ventures.

58. A prima facie case exists for the proposition that this joint venture may tend to substantially lessen competition in a line of commerce. Even if the European companies don't expressly agree to terminate their separate competitive efforts in America, the creation of the joint venture allows the court to imply such an agreement. See *Penn-Olin*, Footnote 56, *supra*. It is here assumed that solar electricity producing devices are a separate line of commerce for purposes of the Antitrust Statutes.

59. Clayton 7 applies to the acquisition of 'any part' of the stock or assets 'of another corporation also engaged in commerce'. It has an expansive reach covering acquisitions of less than controlling interest and less than all assets. Theoretically the purchase of a mere patent is within the act's scope, particularly where as here, it is the Liberian Co.'s major asset. While Section 7 is inapplicable unless one of the acquiring parties and the acquired party (subsidiary) is a corporation, Sections 1 and 2 of the Sherman Act and Section 5 of the Federal Trade Commission Act are applicable without regard to the parties incorporated status.

60. See discussion infra respecting 'tying' and patent misuse.

61. See *United States v. National Lead Co.* 63 F. Supp. 513 (1945); affd., 332 U.S. 319, 67 S.Ct. 1634, 91 L.Ed. 2077 (1947). The trial court did not have jurisdiction over some of the foreign based co-conspirators. To prevent a frustration of American antitrust law, the judge invalidated agreements with the co-conspirators and enjoined the American parties from performing them. The United States Supreme Court affirmed. See also *United States v. Bayer Co., Inc.* 135 F. Supp. 65 (1955), and *General Aniline v. Bayer* 117 N.Y.S.2d 497 (1952).

62. It is conceivable some plaintiff might assert that the joint venture does substantially affect United States commerce even though neither party to the venture had previously marketed in the United States. The theory to support such an unlikely result is described as the perceived potential entry theory. It would require evidence revealing: (1) that prior to the joint venture, a solar unit market existed in the United States; (2) that the American marketers actually perceived each of the two European corporations to be potential entrants and potential competitors in the American market; (3) that the American marketers were more competitive by reason of the perception, i.e.; perhaps they cut prices and profits in order to make actual entry less desirable; and (4) by forming the joint venture, this perception of two entrants is eliminated, and one actual entrant (the subsidiary) has less impact and is to be less feared than two potential entrants. This theory becomes more viable if one of the joint venturers was an entrant and the other a perceived entrant prior to the joint venture, or if one of the joint venturers is an American marketer.

63. While Clayton 7 requires that the parties be 'engaged in United States commerce' prior to formation of the joint venture, Sherman 1 and 2 merely require that the formation or operation of the venture affect United States commerce. See footnote 57, *supra*, for varying views when foreigners are involved. Sherman 1 is relevant because it can be asserted that the European venturers have agreed not to compete in the United States Sherman 2 may be relevant if monopoly power or an attempt to acquire such is evidenced.

64. Necessity or justification are relative concepts. If one of the two parties is a failing company and will be saved by the venture, it may be alright unless a 'savior' presenting a lesser anticompetitive impact should have been chosen. Sometimes technology or effort *must be combined* in order to accomplish a laudable goal, (examples—the Alaska pipeline, or underwriters joint venturing a new stock issue). In the hypothetical, however, even if there is merit in combining the superior unit of each company, it could have been accomplished by reasonable, less anticompetitive alternatives such as cross licensing of patents. An alternative which would have availed the world of the superior product and avoided the evils of a monopolistic joint venture.

65. *International Salt Co. v. United States*, 332 U.S. 392, 68 S.Ct. 12, 92 L.Ed. 20 (1947), *United States v. Loew's, Inc.*, 371 U.S. 38, 83 S.Ct. 97, 9 L.Ed.2d 11 (1962).

66. See Brewster, Antitrust and American Business Abroad (1976, Arno Press, reprint of 1958 edition McGraw Hill), for an excellent discussion and citation of cases involving antitrust patent abuse. Brewster notes that antitrust decrees in patent abuse cases (particularily where there is patent pooling and restrictions) frequently go far beyond a mere invalidation of the arrangement. For example, decrees have: deprived patentees of the right to license exclusively; required reassigning of patents, enjoined transfers, required cross licensing and mandatory licensing. See also *United States v. Imperial Chemical Industries LTD* 105 F. Supp. 215 (1952).

transfers, required cross licensing and mandatory licensing. See also *United States v. Imperial Chemical Industries LTD* 105 F. Supp. 215 (1952).

67. See cases and analysis in Fugate, Foreign Commerce and the Antitrust Laws; 2nd Ed. 1973, at pages 431–437.

68. *Timken Roller Bearing Co. v. United States*, 341 U.S. 593, 71 S.Ct. 971, 95 L.Ed. 1199 (1951).

69. *Continental T.V., Inc., v. GTE Sylvania Inc.*, 433 U.S. 36, 97 S.Ct. 2549, 53 L.Ed.2d 568 (1977). These vertical restraints of trade will be tested by the rule of reason.

70. *United States v. General Dyestuff Corp.*, 57 F. Supp. 642 (1944).

71. For treatment and explanation of contingency payments see Treasury Regulations, Section 1.871-11 (1967) and illustrations contained therein.

72. Compare the State of New Jersey which applies the tort law of products liability even in the absence of personal injury or physical harm to property. *Santor v. A. & M. Karagheusian, Inc.*, 44 N.J. 52, 207 A.2d 305 (1965).

73. *Seely v. White Motor Co.*, 63 Cal.2d 9, 403 P.2d 145 (1975).

74. *Lewis v. Mobile Oil Corp.*, 438 F.2d 500 (8th Cir. 1971).

75. *Greenman v. Yuba Power Products, Inc.*, 59 Cal.2d 57, 377 P.2d 897 (1963).

76. *Russell v. Ford Motor Co.*, 281 Or. 587, 575 P.2d 1383 (1978).

77. Id., 575 P. 2d 1383, at pages 1386–1387.

78. *Golden v. Conway*, 55 Cal. App.3d 948, 128 Cal. Rptr. 69, (1976).

79. Seely, Footnote 73, *supra*.

80. Uniform Commercial Code, Section 2-318.

81. *Randy Knitwear, Inc. v. American Cyanimid Co.*, 326 NYS2d 226, 181 N.E.2d 399 (1962).

82. Uniform Commercial Code, Section 2-316. Note that this right of disclaimer may be limited by federal or state law in consumer transactions.

83. Uniform Commercial Code, Section 2-719.

84. Uniform Commercial Code, Section 2-715.

85. Uniform Commercial Code, Section 2-607.

86. Uniform Commercial Code, Sections 2-313; 2-314; 2-315.

87. *Kasel v. Remington Arms Company*, 24 Cal. App.3d 711, 101 Cal. Rptr. 314 (1972). The plaintiff in this case was a California resident who went to Mexico where he purchased 'Remington' shot gun shells which were locally manufactured by a Mexican company as reflected on the box. The plaintiff was injured in Mexico as the result of defects in the shells. The plaintiff returned to California and sued Remington Arms, an American corporation which does business in California. The trial court found that Mexico had no products liability law and Mexico did not allow recover for pain and suffering, but it concluded California law should apply. The Court instructed the jury on the law regarding agency (on the theory that the Mexican company could be found to be an agent of Remington). The jury rendered a verdict for the defendant. The Court of Appeals reversed, holding that the trial court should have instructed the jury that, as a matter of law, Remington Arms was an integral part of the overall producing and marketing enterprise that placed the defective shell in the stream of commerce.

The facts which were referred to by the Court of Appeal included: 1) Remington assisted in creating the Mexican company and owned forty per cent of its stock and a large part of its bonds. 2) Some of the employees of the Mexican company had been trained by Remington and one was an American who was a former employee of Remington. 3) Remington had licensed the Mexican company to use the name 'Remington,' and Remington had the right to inspect and control the quality of all ammunition upon which its trademark was used. 4) Remington had large sales and did extensive advertising in California and elsewhere. 5) A minority of the directors of the Mexican company were also Remington directors.

88. As an example, Oregon Revised Statutes, Section 14.035 states: '(1) Any person, firm or corporation whether or not a citizen or a resident of this state, who, in person or through an agent, does any of the actions enumerated in this subsection, thereby submits such person and, if an individual, his personal representative to the jurisdiction of the courts of this state, as to any cause of action or suit or proceeding arising from any of the following: (a) The transaction of any business within this state; (b) The commission of a tortious act within this state...' These approaches to establishing jurisdiction are subject to limitations of the United States Constitution. *International Shoe Co. v. Washington*, Footnote 4, *supra*, *Hanson v. Denckla*, Footnote 13, *supra*.

89. *Hapner v. Rolf Brauchli, Inc., et al,* 404 Mich. 160, Z73 N.W. Zd822 (1978), involved an action for injuries allegedly caused by a defective hair dryer which had been purchased in Illinois and taken to Michigan by the consumer. The defendant in question was a Swiss manufacturer which had distributors in New York, Illinois and Californıa. The majority held that the constitutional requirement of minimum contact was not satisfied by the established facts. The defendant had not distributed its product through a marketing system in such manner and to such extent that it could be found to have purposefully availed itself of the privilege of doing business within the State of Michigan. The mere foreseeability that some of its products would be taken to Michigan does not establish a relationship to the State which makes it fair and reasonable to subject the non-resident to Michigan jurisdiction. The dissent took the position that given the nature of the product, the volume of sales and the mobility of United States residents, the defendant could reasonably foresee that the product would enter the forum state and that this was sufficient to establish jurisdiction. While this is a significant decision, a European manufacturer cannot safely assume that all states will follow the Michigan result.

90. *Gray v. American Radiator & Standard Sanitary Corp.* 22 Ill. 432, 176 N.E.2d 761, (1961). See discussion at Footnote 11, *supra.*

91. The general rule in tort cases is that the *lex loci delicti,* or law of the place of the wrong, governs issues of liability. In a multi-jurisdiction problem this is usually held to be the place of injury. (*Restatement (Second), Conflict of Laws,* Section 146 (1971).) Although some cases apply the law of the place where the wrongful conduct occurred, these cases usually involve issues other than products liability. *Schmidt v. Driscoll Hotel, Inc.,* 249 Minn. 376, 82 N.W.2d 365, (1957).

92. *Bernhard v. Harrah's Club,* 16 Cal.3d 313, 546 P.2d 719 (1976). See also, Footnote 87.

93. See generally, Wade, 'Strict Tort Liability of Manufacturers,' 19 *Southwestern Law Journal* 5 (1965); Prosser, 'The Fall of the Citadel (Strict Liability to the Consumer),' 50 *Minnesota Law Review* 791 (1966); Keeton, 'Product Liability and the Meaning of Defect,' 5 *St. Mary's Law Journal* 30 (1973); Donaher, Piehler, Twerski and Weinstein, 'The Technological Expert in Products Liability Litigation,' 52 *Texas Law Review* 1033 (1974).

94. This discussion is focused upon jurisdiction based upon commission of a tort in the forum state. It should be noted that this problem is not applicable to the Liberian corporation which sold both component parts. It should also be noted that alternative bases of jurisdiction over *A* and *B* may exist as previously discussed.

95. *Hall v. E.I. du Pont de Nemours Co.,* 345 F. Supp. 353 (1972); *Ybarra v. Spangard,* 25 Cal.2d 486, 154 P.2d 687 (1944).

96. *Jakubowski v. Minnesota Mining and Manufacturing,* 42 N.J. 177, 199 A.2d 826 (1964).

97. See generally Article IX of the Uniform Commercial Code which has been adopted in all United States jurisdictions except Louisiana and which permits and controls perfection of security interests in such intangible property rights as patents.

98. Robinson-Patman Price Discrimination Act Sections 1 and 3; 15 U.S.C.A, Sections 13 and 13(a).

99. If the Liberian corporation were to bring an action in a United States court to prevent patent infringement, the defendant can raise (in fact must raise or forfeit) its counterclaim for violations of antitrust laws arising out of misuse of the patent.

100. American Bar Association, Code of Professional Responsibility, provides in part: DR 7-102. (A) 'In his representation of a client, a lawyer shall not: . . . (7) Counsel or assist his client in conduct that the lawyer knows to be illegal or fraudulent, (EC 7-6 Whether the proposed action of a lawyer is within the bounds of the law may be a perplexing question when his client is contemplating a course of conduct having legal consequences that vary according to the client's intent, motive, or desires at the time of the action. Often a lawyer is asked to assist his client in developing evidence relevant to the state of mind of the client at a particular time. He may properly assist his client in the development and preservation of evidence of existing motive, intent, or desire; obviously, he may not do anything furthering the creation of preservation of false evidence. In many cases a lawyer may not be certain as to the state of mind of his client, and in those situations he should resolve reasonable doubts in favor of his client.'

101. On 26 June 1979, the Supreme Court reversed *Great Western United Corp. v. Kidwell,* 577 F2d 1256 (1978), *sub. nom., Leroy v. Great Western United Corp.,* 47 U.S.L.W. 4844 (1979). The reversal was based upon lack of venue. With respect to the jurisdiction issue, the court stated: ". . . the question whether personal jurisdiction was properly obtained pursuant to the Texas longarm statute

is more difficult. Indeed, because the Texas Supreme Court has construed its statute as authorizing the exercise of jurisdiction over nonresidents as authorizing the exercise of jurisdiction over nonresidents to the fullest extent permitted by the United States Constitution, resolution of this question would require the Court to decide a question of constitutional law that it has not heretofore decided. As a prudential matter it is our practice to avoid the unnecessary decision of novel constitutional questions. We find it appropriate to pretermit the constitutional issue in this case because it is so clear that venue was improper under either §27 of the 1934 Act or under §1391(b) of the Judicial Code." (footnote omitted) 47 U.S.L.W. at 4846.

INDEX TO MAJOR TOPICS